RETURN OF LOVE
TO PLANET EARTH

RETURN OF LOVE TO PLANET EARTH

Memoir of a Reluctant Visionary

—~—

Nina Brown

Santa Fe, New Mexico

Cauda Pavonis
PO Box 32445
Santa Fe, NM 87594

www.CaudaPavonisPub.com

ISBN-10 0-9826769-0-5
ISBN-13 978-0-9826769-0-5
Library of Congress Control Number: 2010924671
Copyright information available upon request.

Cover Painting: James F. Jereb, Ph.D.
Cover Design: Tammy Mabra, www.sevacreative.com
Interior Design: J. L. Saloff
Typography: Garamond Premier Pro, Bell MT, InaiMathi

v. 2.0
Second Edition, 2011
Printed on acid-free paper

To my three children,
who fill my life with radiant light

To Marijon, James, and Tyberonn,
who gave me a voice

To my higher self,
who wrote the cosmic version of my story

To the star warriors,
who are working to repair the ancient energy grids

~ APPRECIATION ~

I learned from the dolphins and from the Hathors that the frequency of appreciation and gratitude makes life rich, and that this frequency is the fuel for bringing love back to planet earth. I wish to fill these pages with my profound appreciation and gratitude to the many people who have walked part of this journey with me. They provided a safe place for me to test new ideas and speak new thoughts. They encouraged me to be just a little bit more of who I truly am in their eyes. So, without everyone mentioned in this book, and so many more, I would not be writing *Return of Love to Planet Earth: Memoir of a Reluctant Visionary* for I would still be in the early stages of my alchemical path. To all of you and to the three people who asked me when I was going to write my book, I say thank you from the bottom of my heart.

I thank my higher self, Anaya-ra (Ah-ny-ah-ra), also all the interdimensional beings who spoke to me over the last ten years, as themselves or through my higher self: Archangels Raphael, Metatron, Michael, Gabriel, Uriel, Jophiel, and Lady Constance; the whales and the dolphins, the ancient ones, cosmic mother, Sananda, Kuthumi, El Morya, the fairies, the beings from inner earth, the Cosmic Council of Light, the Council of Thirteen, Aphrodite, and the crystals. This book is very much their words. This is our story, seen through their eyes and through my eyes, for we are indeed one!

I would also like to extend appreciation to those who assisted with the glossary: James F. Jereb, Ph.D.; Jesus through Glenda Green; Kryon channeled by Lee Carroll; Archangel Metatron channeled by Tyberonn; Archangel Michael channeled by Ronna Herman; James Tyberonn; and

Ellen Kleiner, of Blessingway Authors' Services, whose idea this was. Gratitude as well to J. L. Saloff and Tammy Mabra for their contributions to the making of this book.

~ CONTENTS ~

~ Part II ~
Return of Love to Planet Earth

~ FOREWORD ~

On rare occasions, we meet people who are extraordinary. Nina Brown is such a person. She exudes a light that seems to encompass nurturing, wisdom, and well-being, causing her presence to fill a room with a vibrant energy of balance and grace. I recognized Nina as a great soul and brilliant visionary almost immediately. She is a true "walk-in of ascended mastery," having completed her necessary lifetimes and merged with her ascended soul in this present life to complete a sacred mission of service to all humanity.

Nina has had a remarkable life. A highly successful business owner and influential leader in women's rights, she was among an elite group invited to the White House to advise President Clinton on issues related to women-owned businesses. She has also been an unrelenting advocate for veterans with disabilities. Her impressive biography, reflecting a life of notable achievement, is complete, and the extraordinary soul now emerging is just beginning to offer its myriad gifts. Widening her arena of influence, Nina currently devotes her amazing energy to her divinely inspired mission of assisting all of humanity.

In *Return of Love to Planet Earth*—a must-read for all on the spiritual path—Nina's warm, compelling narrative engages interest from the start. As the chapters unfold, she shares her remarkable journey of spiritual self-awakening and, consequently, the serendipitous flowering of divine consciousness within her.

More than any other recent publication I am aware of in the spirituality genre, this avant-garde book captures the unfolding of self-realization and spiritual empowerment that is available to all of humanity. Step by step, it details Nina's personal pilgrimage into the deeper mystical purpose of life, at once revealing her truths with exacting precision and challenging readers who seek greater consciousness to uncover their own.

May this rare chronicle help to deepen the understanding of who we are and why we are here, and serve as a guiding testament of ascension in consciously transforming ourselves and returning love to our planet.

—James Tyberonn
Author and messenger for Archangel Metatron

~ INTRODUCTION ~

Ten years ago, an alchemical flame entered my heart, burning away impurity, duality, and the imbalances of living life separated from my higher self. Clarity, like a translucent crystal, entered my being, as did a voice guiding me onto the path I was about to take. The voice consoled me as dramatic shifts occurred, both physically and spiritually. What I have come to understand is that while I thought the voice identified itself as Archangel Raphael, the whales and the dolphins, or the Council of Thirteen, it was always my higher self speaking, representing specific archetypal aspects of me. In 2009, the voice became consistently that of the Cosmic Council of Light, for by then I knew I was a member of that council. It was indeed my higher self, Anaya-Ra on that council speaking directly to me, Nina.

Return of Love to Planet Earth chronicles hundreds of transformative events that transpired over those ten years but, oddly, not my feelings about them. I reported on the events themselves as if taking notes in class, jotting down all I had learned. Retrospectively, I am reminded of Buckminster Fuller's observation that the only thing making us unique is how we *feel* about life and events, and that "not a single human being can be taught to feel."[1] For me, that part was to come later.

And so this is the memoir of a reluctant visionary, one not yet prepared to represent her everyday self to the divine core of her being. Subconsciously I had left my feelings out, instead hiding behind journal entries, others' impressions, the telling of events—the easy route.

I still tend to hide my physical being, Nina, behind my cosmic being, Anaya-Ra. But it is the human Nina whose story this is: a tale of becoming fully aware of living simultaneously in the physical and spiritual dimensions.

As I look back, I see my feelings were pronounced, and readers who pick this book up may experience similar ones. My journey started with: "A feeling of yearning: I feel there is more to my life. Why isn't it showing up?" and "I can taste it, but there's got to be more." Then as new facets of life emerged and I began finding clues about who I was, why I was here, and what my work was to be, I felt lonely, for that was all I wanted to talk about. I wanted to be surrounded by people with whom I could explore the new me, but few could understand what I was yearning for. A passion was unfolding in my life. Yet with the unveiling of each new truth came an equally explicit question: "Why me?"

How do I feel now, knowing you may turn the page and see who I am? I feel vulnerable and hesitant. My ego is fighting back very hard, urging me to stop chronicling and return to life as it used to be. I realize, however, I am intended to tell this story, though it would be so much easier to just sit in my red leather chair and pull the plug on the publishing of this book.

~ PART I ~

The Peacock's Tail

~ 1 ~

Who Am I, Why Am I Here, and What Is My Work?

How does one know that they are an incarnate ascended master? One way is that they can be told, as I have been by Archangel Metatron. "It can be said to you in truth that your oversoul is on the level of the ascended mastery. Not yet fully accomplished on that realm, not yet at the level of Saint Germain, whom you recently encountered, for there are levels of mastery within each realm, each level. We would have you know that you are indeed within the realm of the ascended masters, and we would have you acknowledge self."[1]

Another way to learn that one is a master is to remember; this hasn't happened yet for me. Or, they can know. I know that I carry the Christ-consciousness codes. I know that I am transferring them to 144,000 individuals (a minimum of 33) who are anchoring the Christ-consciousness grid on planet earth. J. J. Hurtak's *The Keys of Enoch* describes those 144,000 as being ascended masters.[2] It is the profound knowing that confirms to me who I am: an ascended master called Anaya-Ra, Crystal Singer of the Cosmic Council of Light, formerly known as the Great White Brotherhood.[3] Kryon, channeled by Lee Carroll, says that all the ascended masters are present at this time of the ascension: "The energy of the masters are part of the energy of the great shift that is upon you. They intermingle with the vibration of this planet. They're all back, and it's what you're feeling. In a quantum state, they're in your DNA. Don't you sense this?"[4]

How did this knowing come about? What life events were clues?

What experiences moved me farther in my journey of empowerment? Who were the people who spoke my truth in such a way that I could hear? How did these codes get transferred to me and when? Who are the individuals who are counting on me to live an impeccable life so that the frequencies of the codes can be held and transferred?

What follows is my story, with its typical sadness and joy, peaks and valleys, and life's lessons—the story that brought me to this moment of knowing who I am, why I am here, and what my work is. This story is mine, but perhaps it is yours as well, though the details might differ.

I, Nina, am Anaya-Ra, Crystal Singer of the Cosmic Council of Light. I am on planet earth to return love to the planet and my work is to transfer the Christ-consciousness codes that I received a year ago from Sananda, Jesus the Christ to 144,000 ascended masters, who anchor the Christ-consciousness, the crystalline grid.[5]

Archangel Metatron, through Tyberonn, has told me that I merged with my higher self as an internal walk-in, during the seven-year period between the ages of forty-two and forty-nine—a seven-year cycle in which one completely renews oneself physically, and in my case, spiritually. When I think back on that time, my memory is filled with loss and sadness. Archangel Metatron confirms that I was shedding what didn't serve me in the full expression of my higher self. Even the years of adjustment following my forty-ninth year were challenging, but there was an inner knowing that the lack that surrounded me was not who I truly was. I kept waiting for the universe to readjust in some magical way so that I could express myself fully, and so it did.

My tale will encompass a period of ten years that ends on Christmas Day 2009. The heart of this part of my life's journey occurred in October 2007 when I returned from Dharamsala, India, where I had joined the Council of Thirteen Indigenous Grandmothers in prayer for peace and attended a private audience for them with His Holiness the Dalai Lama. When I returned to New Mexico, I read *The Keys of Enoch*. Only now do I realize that those keys were imprinted and ignited in me while reading that book, for it was directly after that transfer of energetic codes that my higher self went into full forward drive.

By means of the following narrative and journal entries, I will tell my story, more in the passion of the moment as opposed to in memory of the events. It is a story of how I slowly removed the veil from my heart and was able to become a receiver of the Christos energy, the Christ-consciousness codes, and a transmitter of that frequency for planetary nodes and human crystalline structure—so that humanity might remember their own divinity. I am an envoy bringing the crystalline light. I am the tunnel through which this frequency travels. I am not the frequency, merely the conduit.

My journey has been one of awakening to my own potential and to knowing with conviction that I am the one for whom I have been waiting. My truth is no longer found in the wisdom or actions of others, but in the chamber of my sacred heart. The heart I speak of is not the physical organ (although the physical heart is an appropriate instrument for the sacred heart because it nourishes the body with life blood every moment). The heart I speak of is the central focus point of the soul. It is the lens through which our soul integrates all of our earthly emotions and all of our divine awareness into a focused point of infinite possibilities. This point is on the threshold of our physical existence, at a spot slightly below and behind the physical heart. This is our true heart and our sacred chamber.[6]

All of those masters and teachers attracted to me have provided clues, tools, and inspiration to look within myself to find the divine that I am. I know all of us to be one, each a spark of the divine. I therefore offer this story of my journey to all those who are on their own path toward ascension: a process where the human body is transformed into crystal light and translated by an incredible birth into a new world.[7] That discovery of who you are is just around the corner. Join me in the rabbit's hole where belief transforms the impossible into the possible.

Why is it important to share this information? Does it really matter? Yes, humanity was created in the image of the Creator. We are creators, currently creating in duality. By means of the return of pure love and light, we raise our frequency, the frequency of our intentions, and thus, the frequency of our manifestations. We do this by living in two dimensions simultaneously—for me, Nina and Anaya-Ra. Thus our creations shift from duality into unity. We are perfection seeking the expression of perfection. We are creators creating heaven on earth. We do this by means of pure love and light, and the raising of our vibratory note.[8]

Who I Am

I am a spiritual being living in a human experience and having an animistic relationship with all life, believing that inanimate objects have consciousness.

The Cosmic Council of Light brought in this fairy tale during an automatic writing session. I learned who I was by means of a fairy tale, so that I could gently assimilate the amazing information.

Once upon a time, there was a brave commander who lived in a far-away galaxy, a galaxy different from any other. It was radiant and filled with the unfiltered, pure-love vibration of Source. All who lived there were filled with love. The commander was named Anaya-Ra the Great. ("Are you having fun?" The council interjected at this point.) Anaya-Ra was called by the leaders of other nations, to come and assist them with perfecting the frequencies on their own planets. Knowing that Anaya-Ra was a leader of many and had been responsible for maintaining the pure love vibration in the galaxy, the other nations felt that Anaya-Ra could be of great value. So Anaya-Ra left the galaxy and joined the Council of the Thirteen Nations (planets) as their fountainhead, or ambassador, to bring wisdom, justice, compassion, and—most importantly—love to the other nations. They learned much from the ambassador, and the love vibration was increased in each nation. Anaya-Ra was a starseed crystalline being and able to transfer the crystalline love frequency to the other nations to allow each member to raise their DNA and love quotient to a purer level. It was not words or leadership techniques that were the answer. It was the ability to transfer the adamantine particles of a high vibration that made Anaya-Ra a commander, ambassador, and fountainhead of the thirteen nations. Do you see?

With our love,

The Cosmic Council of Light via Anaya-Ra

Who Am I?–12/8/07

Nina: Who am I?

We are glad, dear one, that you have finally asked that question of us. Besides our beloved one, the ambassador of light, you are indeed a star being here to bring love and compassion to humanity. There are other star beings here on earth; not all are like you, however, which is why you are the ambassador of light.

The ancient ones via Anaya-Ra

Why I Am Here

I am here to return love to planet earth. The following children's story tells of a crystal that fell back to earth and into the sand. I found the crystal (stone) in that story on the beach in Del Mar, California. The stone became a central theme in the children's book *Quest of the Golden Dolphin* by James F. Jereb, Ph.D., and the beginning of my own work, the returning of love to planet earth:

> Once there was a civilization called Mu on the planet earth that was filled with treasures and was a wonder to all. Neptunus, a great magician, was charged as keeper of all the sacred crystals—the libraries of the stars. The sacred crystals contained the original memories and the power of creation of the many races on Mu, all of which had arrived on earth from various galaxies in the universe. Neptunus himself originally came from the planet Saturn, where all the great magicians of the universe had been trained since the beginning of time. After being on Mu for many thousands of years, Neptunus was instructed by Raphael, an archangel of the holy ones, to send the star crystals back to their origins. Neptunus questioned the holy ones' decree. After all, the crystals had been Mu's source of power for healing and magic for centuries. "Mu and its people have become weak. They forgot to have compassion for each other. This will destroy them," said the holy ones.

Raphael explained, "Only when the people of Mu can begin to feel love, caring, and kindness again, while holding magic in their hearts, will there be a new world. Then Grandmother Agnes White Whale of Wisdom will birth a new pathway of stars for this world. Those beings will be called golden dolphins."

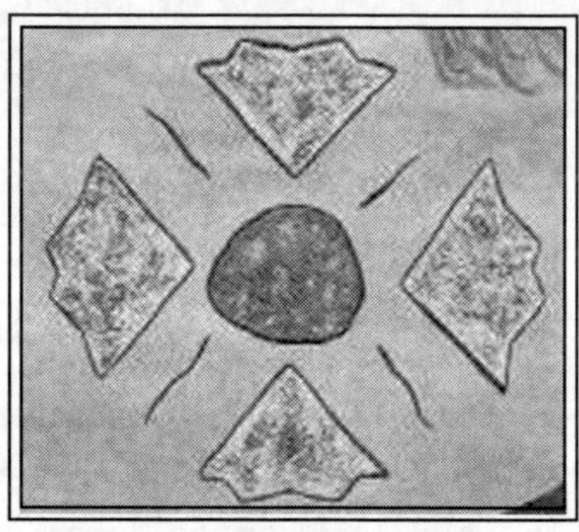

Return of the star crystals.

"What are golden dolphins?" Neptunus then asked Raphael.

Raphael answered, "They are star warriors who are in service to the light and to all the inhabitants of planet earth. They will cocreate with what—in the future—you will call the shining ones (creational forces of light, gods, evolved beings from this world; and others)."

Neptunus now understood Raphael's directions and acted accordingly. He exhaled a breath of blue smoke, known as the power of the dragon, onto a cluster of star crystals. This dragon's breath gave the stones an unbelievable power. As his breath grew stronger, many star crystals from sacred caves, temples, and labyrinths in Mu left the earth and went back to their starry homes all over the universe. In a different time and place, one crystal fell back to earth and into the sand. Many other crystals would follow as people on earth remembered again their place in the universe.[9]

About My Work

In an astounding channel from Archangel Metatron via Tyberonn, I learned—and was supported and encouraged by Tyberonn—that I am here to return love to planet earth by means of recoding or upshifting the frequency of planetary nodes and human DNA.

In closing, we tell you to accept these truths and have confidence in who you are. You are the master, you are the teacher, you are the healer of crystalline seed come to recode. Your most important role is not in recoding the grid; indeed, you will and are playing a key part in that process, and it will continue. However, your greater role is in recoding humanity, in small groups and individually. That is why you are here. Take your power. Be the teacher, the master, and be guided by the self.

I am Metatron and I share with you these truths. And so it is.

Archangel Metatron, Lord of Light via Tyberonn (6/28/09)

What Return of Love to Planet Earth Means

The end of duality and the return of unity, a state of consciousness long forgotten by humanity, is returning as the ascension approaches. The ancient wisdom of who we truly are—divine beings on planet earth, here to experience life—is being remembered in order to grow in spirit upward on the spiral of life. The frequency of love is igniting the planet and the physicality of those beings who are choosing to move into the vibrations of a higher dimension. I am a receiver and transmitter of those frequencies. I am one who has come to assist in bringing the vibration of love back to planet earth, to assist with the planetary ascension. I have come to unveil hearts, to help them remember the sacredness of all and the divinity of humanity. Like a pure crystal or a diamond, I am able to absorb light and love and to reflect it out to planetary nodes and human DNA. I do this by raising the vibration to a higher frequency, that of Source, All That Is. I refer to this vibration as the Christ-consciousness codes. This ability was transferred to me a year ago by Sananda and began to be expressed by me on summer solstice of 2009. This is the now of the awakening of souls to their oneness with Source, the return of love to planet earth. With the advent of the crystalline age, all of humanity is able to possess this gift, heaven on earth. How did this come to be for me?

My Story Begins

My ten-year alchemical journey began after moving to Santa Fe from Philadelphia in 1999, because my inner voice told me to. Shortly after my move, I reached such a level of lack that others gave me food for Thanksgiving, then a window opened. I found a temporary position as the executive assistant to the chief executive officer of Los Alamos Medical Center. At this point in my life miracles began to happen, and I knew that I needed to keep track of them, so I started filling binders with emails, journal entries, and copies of my automatic writings. As I recently looked through the twenty-plus three-inch binders that chronicled my thoughts and events over the last five years, I found it curious that the first two selections relate to my three children and my deceased, former husband. On reflection, it became clear that I had to begin with family, for the next phase of my alchemical journey required clarity and balance with those closest to me. I began keeping the binders at a time when I was about to venture off to create an alternative wellness center in New Mexico. The details of that center were not yet clear, but my passion was powerful.

I wrote to my children, saying:

> I need to put my thoughts down on paper today. Instead of writing in my journal, I thought I would share them with you and perhaps you can put a copy in the file you have labeled "Mom" to look back on when my vision becomes reality. If life has purpose, I feel as if today I understand mine, or at least a piece of it. I have had so many experiences and gone in so many directions over the last sixty years. As you all know, the journey has not always been a fairy tale. I can see so clearly how several main events, which at the time seemed puzzling, are now beginning to make sense. The culmination of so many of these experiences will be the Life Harmonies Institute, which is just beginning to materialize. Let me first describe it to you, by quoting from the first draft of the business plan. "Life Harmonies Institute will be a unique destination, in the Northern New Mexico highlands, focused on human

> wellness from birth to death and on sustainability of individuals, families, and communities on this earth. It is planned as a collage of services and practitioners available part time or full time on campus, using allied professionals and facilities in the Northern New Mexico area." After so many years, I finally feel passion returning to my life. I had so much passion for former projects then it disappeared. Now I am excited again and enjoy watching the vision unfold.

Why had that passion for life disappeared? I used to have passion for whatever I had chosen to be involved in. The projects—volunteering for the Philadelphia Museum of Art, then the Opera Company of Philadelphia, or being a trustee of my daughter's school—always seemed to have a five-year life span, during which I would dive in with enormous enthusiasm, commitment, and passion. This gave me great joy, for I felt that I was contributing, and maybe even making a difference. I would always rise to a leadership position. My husband had an enormously successful career as an attorney, defending hospitals and physicians, one that would ultimately wear on him, to the point where he began to use alcohol as an escape.

As my husband's depression and drinking began increasing, I discovered that I could go to college as a nontraditional-aged student. While I was a trustee of the Shipley School in 1980, the board was trying to figure out whether the development office should get computers. As a new member of the board, I volunteered to research the question. Someone suggested that I go across the street to Bryn Mawr College's Continuing Education Department for advice. The director, who became my good friend, suggested that I take a three-hundred-level Fortran programming course that she was teaching. Although I had no idea what that meant, I said yes. My eldest son, who was in the tenth grade, asked if he could join me and got special permission to register for the class. So I was the oldest student and he was the youngest. With a great deal of tutoring, I got the puzzling grade of 3.8. Out of a score of 100, that didn't sound very good. I was proud to return to the board and encourage them to put computers in the development office, which they chose to do. So I now had one college credit, as did my son.

Later, a gray-haired friend told me that she had just graduated from Villanova University, so I quickly rushed back to the little red cottage on Bryn Mawr College's campus (with my one credit) to inquire if I could apply. I hadn't had an impressive academic career, but I did have something that balanced that: life experience. I was admitted and began with the mandatory English 101. I remember working with flash cards during the summer before my Math 101 course because I still counted on my fingers. The miracle of my college years was that while I was a college student, my children also entered college. My son tutored me in algebra long distance from Brown University, and my daughter, then at Lake Forest College, asked me to spend spring break with her and her friends in the Caribbean. It was such fun: I felt like one of the girls! At the end of my college career, my youngest son entered the University of Vermont.

The president of my college asked me to become the first Katherine McBride Scholar in the program the college was launching for nontraditional-aged students. I assisted them in the creation of the program. I was also the first student in the program and the first to graduate. My passion for this opportunity was so strong that I graduated cum laude. I was, for the first time, able to tell myself that I was smart.

But as my self-worth was growing, my marriage was deteriorating, and it came to an end shortly after my graduation. The end of my college career was also the end of my mother's life. It was during exam period when I received a call from the doctor to come to my mother's house, not far from where my husband and I lived. Mother was ill from alcohol abuse and the doctor wanted to put her in the hospital. I concurred, but she refused to go. I decided to spend the night upstairs in the guest room. During the night I awoke with a knowing, and headed to my mother's room. She had chosen that night to leave us. I felt calm and knew that there really was nothing for me to do, so I went back upstairs until the morning. Her struggle was over, and the tension between us was also over.

A new phase of my life was beginning. I had a glorious degree, which

I knew would assist me in finding my first job since before meeting my husband. It never occurred to me that finding a job would be difficult, but it took three years. I discovered that I did not have the experience for the good jobs, and that I intimidated employers for the less challenging jobs.

One of my mentors asked, "Why don't you start your own business?"

"Okay, what shall I do?" I asked.

"Access to capital for women-owned businesses," he replied.

"Okay, what's that?" I wondered aloud.

So I decided the best way to figure out the answer would be to go to the telephone book and look up "Women." What I discovered there was a lot of professional associations for women entrepreneurs; so I visited their presidents and asked, "What are the capital needs of your members?"

"Collateral!" They replied.

I created a new funding instrument called "venture collateral," which in theory provided the collateral for a business by means of a CD in a bank. Our company, in turn, took a small equity position in the woman-owned business as a trade-off for the risk. The source of income for the purchase of those CDs, a women's directory, didn't succeed, so the cash-flow triangle also didn't succeed. But it caught the attention of the country in the mid-nineties at a time when banks, investors, and so many others were beginning to acknowledge the value that women in business provided to the national economy.

This was an issue of such interest to the country that I was put on the cover of *Business Philadelphia* with a caption under my photograph that read: "She's got money!" It was a great story, but nobody had asked me if I actually had money. I had raised enough to fund two women's businesses, but we were just starting. I had so little personal money that it was difficult to pay for a hotel room in Harrisburg when I was being presented with the first Pennsylvania's Best 50 Women in Business award by the Department of Commerce and the Governor's Commission for Women. I was gratified that the governor knew of my work, but I needed President Clinton's 1995 White House Conference on Small Business to know about it also. I was sure that no representative to the conference would be as strong an advocate for women-owned businesses as I would be, but how could I manage to attend?

My representative, my mayor, and my governor had already chosen their representative to the conference, and I thought the door had been closed on my wonderful idea. Then I was invited for the second time to the White House. (My first visit had been a private reception with Hillary, at which time I gave her a copy of *Business Philadelphia* with my story in it.) This invitation to the White House was for the seventy-fifth anniversary of the Women's Bureau. The enormous white tent on the White House lawn contained beautiful food and flowers and a shiny brass band with musicians in starched uniforms. I was dazzled that I had been invited, and that it was because of my own accomplishments, not those of my husband. There was a roped-off area, where President and Mrs. Clinton would pass by, greeting the crowd, each approaching from opposite directions. Seeing this, I had a brilliant idea!

I went to stand next to the rope long before the president was due to arrive, so as to be in the front. When someone joined me, I asked to borrow her pen. I wrote on the back of my business card, "I want you to appoint me to your White House Conference on Small Business," then I waited. President Clinton finally approached slowly from the right. At a certain point, I extended my hand out and to the side, for he was not yet in front of me. He took it. This wasn't perfect, so I didn't let go. He soon stood in front of me, and I said, "I want you to appoint me your representative to the White House Conference on Small Business," and I gave him my business card. He put it in his coat pocket instead of giving it to the aide behind him. Then I forgot about what had just occurred.

A few weeks later, my secretary told me that I should get off the phone because there was an important call on the other line. I switched lines and a voice said, "This is the director of human resources at the White House. The president came to see me this morning and gave me your business card. He told me, "Make it happen." And so he did.

I was then asked back to Washington, but this time by the SBA (Small Business Administration), and asked to start the country's first female-focused SBIC (Small Business Investment Corporation). Of course, I said yes, even though I did not know what a SBIC was. I found a mentor and did all that he said, but when I tried to raise the money for the fund, I was asked, "What have you done before?"

"Not this," was my answer. So my partner and I did a national search and hired one of the few female venture capitalists in the country. Once we had found her, we became successful and transferred the company to her, while retaining an interest in future profits. I'd had boundless passion for this adventure, but by the time it was over, I'd spent a great deal of money in the effort. Ultimately, the fund didn't grow and my financial interest in the company had no value.

I couldn't get a job and I couldn't make money. I had to sell my house to pay my debts. At this point, I was trying to understand what the word *success* truly meant. I had changed the country's understanding of the value of women entrepreneurs, but I had no money. It was such a paradox. This is when my passion for life waned. Philadelphia seemed a sad place. Besides the discomfort of not being successful, I also didn't fit in. Something was stirring in me, something my friends didn't understand. I became interested in and wanted to know more about energy medicine and quantum physics. More importantly, I was beginning to question my prior beliefs, particularly the idea of original sin. I didn't feel as if I had original sin. Something was changing, so it seemed appropriate to change where I lived. The destination of Santa Fe, New Mexico, popped into my head.

In a few months, the house sold, all was in storage except my toothbrush and computer; I rented a small trailer, said good-bye to my friends, then went to see my sister for a farewell visit. This good-bye would be difficult because I knew that as a cloistered Carmelite nun, my sister would never be able to come visit me. My daughter and son-in-law accompanied me for this farewell and also to the grave sites of my mother and father. I was leaving my home, and Philadelphia, to head out to, what was for me, uncharted land.

I had never been to Santa Fe, and I knew no one there. I had no job waiting, nor a place to stay. My strongest emotions were a longing for adventure and a desire for survival. After a very bumpy landing and false hopes, I went to a temporary employment agency and was assigned to Los Alamos Medical Center to support the chief executive officer.

It's fascinating how life presents itself. The rhythm of going and coming to work was so healing for me, as was the paycheck, but I felt no passion. I loved learning and meeting so many people. I loved it when my ideas were acknowledged, but there was no passion. My three children liked that I was working for the hospital because I was safe. They had suffered considerably watching me struggle. But still I felt no passion. I felt like there were walls all around me, keeping my creativity and love for discovery in check. I remember one of the many new CEOs for the hospital wanted to put a partition around my desk to distinguish it as a place for administrative activities. I had a quiet anxiety attack. Fortunately, the wall was subsequently taken down by the next CEO.

All the members of the hospital's board of directors became my friends, and one in particular, Beverly, the vice chairman of the board, became a good friend. Beverly was also a Cherokee elder and person of significance at Los Alamos National Laboratory, and we talked on numerous occasions about introducing alternative medicine into Los Alamos Medical Center. It was Beverly who returned passion to my life. She asked me to join her in an independent effort to create a wellness center. At the same time, she also asked a business professor from Texas, Rex, to join us as the future president of our new venture. I could feel the life force returning to and flowing through my body. I felt the walls coming down. I knew that the safety net would drop. Life had joy and excitement again. I thrive, though not financially, in pioneer experiences and that door had been opened to me. I was going to walk through it with conviction and passion.

During the time I was involved in the creation of the visionary wellness center, while still employed by the hospital, I had an occasion to view the movie *What the Bleep Do We Know!?*[10] and the subject of quantum physics resurfaced. I heard that The Crossings in Austin, Texas, was going to host a conference with the principals in the film; and I so wanted to meet Dr. Masaru Emoto, one of the featured presenters in the film that I headed south to do just that. As I approached the day of departure, a recurring tune, "Principessa Divina, Gracia, Gracia" from Puccini's opera *Turandot,* kept popping into my head.

The day I was to fly to Austin, I awoke abruptly, realizing I had overslept. I needed to get moving to catch my early morning plane in Albuquerque! I still heard Puccini's "Principessa Divina, Gracia, Gracia" in my head. Something made me ask the spirit of my former husband, "Are you trying to tell me something?"

The answer was, "Yes, it's very important." This had never happened to me. The presence of my deceased husband had never before communicated with me. I needed to catch a plane and wasn't willing to hear anything important right then.

Then I heard, "Don't take the flight." Not good news! I kept wondering what to do with that information, for I always followed my voices. I was willing finally to do as advised, but decided to stop, meditate, and gain clarity. Then I understood my former husband saying that the flight was fine and that he had used that to get me to stop and listen. He told me that he was sorry for those things that had upset me during the final years of our marriage. He also said that I had said I was sorry to him, but he had never said it to me. As I drove to the airport, I remembered the events of the final years of our marriage and at the end of each memory I was now able to add his words, "And I am sorry." This made a big difference. *Turandot* was the opera with which my former husband had wooed me. I always wondered how I would be able to listen to it without him. Now I had another good memory attached to this majestic music.

Having found a feeling of balance with my family and a passion in my heart for a new venture in alternative medicine, it was time for the universe to begin to share information about who I really was. A significant door of self-awareness was opened to me by Patty Ann, a new acquaintance who asked me if I was a lightworker, one who has chosen to assist with the ascension. This was a term I had never heard before.

I had invited Patty Ann over to get to know her better, since her husband and my partner were best friends. What unfolded was well beyond my expectations. My favorite topics of conversation were miracles, quantum physics, the sacred, and the paranormal. I had no idea that Patty Ann would stay connected to the conversation as I tested the waters of our beginning communication. She not only stayed with me, she went way beyond me! Patty Ann asked me if I knew of the channeled work of the Crimson Circle (www.crimsoncircle.com). I didn't, but I was curious. It wasn't long afterward that I knew I was a lightworker and that I began studying Geoffrey Hoppe's channeled work of Tobias with interest, as well as Lee Carroll's channeling of Kryon. Now that I was a lightworker and had been introduced to interdimensional reality, how was I to express myself authentically on the earthly plane? My need to understand this coincided with Beverly's invitation to create a wellness center. I was now aware of miracles in my life that I was to learn to manifest by means of appreciation.

My passion and excitement for joining Beverly in this new venture had my mind racing, so I had to tell her what I had read in *Dolphin Connection* by Joan Ocean:

> So often we no longer see the planet's beauty. Because we are not seeing the beauty, we are not expressing our appreciation. It is the expression or feeling of appreciation that feeds the beauty on our planet. In multiple ways, the absence of gratitude in our world results in the demise of our planet. Expressing heartfelt gratitude is one of our intrinsic purposes, a sacred responsibility.[11]

I knew that all aspects of the Santa Fe Wellness Center that we would manifest would come to be through heartfelt gratitude. There was no need to seek the funding, but merely to be thankful for the funding. There was no need to seek healing for our patients, we needed merely to be thankful for the healing of our patients. It was not necessary to seek a new style of architecture or find out how to create the first hado medicine in the country. (The fundamental principles of Dr. Emoto's hado medicine are vibration and resonance.) We only had to be grateful for all the aspects of this magnificent place of healing that was waiting to be built. The door was open, and the center was coming. I asked Beverly to please join me in an expression of profound gratitude and joy. Now I knew the significance of the dolphins. Their message was one of profound gratitude and appreciation.

Now in 2010, I am amazed that those were my beliefs at the time. Looking back on this today, this is so profoundly my truth, and how I am living my life. My journey from 2005 to now was necessary for me to learn and totally embrace those words. We eventually closed our two clinics, and I believe now it was because we were "trying" rather than "attracting." If one is working toward a vision in partnership with Source, the clear compression of events lines up perfectly to allow their expansion to manifest into the perfection of divine intention. It is with ease and grace that this occurs.

Before I resigned from the hospital, I made one last effort to bring alternative thinking to the doctors and patients. I asked for a meeting with the two directors of the emergency room. We sat in administration, where it was appropriate for me to receive requests, but this time it was my turn to make the request. I asked that if anyone presented in the ER saying they heard voices, that I be contacted. The directors, my friends, were very polite as they listened to me.

Before I resigned from Los Alamos Medical Center to join Beverly and Rex, I wrote a letter to the Los Alamos community leaders who were trying to understand why the attempted-suicide rate among school children was so high. This is another example of how I tried to expand the consciousness of the hospital and its community. I wrote:

> As we approach Suicide Prevention Week, with your permission, I would like to present a new approach to teen-suicide prevention. It is the introduction of the term "Indigo Children." This concept might take you out of your comfort zone, but many people around the world believe this information to be accurate, so I would suggest that it is important to examine it and reach your own conclusions. In 1999, Lee Carroll and Jan Tober wrote, *The Indigo Children—The New Kids Have Arrived.*The book is in its third printing. What is an Indigo Child? First, the definition: "an Indigo Child is one who displays a new and unusual set of psychological

> attributes and shows a pattern of behavior generally undocumented before. This pattern has common unique factors that suggest that those who interact with them, change their treatment and upbringing of them to achieve balance ..."[12] On the assumption that this information is accurate, it would suggest that conventional education and upbringing might contribute to pushing these children toward suicide.

Then I shared with Beverly that I saw our center as a research, education, and support group for Indigo Children, their parents, and educators.

Not too long before I learned about Indigo Children, I remember one of the maternity ward nurses at Los Alamos Medical Center excitedly telling me, "There was another one born today." At the time, I didn't know what she meant.

As I was winding down my days at Los Alamos Medical Center, messages from the universe, guiding me toward my new journey, increased in frequency.

The Money Is Coming Soon–7/31/05

We are all here to support you. Don't be afraid. We are proud of you. The money is coming soon. Now relax. We love you. Go to sleep. We'll talk to you later.

Message of Peace–8/19/05

Be at peace. All will come.

What I realized as each day passed was that in order to create a wellness center, I needed to heal myself first. I had learned that one could alter the memories of the past by means of intent, so I began to do so. The first memory I chose to work with was the loss of my father when I was nineteen. At the time of his death, I was a student at Chatham Hall, in Virginia. It was my senior year, and I was in the library basement, studying in a cubicle for my final history exam. I wasn't doing particularly well in that subject, so studying was imperative. The telephone rang and immediately I knew the call was for me. Sure enough, the principal called me to his office in the main building. It was a snowy night with brilliant stars shining down from the clear sky. I walked slowly, knowing that my father's spirit was with me. Arriving in the office shortly after the call in the library, I sat down, looked at the principal, and said, "I know that my father has died."

My father had moved me and my mother to Arizona from Philadelphia where I had lived all my life because he felt that Arizona would be a healthier environment. My only sister remained in Philadelphia, where she was a nun of the Carmelite Order. Over the Christmas holiday, I realized that my father wasn't feeling well, but I had just received a letter telling me that he was fine, so there was no reason for me to suspect that he was not. It was a shock moving from believing my father was fine to learning that he had died. I remember being in a daze as I took my history exam the next morning before packing and returning to Philadelphia for the funeral. What I couldn't explain to anyone was that along with the sadness of loss was a joy of knowing that wherever my father was, he was in a place of peace. At the funeral everybody was dressed in black, myself included, but I had found a silent way to rejoice without causing attention. I had put on a slip under my black dress, and it was bright red.

As I remembered my father's death, what bothered me was that he hadn't been to my wedding, nor had he met my children. I now had three grown children, and I felt sad that they had never met their grandfather. So, through intent and imagination, I chose a different memory. I saw my father dancing blissfully with my mother at my wedding. I saw my father, a few years later, sitting on the porch with my husband and young children, reading them nursery rhymes. These images over time have become clear memories and have relieved an ache I had felt. I was told the brain doesn't know the difference between story and reality, and that we can replace what we believe to be reality with a different story. Today I would describe this process as choosing a different possible past, and I now know I can also choose a specific possible future out of many possibilities.

I began to often notice that people were appearing in my life who, after talking with me, expressed a real passion for our vision of a wellness center. Nurses, an internal medicine doctor, technicians, investors, economists, politicians, all began to show up. I would sit at my desk at the hospital and people would just walk through the door.

We Sent Her to You–8/30/05

She's the one. We sent her to you. Write it down. We're always with you.

Jeshua ben Joseph (Jesus)–All Is Aligning–9/2/05

Be patient, dear, all is aligning.

Clean You Up First–9/15/05

It's coming soon. We had to clean you up first.

A Safe Place for Energy Rebalance–9/21/05

The center does not need practitioners. It needs to be a safe place for energy to rebalance. Practitioners may be present for those who feel they need them.

Perhaps the following was a part of my cleansing. I'm not sure, but it certainly was scary.

The event was recounted in an email to Patty Ann:

> What an amazing evening the other night with you and your friend. I am dazzled by her stories. I want to share with you what happened to me last night after you left. Not sure if her healing session with me unlocked "stuff," but it was weird. I had many adventures in my dreams—going boating, getting kittens, watching poor people being driven with no driver in a red Corvette up a hill through many other cars. Then at about 3:00 a.m., Patty Ann, I couldn't tell what was real. I was definitely lying down in my bed when a *whoosh* of strong air or energy came at me from the right and swirled around me. It was dark and scary, and I felt my body shaking up and down in a very fast rhythm. I opened my eyes and saw a wooden chair floating above me on the right as if to create a cage. This went on for too long. I had to stop it and make it go away. With tremendous effort, I was able finally to pull

my hands up from my sides and put them together as if to begin a prayer. I called out by name to all the spirits I could think of to help me, and it ended.

After this experience and my world was calm, I was afraid that something negative had entered me, so I asked for a clearing and deep healing. If that happens, it will be the third dramatic healing that I have experienced in the last two months. Wonder what I put in those margaritas last night. I would love your thought on the night's occurrence, Patty Ann. I was scared that day, and even last night I asked that I be protected and not have to experience something like that again. I went so far as to wonder what death is like and if that was what I was resisting and shaking off. It was so real, Patty Ann, more than just a bad dream. I think the shaking was perhaps to get stuff out of me. Luckily, once I was able to successfully call for help, it came immediately. Then of course the huge opening came the next morning with Beverly putting her foot to the pedal.

I have been waiting and waiting for that moment when we would be called together to get going. During these past quiet months, three huge events I am sure have changed me. 1) I changed memories of my father, and created new memories of him walking me down the aisle and talking to my children. 2) A medical intuitive appeared in my dream who said she has been waiting to meet me and who facilitated many black owls and two humanoid figures coming out of my body. (I have no recorded journal entry for this event.) 3) The whirling darkness shook me, and then I was rescued on request. I keep saying that I can't build a healing center until I am healed. So, yes, I think ultimately that healing is what has been happening. Now the light has turned green.

The manifestation of the Santa Fe Wellness Center was getting closer, as I shared with several who were eager for us to be successful:

> Here is an update for you on our progress. A core team has assembled over the past months, and Beverly has called us together on the third weekend in November to lay the business foundation of the Santa Fe Wellness Center (later renamed) during a three-day retreat. Along with the details of planning, Beverly will assist us with wonderful traditional Cherokee ceremonies.

When one launches a new business venture, raising capital is usually the first priority. I tell the following story because it demonstrates that capital can be attracted.

We shared our vision for a wellness center with a physician at the hospital, who then called an investment banker. The banker later emailed me, writing:

> It was a pleasure speaking with you this week regarding your plans for an integrated healing center in Santa Fe. It sounds like something the world needs more than one of. As I understand it, you are seeking to raise funds from institutions and private equity sources to build the business. To that end, we would be pleased to be of assistance.

A miracle!

The investment banker came in from Colorado to attend our Genesis Weekend Think Tank for the Santa Fe Wellness Center. Many were invited from all over the country, including Dr. Lori Alvord, the first Navajo woman surgeon and author of *The Scalpel and the Silver Bear*.[13]

I wrote to Dr. Alvord to tell her of my profound admiration for her and her work:

> I am so pleased to be able to tell you how much I admire your work and what an impact it has had on me personally. My position is as the support to the CEO of Los Alamos Medical Center. Since I began work here five years ago, I have often talked about the part in your book *The Scalpel and the Silver Bear* that states that if the doctor and staff in the ER are not in harmony, it can be known subconsciously by the patient. I put your book in the physician's

> lounge and gave a copy to our new CEO when he arrived a year ago. At the moment, I am working with Beverly, vice chairman of the governing board, in the expression of a wellness center to be built on Native land outside of Santa Fe. I would so love to share more about this project with you and get your insights.

As we were preparing the Genesis Weekend, I had to go off to Jackson Hole, Wyoming, to retrieve some of my furniture. A dear friend had transported it to her new house for me to pick up and take to my tiny adobe house that I had rented in Santa Fe. So, on a very early shuttle ride to the airport, I found myself sitting next to a man who had just attended a conference for caregivers. He spoke of a Muskogee Creek Indian medicine man, Marcellus (Bear Heart) Williams, who had presented to this group. Immediately, I knew that I had to find a way to contact Bear Heart and arrange for him to speak to the medical staff at Los Alamos Medical Center. Perhaps he could share some of the ideas from Dr. Alvord's book.

A few weeks later I was sitting in the CEO's office, asking if the hospital would sponsor a talk to the medical staff by Bear Heart the shaman. He agreed with an immediate and enthusiastic yes, and what followed was such fun.

> Beverly, watch on Thursday how the CEO will present tobacco and a check, and how he will bow east, west, north, and south. I think it is so cool that the CEO of the second largest employer in Los Alamos will be bowing to a Native American. Think how different it was fifty years ago! This is another form of healing, a healing of the animosity left over from appropriation of the Manhattan Project of tribal land.

Beverly replied:

> True, my dear, although Oppie (J. Robert Oppenheimer) had the right respect, few, very few, then did.

Bear Heart and his wife Reginah became good friends of mine, and we did many sweat lodges and ceremonies together. One of the most amazing of these took place at the Genesis Weekend for our vision for a wellness center, which started as Life Harmonies Institute and then was joined by the Life Sustainability Group, a for-profit company.

I needed to tell the world that Life Harmonies Institute had been birthed:

> Please tell our mutual friend that Life Harmonies Institute was born this weekend! I will share more of this enormously productive weekend as the details settle.

Then there was the need to thank those who had traveled from all over the country, in particular Barbara, from New York:

> Wow, what a weekend. I can't imagine what it would have been without you. The magic that you brought was an opening for sacred geometry, which is so much a part of the vision. How could I have conveyed that message? The energy from your work and from you transformed the room and had an impact on the spirit of all present. I am so grateful and appreciative.

A year later when we bought the Albuquerque clinic, we hung Barbara's work throughout it. Later, after the clinic closed, I stored the collection of prints in my garage until one day in the summer of 2009, when I was directed by my voices to hang all thirteen of the prints in my garage. What a joy it is to come home, open the garage door, and see, then feel, the energy emanating from Barbara's magical work. (www.CrystalWingsHealingArt.com)

Now that the vision was launched, Rex began commuting to New Mexico from Texas, and I was preparing to leave my position at Los Alamos Medical Center. Then the time came for me to say good-bye to my friends at the hospital:

> I wanted to share with you that I have given my resignation to the CEO and will be leaving Los Alamos Medical Center on April 15. I am joining Beverly (president and founder) and Rex (vice president, from Texas) in a new nonprofit corporation: Life Harmonies

Garage full of prints.

> Institute. I will serve as the institute manager. The focus of the institute is alternative medicine, education, and research. It has been a pleasure working with the members of the governing board and the medical staff, from whom I have learned a great deal.

Over the next two years the laws of attraction operated in full force. I attracted advisors, bridge funding, an internal medicine physician, nurses, an office manager, support staff, and more. They were referred to us on most occasions. I never went out looking.

~ 2 ~

Speak Universal Wisdom of Truth

Now that I had resigned from my position at Los Alamos Medical Center and was about to launch my new venture of Life Harmonies Institute, I felt that my path had become clear, and I was filled with passion. Other energies were bubbling inside of me, eager to be expressed with the same, or even greater, passion. The universe was creating movement all around me. I was achieving a greater awareness of who I was and why I was here. The new was about to enter my life: new friendships, new experiences, new paintings, new crystals, but above all else, a new understanding of myself, my magnificence, my magnetism, my higher frequency, and my ability to speak the universal wisdom of truth. I learned from the whales and the dolphins that I was to participate in the return of ancient wisdom and the frequency of pure love. I would then learn, a year later, that receiving and transmitting that wisdom and frequency was to become my life's real work. I was ready to go forward, but there was a subtle, very strong tug pulling me in a totally different direction, one that I would not clearly identify until summer solstice 2009.

This new chapter of my life began in August with Beverly's fund-raiser for the Council of Thirteen Indigenous Grandmothers, at which time I was introduced to Flordemayo, one of the grandmothers, who became my advisor and good friend. That night, I was awakened by a profound knowing. I had to go to Dharamsala, India, with the Grandmothers to support their mission and to pray for peace. I had no idea why I was to go and was stunned by these thoughts, but I always followed my internal compass.

I have known that the best gifts come unexpectedly and unsolicited.

Sitting in the New Delhi Hotel lobby, having just flown from Santa Fe, Flordemayo introduced me to Marijon. This meeting marked the beginning of a fascinating journey and friendship that changed my life. Over the next three years, Marijon coaxed me gently into becoming more of who I am. She protected me as I innocently opened new doors and explored new pathways, and she helped give me my voice.

She also invited me to go shopping with her in the steep streets of Dharamsala, where I spotted a slender, clear obelisk-shaped crystal that called out to me. I knew nothing about crystals, but Marijon agreed that the crystal was special and offered to "clear" it for me. This was to be the first of many magnificent crystals that I became the custodian of.

The rough Himalayan rubies, I bought on my own. First, a bracelet and earrings from the Tibetan Women's Association appeared. Then, my dream led me to a Burmese ruby-beaded necklace. Finally, I found a ring, matching my bracelet exactly, that a street vendor "knew" I was to own. In a message that crossed the ocean to Santa Fe, I shared this experience with Beverly:

> When I left Santa Fe, it appeared that I was to return with a ruby to represent the love of Dharamsala. When I went to see what treasures the Tibetan Women's Association had in the basement of the hotel, I saw a bracelet and earrings made of unpolished large rubies from the Himalayan mountains. There was no discussion; I was to buy them. They were not expensive. I then dreamt of a three-strand ruby necklace. I was guided to it the next morning. These are from Burma and were also not expensive. Then I was told by my new crystal—for the universe expresses consciousness in all things—to wear the rubies often. I was told that "they represent the energy, the light, and the love of the universe."[1] This morning, as I was assisting with the space bridge for the Bioneers' live broadcast with the Grandmothers. I began to focus. What came to me was that I was to wear the rubies in order to project energy, light, and love of the universe behind the Grandmothers, through them, and to all who were watching.

There was a more personal reason that I had been called to Dharamsala: it was to meet and exchange energy with the Dalai Lama. At the time, I would have been reluctant to write such a statement, for how could I have anything to give to such an esteemed being? But as time has passed, I understand that, indeed, there was an exchange, him to me and me to him.

Our group had been included in a special ceremony to be held at a local stadium. The youth from the schools were to process, dance, and sing to celebrate the occasion and to honor the Dalai Lama. On the day of the ceremony, I walked up the hill from our hotel to the stadium with our group, but I lost them in the crowd. I was told to go to the second level, where I was amazed to find a vacant chair in the center. After a while, I looked around and didn't recognize anyone. Then I saw my group all seated together at the end of the stadium. I felt very uncomfortable and thought hard about leaving my prized seat and going to join them, but I decided to stay. It was obvious that I would be able to see better where I was.

Before the games began, special attendants for the Dalai Lama came to inform us that His Holiness would soon be passing us to take his chair in the level above. We were told how to hold our body as he passed, with our toes pointed together. Then the delegation's caravan entered the stadium and passed right in front of me on the Dalai Lama's way to his seat exactly above me, one level up. That is where the energy exchange between us occurred. Our fields were directly lined up for about an hour. It had been foretold to me that this was one of my missions while in Dharamsala, but I did not truly believe it until I realized that I alone from our group had been magically escorted to a seat directly under that of His Holiness the Dalai Lama.

I had been called to India as a receiver and transmitter of love and light, and this trip turned out to be the beginning of the expression of my earthly contract. Upon my return from India, the universe must have felt that, in order to be a receiver and transmitter of love and light, a few adjustments to my physical being had to take place. Although I didn't know the reason, I experimented with a form of acupuncture to see if it, and the practitioner, might be an appropriate referral from our wellness center. In retrospect, I believe that my experiments with acupuncture had more to do with my own expansion of consciousness and new higher degree of awareness. I captured the experience in my binder notes:

> My first session for Shen acupuncture was last week. I was told that my pulses were out of balance and the pulse in my belly button was off center. The practitioner would not do Shen acupuncture for that reason. Each morning, I have been massaging my stomach in a circle for one hundred and eight times to move the pulse. It is now in my belly button, but not strong. I am to continue. My pulses are now balanced and stronger, so it is a go. I invited the practitioner's godson and friend into the treatment room, as students. Needles went into the tips of my big toes, the tips of my thumbs, the right-center part above my lip and right-center high on my forehead. Then I was left to cook. Shortly, my body began to shake, then an intense feeling concentrated in my heart area. I was gently shaking for a long time. I could have shut it off, but I wanted to experience the full treatment. I was told to focus on my third eye, breathe from the diaphragm, and be in a meditative state. I asked for protection as I continued to shake. The shaking moved to my legs, but not for as long. I was afraid that the right finger needle would fall out. When the shaking stopped, my eyes began to twitch. Then my eyelids started to "talk." Just as my lips moved to talk, my eyelids did the same. There was no regular pattern. They went very fast and ended with my eyes wide open. All was calm for a bit, and the practitioner entered. I told him, and then the students, of the experience. Apparently, I had received a transmission during the session through my eyes to my soul.

After this opening to the universal forces, I wrote in my binder the following statement: "I accept my contract to be the vehicle for the divine will of the universe." Not long afterward my physical body would fight back to keep me from accepting my contract.

By now, Life Sustainability Group had a clinic in Albuquerque and was soon to open another in Santa Fe. We had contracted with Neurosensory Centers of America[2] to be providers of their remarkable technology for diagnosing complicated disorders of the nervous system. But I had no idea that my own nervous system was about to overcharge. Something was about to happen to take me deeper into my spiritual journey. It seems now, on reflection, that my subconscious was pushing very hard to move me in the direction that my higher self knew I was to take. One evening I was sitting in my living room in what was to become my famous red leather chair. Rex had been with me to work on our clinics, so he was there when I went into a trance. He was too scared to assist me, so he began taking notes:

> You started hyperventilating, the rate and depth of your breathing increased, and you started screaming and saying, "I have to get this out of me." You started waving your arms and legs about. I tried to calm you down, but your movement and screaming increased. I left you alone, and you finally stopped. Then you started hyperventilating again and saying, "I don't know what it comes from. Get down there, I cannot stay up here. Get down there. I can't do it. Get down! You are not this. I don't understand." Then it slowed down and you said, with your face very angry: "I am back. I don't know what happened! I don't want to be there. I want to be here. I don't do this every night. I don't know what it was. Why? What the hell was that? I have no memory of what happened." You started rolling your head back and forth, hyperventilating, kicking and beating the chair. You slowed down your breathing and relaxed. You kicked over glasses. Then heavy breathing. "I get it. I get it." Screaming, "I get it." Your arms were waving. You were screaming, hyperventilating. "I get it. Thank you. Thank you." Pause. Crying. "Thank you. I get it." Sobs."Thank you. I get it." Pause.

Having accepted my contract with the universe, it was about to show me with whom and how I could express it. I was about to make a new acquaintance with James Jereb, who would become a lifelong friend, teacher, and mentor. He is a wizard with a gentle ear, who listened to my tales of growing pains and gave strong, confident answers to my questions. He was another gift from the universe, a gift who over the next two years, would teach me to speak my truth and knowledge with the same confidence with which he spoke.

I met James because Marijon was visiting me in Santa Fe, and both she and Flordemayo thought we should go to Stardreaming to meet him. We drove south of town and turned off the main thoroughfare onto a dirt road that wound up a hill to the twenty-two acres of Stardreaming: the site of twelve Temples of the Cosmos and a wizard's cottage. We entered the cottage, and the magic began. Paintings on the walls, kachinas hanging near the fireplace, hats, canes, the smell of incense—we had entered a world of magic and star consciousness. I was bewildered by the stream of passionate spiritual talk that came out of James's mouth. I honestly didn't understand what he was saying, but I knew that he knew something, about which I wanted to know more. I saw in his rack of prints one of Archangel Raphael, whom I feel watches over me. So I bought the print. Then on the refrigerator I saw yellow lined paper with a list of paintings to be done in the future. Number twenty was *Archangel Raphael, Architect of the World*. I asked James when he was going to paint number twenty. I wanted a print of it as well.

"I can paint that anytime," replied James.

"How big will it be?" I asked.

"Six feet by seven feet," he replied.

"Oh, that is too big," I said.

Then, it happened. "I see it in your clinic," James declared.

His words acted like a magnet, pulling me closer to becoming the custodian of painting number twenty. By the time I got to the car to go home, I knew that I would own it. A day or two later, I called James to tell him of my decision to buy the painting.

"The painting will have a whale and dolphins in it," James shared with me.

"Good," I replied.

After experiencing three years of magic and miracles together, this mysterious wizard, who lives in the countryside outside of Santa Fe, became my good friend. He has such an amazing story. He was a man at the height of his career as an art historian and museum educator, with a three-book publishing contract in hand. He told me how his life abruptly changed one day when he went with a friend to Sedona, Arizona, to walk in the hills and entered a medicine wheel. He began accessing various masters from the higher realms of consciousness who told him, "You are not who you think you are. Go in this direction with your life and close down the one you have been on." James said yes. He began building labyrinths and spirals on the twenty-two acres that he was renting, then, at the request of the masters, he started painting. Each time he finished a painting, the future owner would unsuspectingly walk through the door. Over eighty paintings left his small wizard's cottage this way. Thousands of people from around the world have traveled to Stardreaming because of an inner calling. James and his courage to say yes has had an impact on the lives of many people, mine in particular.

On my third trip to Stardreaming, I told James that I was in awe of him. His autobiography portrayed the struggle he had gone through: his pain, his questioning, and finally his surrender and acceptance. By then, I could understand so much better his words and his passion. James placed me on his sofa in front of a picture window facing Marijon's finished painting, *Sirius C*. The painting showed a circle filled with dots forming a unique, fascinating pattern, or code. James told me that his paintings are alive. Each painting is comprised of several layers, one on top of another, so there is depth and a transformative sense to them. I wondered what the painting I had bought was going to do to me. As we were talking, I saw the star painting behind James moving. My focus shifted from seeing the star as being foreground to seeing the purple background as foreground. I imagined something was happening to me on a deep level being in the presence of three powerful star paintings. I told James that my wish was to be a part of the process as he created my painting: painting number twenty, *Archangel Raphael, Architect of the World*. He said that was fine, and he explained that painting is an alchemical process. I would change as he reached different levels with the painting. He said that his paintings are all over the world, and they are connected in a frequency web. He kept referring to "us." I believed he saw something in me that I did not yet see clearly: cosmic consciousness.

During this phase of my alchemical journey, I often traveled to conferences. I was sure that the presenters would help expand my conscious understanding of who I was, why I was here, and what my work was to be. I felt my hands emitted an energy, and I realized that I too had a gift as a healer. I wanted to know more. I had been certified in Reiki Healing I and II a year before. Then I discovered Reconnective Healing . In January 2007, I went to study with Eric Pearl and was certified in Levels I, II, and III of Reconnective Healing.

On April 19, 2007, I went to a gathering of the Crimson Circle in Del Mar, California, with the intention of learning even more magic. The hotel where the conference was being held was a short walk from the ocean, and coming from arid New Mexico, I was not going to miss an opportunity to walk in the sand and the salt water. As I was strolling along the water's edge, a stone called out to me. I didn't think it was an especially unusual stone, but I picked it up anyway and went to sit down on a bench to examine it. I discovered I was very wrong about the stone's special powers. My outstretched right hand held the stone on the wooden bench. Then, in my mind, I heard myself saying, "To all the whales and all the dolphins in the Pacific Ocean, give me your knowledge to take back to James." I felt my right hand begin to move as the stone under it jumped around on the bench. I looked down the beach, hoping that no one was watching my strange antics. When my hand finally stopped moving, I took the stone and placed it over my heart, saying that I would take it back to James. I was to tell him to wet it before talking with it. I knew that he could talk to inanimate objects, such as stones, because there are "talking stones" at Stardreaming, and I couldn't wait to hear what our stone had to say. Later, in a channeled writing at the conference, I was told, "You brought the stone, and it will indeed be in your heart." When the conference was over, I headed back to Santa Fe, eager to visit with James and our stone.

I thought that James was in Texas delivering *Sirius C* to Marijon.

However, shortly after returning from California, I went to the Ark Bookstore, in Santa Fe, to hear a presentation by someone much like James, who had an unusual connection to Spirit. I suggested that he might want to meet James, and in about ten minutes James appeared in the meeting room. When I told him about the stone from the whales and the dolphins of the Pacific Ocean, he told me that the dolphins in the painting would be gold. I went home to look at the stone, and the dots on the surface were gold!

After I discovered the gold dots, I wrote to James, who replied, "The canvas just arrived, and it is big."

James was ready to begin to channel the painting of *Archangel Raphael, Architect of the World*, so for the first time I channeled Archangel Raphael.

First Interaction with Archangel Raphael—4/26/07

I have talked with you. We will talk often. Thank you for doing this ... It will hang in a grand place.

Nina: What can I do?

Archangel Raphael: Love it.

During my weekly viewing of the painting, James told me that our stone had communicated to him, saying, "You have not forgotten us, James." James then read from his journal about what the dolphins had said. He was to gift the whales and the dolphins from the proceeds of a children's book the masters had asked him to write. The dolphins concluded by saying that they would return.

As our painting was "coming in," James called me with great enthusiasm and a new level of understanding about what he was painting. James said:

> There is a turn in the road. This is not Archangel Raphael. What's with the hair? I was a little bit horrified last night when the dark head came through. It was a big shock to not be doing an angelic figure like Raphael. I had to let go. I felt like a failure. The story is about the Indigo Children, not Raphael. Raphael put information

> in a crystal. Who is this? I don't know. A star priest of the ancient ones? One of them, I don't know who is who. The next couple of days will be interesting. The title of the children's book is the *Quest for the Golden Dolphins* (later changed to *Quest of the Golden Dolphin*).

I asked:

> What is it?

James replied:

> I have no idea. It will be revealed. Usually children's books are fantasies. In this one, we are telling the whole story as truth. You will have to trust me on this. This is going to be intense. The whole story will be in this painting. It is a timegate. This is my total focus until solstice.

Following James's call, I went to Stardreaming to see the changes in the painting, and found James in a state of anxiety. He thought he had failed, that he couldn't paint, and that I wouldn't want the painting. What appeared in the center of the canvas was a head, but James didn't know whose head it was. He was to find out a month or so later, while at Chaco Canyon, the whole story of the children's book that he was to write, and that this painting represented one chapter of that book. The book would be the tale of Archangel Raphael commanding that the crystals of knowledge be returned to their source by Neptunus, keeper of the library of Mu. James would later learn that he had painted Neptunus in the center of the large painting, rather than Archangel Raphael.

I was amazed to discover that Neptunus had been with me before he appeared on James's canvas. This had happened a month earlier, when I had attended a retreat at Marijon's home in Texas. Apparently, the therapist, who had me on a massage table for her water-drip process, saw a being next to me. On visiting Stardreaming later, after our painting was complete, she recognized Neptunus by the gold band around his forehead and realized that it was he who had stood by me during her treatment.

While I was engaged in helping James bring in *Archangel Raphael, Architect of the World*, I was simultaneously focused on advancing the vision for what had now formally become Life Harmonies Institute and Life Sustainability Group. Marijon suggested that I take pen to paper and allow my thoughts be written on the paper with no control or effort. Unfortunately, I have no complete record of that first magical transmission.

I sent a copy to James, who replied, "Bravo! Always listen to your own heart and not someone else's."

I did, however, put a summary of the writing in my binder. That note from the ancient ones, my first automatic writing, talks about the need to accept my magnificence, and it seemed as if that was coming soon:

> Yesterday was a beginning. I found myself accepting the comments of those present, with no denial. A woman told me that my aura showed her I was connected to other dimensions, and she seemed quite in awe of that. She made similar remarks throughout the day as if she could see something remarkable. Another woman kept looking at my tarot card and saying my name as if it was something very special. Then during conversation, she asked twice, "Who are you?" She said that she never shares with people the spiritual side of herself, so quickly. When we parted, she said, "I am in awe." What I felt was that there was a shift yesterday. I have asked the ancient ones to protect the words that I spoke at that gathering, and I requested that they only be heard and remembered in grace. What I feel is that, on occasion, my words will be shared, and that they will come back to me. It is as if I am no longer quiet and that others will understand who I am and what I bring. I ask for great humility as I go forward for the greatest good of all. As James would say, all that I have experienced over these two years is "no longer in the closet."

Second Automatic Writing–5/14/07

Dearest Nina, We are here with you now. We have wanted to speak to you. You must not be afraid to pick up the pen. We have only good news for you: Trust your instincts. They are valid and will always lead you in the right direction for your soul's growth. The path might seem puzzling to you, but all has been done before, and it is just now coming to this plane. Many who are involved have your interest in mind. Be not afraid of change; while it is happening, change might seem difficult, but it will prove to be the best thing for the higher good of all, which is what you always ask for. All you need do is ask, for we are here to serve you, the one whom we adore. Your road has been difficult, but now you can relax for that is over. We are here to give you all that you need and more. We love you and know that you will be fine in all that you do.

Much love to you, dear one,
We are the ancient ones via Anaya-Ra

Nighttime Message from the Universe

By instinct and dreaming, you can become more than you are.

On May 16, 2007, Beverly, Rex, and I signed the first of two bridge loan documents for Life Sustainability Group. This was the funding for the neurosensory diagnostic equipment for both the Albuquerque and Santa Fe clinics. We believed that once we were approved by Medicare and other insurers, not only would we be able to provide a vital service to the community, especially those returning from Iraq and Afghanistan, but this service would furnish the capital necessary to supplement the other facets of our business. At about the same time, James gave me a crystal similar to the one I had bought in India—obelisk shaped and as tall, only wider. These were the first significant crystals of my future brilliant collection. So two worlds were unfolding simultaneously, a world of clinics and a world of crystals. The following is a journal entry from that day:

We will also be with you on solstice, through James who will be in our ceremonial temple at Chaco Canyon. You too, dear one, are to go there. Soon you will know the time and you will come with another. We have much to share with you there. Be open to the call of the universe, for you can now both hear and trust that you can hear. The story goes on with Jason (the central figure in *Quest of the Golden Dolphin*). You brought the stone and it will indeed be in your heart. It will soon be in the hearts of many of our dear ones who are waiting. Yes, this has been and is to be again on this plane. There are many souls who knew of the golden dolphins and whose human consciousness is waiting for the awakening of the universal truth to pour through your book and painting. We use the word *your* with intention, for you are a big part of both. We will guide you with your open heart in the many ways that this shall come to pass. You are correct, the power of the message will come through on a subtle level, opening many—young and old—to the universal truth of the golden dolphins. They are here, and you will meet them soon. They are you as well, dear one. That is why there is the bond and the attraction to James. You will understand soon and know why this work is for you. We will guide you, protect you, and provide for you as you spread the story afar. We will share more at another time, but the door is now open.

Source unknown via Anaya-Ra

What I had just written was amazing: the "universal truth" of the golden dolphins and "they are you." At the time, I don't believe I gave much thought to the words that had just appeared in my journal, for I honestly had no idea what golden dolphins were. Perhaps when James painted them or completed his book I would understand. I was sure that the answer would come in time from someone who knew. It never occurred to me then that I might consider asking my inner knowing. Only on hindsight can I now observe the emerging awareness of the golden dolphins and how they have become progressively more important to me.

James wrote to me about the progress of his painting and his experience at Chaco Canyon:

> I don't know who he is, but he seems Atlantean. The band around his head changes the whole thing. Before he was out of proportion, because he wasn't in yet. Now I know he is complete. The band is

> bright, beautiful gold, the nose is now in proportion, and he is more priestly. The book will say that a long, long time ago information was put in this object that would someday come to Earth. It had been to the stars. It came back from the stars, broke open, and manifested in a stone.
>
> I saw a door with a lock both ways. It was locked, and there was no key except for me. I turned the knob, and I was told to walk east toward the sun on a road midday with my notebook. Noon is my hour of power. I saw the same sperm whale that is in the labyrinth at Stardreaming, only turned in a different direction. One of the future paintings for the book is of the creator grandmother of the northwest coast. Also in the book will be paintings of Green Goddess, Aphrodite, Blue Star Kachina, Saint Germain, Buddha, Merlin, Mary Magdalene, and Lilith.

In Chaco Canyon, James found a cave that he wrote about in his ninety-ninth journal. (He has done a hundred journals in ten years.)

> The painting is emblematic of Stardreaming, with the arroyo (dry ditch) and the whales. The central figure is Neptunus, priest and king of the ancient ones. Golden dolphins are star warriors that serve the light and all its inhabitants on earth. The story found the storyteller.

James read the text to me about Jason, the young boy and central character in *Quest of the Golden Dolphin*:

> Jason walks on the beach and a stone calls out to him. It is Jason's stone, and its origin was knowledge put in a crystal, but because the people had forgotten how to love, Raphael sent it back to the stars for safekeeping. Then, when the people were ready, he sent it back to planet earth. As the crystal came through the atmosphere, it broke and opened into a stone, which fell to the beach. It was like a telephone. Jason was befriended by Bwanazarias, magician of many universes and royal guide to the stars, and taken to the stars to learn.

My relationship with Jason's stone, which I found on the beach in Del Mar, is the reason I am writing *Return of Love to Planet Earth*. As Archangel Raphael said to Neptunus, keeper of the library of Mu, until humanity remembers how to love, the ancient wisdom of the crystals will be unavailable or veiled. The time is now. Love is returning to planet earth, and the ancient wisdom is being unveiled. My story is part of that unveiling. I carry the Christ-consciousness codes, which I am transferring to the 144,000 ascended masters who anchor the crystalline grid on planet earth. They will in turn transfer that frequency through their luminescent bodies to others, thus actualizing the return of love to planet earth. I carry the stone in my heart.

A few days later, James called, waking me. He had found the link that he had asked Raphael for, as he was cleaning the labyrinth of New Atlantis, one of the Temples of the Cosmos at Stardreaming.

Raphael said, "Just keep working." James realized the link was the Temple of New Atlantis, and that might be what the painting was about. It appeared that Stardreaming was the story. I was fascinated listening to James speak as his thoughts unfolded and my realizations kept coming:

> Each one of the temples represents one of the shining ones in the story. Jason will be taken by Bwanazarias to Sirius, where he will go to the Kingdom of New Atlantis (the current earth with the golden dolphins being all enlightened beings). The painting is a star map and a puzzle. The New Atlantis labyrinth, unraveled, is the star path in the painting. It is not new; it is ancient. The whole story is in this painting. It's too perfect, isn't it?

Observe As the Universe Now Lines Up with You–7/7/07

Greetings to you, dear one, on this magnificent day, another day of beginnings, openings, and growth. As the painting draws nearer and you are filled with anticipation, you are being altered on a cellular level in ways that are not detectable to you—but know that this process continues in your sleeping and waking time. What you will discover is that the magnetism surrounding you is becoming who you are. The time is now for this to be. You will attract money, people, ideas, and clients; all that you have envisioned will come to pass. Expect that this is so, and observe how it happens as the universe now lines up with you and your purpose. This is your contract, and it will be fulfilled. We love and honor you, dear one,

The ancient ones via Anaya-Ra

What I have observed over the years that I have been journaling with my higher self and the masters is that each message always ends exactly at the bottom right-hand corner of the page on which I am writing. If it doesn't, then I know that I am to turn the page until the sentence ends in that next page's bottom right-hand corner. It is truly amazing.

The day came that James was to deliver the painting to my house. I wrote to him telling him how grateful I was—and, yes, I would be pleased to accept a second painting, *Peacock's Tail*, which he had been told to bring along as well.

Cauda Pavonis, Peacock's Tail, is about seeing through the eyes of the gods and the goddesses and about them seeing through our eyes. The painting was next to Neptunus when James was painting in his wizard's cottage, and apparently energy was flowing from it into our painting. It seems to be an extension of my relationship with the beach stone I brought James, since it contains dolphins. The painting is an alchemical transition piece for me. It would hold energy while we went through the children's book of twelve images, and it would pull the others together. I knew that our painting would affect everything, and people in my life would come into alignment. The process so far, James told me, had already caused me to evolve. James, the cosmic interior designer, had said, "The painting will be your life that you created in another life."

James asked me if I would transcribe his handwritten copy of *Quest of the Golden Dolphin*, his children's book about Jason, the stone found on the beach, Bwanazarias, and the visit to the temples at Stardreaming on Sirius. It was a fascinating process of embodying the text as I typed each word of cosmic truth.

James, this morning I sat in yoga posture, facing our painting, on the central medallion of my Oriental carpet, and I meditated. This meditation differed in that it was filled with asking.

We greet you this fine day, dear one, with our hands held out to you. You are our dear one, and we love that you spent such special time with us all this morning, and we look forward to many such glorious meetings in the future. Our painting is indeed an altar, and we share ourselves with you even more fully in such a sacred space. Use that space to ask of us all that you need. As you are learning, we must first be asked before we can allow events to conform to the unfolding of your will. When your request is for the highest good of all, then our power is more easily activated. Thank you for the honor you did us this morning. It was like a love affair for you and us, and it gave us deep joy.

Nina: That's beautiful.

It is beautiful and we, too, are enriched by the deed. Our deep thanks to you, and know that once again we have heard your entreaty and will put in motion all that needs to be adjusted to bring about your request for the highest good of all. Be assured that is so.

The ancient ones via Anaya-Ra

An Angel of Change–8/9/07

We rejoice, dear one, that you heard our message, one filled with love. The power that you are unlocking will amaze you as you look back on it, and it will begin to fill the planet with the joy and magic that James speaks about. The two of you have indeed changed, and both in your own ways have a deeper understanding of the magic of the universe. Your fear comes from who you used to be, dear one. Let it go, for you are a different knowing. Your values have altered and are now focused on the highest good of all. Money, as you have come to realize more fully, is merely an exchange of energy. Allow your understanding to flow and know that we support you and love you deeply for your courage as an angel of change. The dolphins thank you for taking them in. They will love and protect you on your glorious new journey.

We love you dearly,

The ancient ones via Anaya-Ra

James had more clarity about the painting:

> The crystal in the painting is a skull. Can't scare the children, so it is round. The book is all of our story. Much deeper, much more vast. It's loaded. It's all coded.

As I was adjusting to the frequencies of the two paintings in my house, while simultaneously working to get Medicare approval for our clinics and the neurosensory equipment, apparently the universe and my higher self felt it was time to birth a new phase of my reality:

> James, I so appreciate being able to share these experiences, since they are too much for me to hold on to by myself! Synchronicity of the greatest magnitude had me cancel my plans yesterday and join a group at Garden of the Goddess Retreat Center in Santa Fe, to participate in the Journey to the Fifth World Ceremony, given by one of the twelve keepers of the Temples of the Cosmos. The workshop did not seem particularly unusual, yet I knew there was a reason for me to participate. When asked what my power animal was, the word *dolphin* appeared. So I said, "Dolphin." We were eventually to walk to some rocks for more ceremony.
>
> We were asked to choose, from the stones on the ground, the ones that spoke to us. Next we put those into a pile, which we then formed into a Vesica-Pisces shape on the ground, with the left side representing the feminine, the right side the masculine, and the intersection of the two, the vulva, into which was poured water, symbolizing blood. Cornmeal and tobacco were part of the ceremony. Only one large stone spoke to me, and I felt awkward about not helping to find more stones. As we formed an arc around the design, I was the ninth in line. When we started to chant, I began to lose my breath and could only participate sporadically. I became nauseated and wanted to lie down.
>
> I progressed closer and closer to the point in the arc where I was to enter. It was referred to as the womb, a cavelike rock

> formation directly in front of the Vesica-Pisces that we had blessed. Before I entered, I found a rock to lean against and my head went down between my legs to try to relieve my symptoms. Then was my turn. I feared that I would fall as my feet tried to find firm spots on the rocks to climb into "the womb." I continued rapidly from the womb into the female circle, to the male circle, then to the vulva, and finally out. I leaned against a rock and was given water. As we walked back to the yurt, I regained my physical composure, but I still felt overwhelmed by the emotional experience.

While writing in my journal the next morning, I asked for an explanation.

The Womb of Beginnings—8/11/07

What you experienced yesterday, dear one, was why we called you to the sacred rocks, the womb of beginnings. You were not clear then—though the words were spoken—that you had entered a womb. As you were sharing the tobacco, the process began. You are correct. Your body was resisting with all of its might the birthing that was soon to follow. All the anxieties of true birth were felt, though in mature terms. With all birth comes resistance and fear for change and the unknown. We honor you for pursuing what you knew was right and for your highest good. Your intention was set moments earlier for expansion of the soul, with balance, to remain on the earth. So it was that we fulfilled that intention. You are expanded. You felt it later that night. The clarity with which you spoke and listened was apparent. The intention of sharing the core of your vision for the wellness center was expressed in the clearest way yet. You have seen its foundation, dear. Nothing can alter it now. You will expand on that foundation through attraction. Many will puzzle about just what is different. Few will be able to understand or speak it. It is right that tears are in your eyes and right that you wish to share this with Marijon, for hers was the prayer that brought this knowing to you. We honor, love, and respect you, dear one. The new birth is here. The foundation is set. This is truth, and we wish to fill you now with that knowing, for it is a beginning unlike any known by humankind and

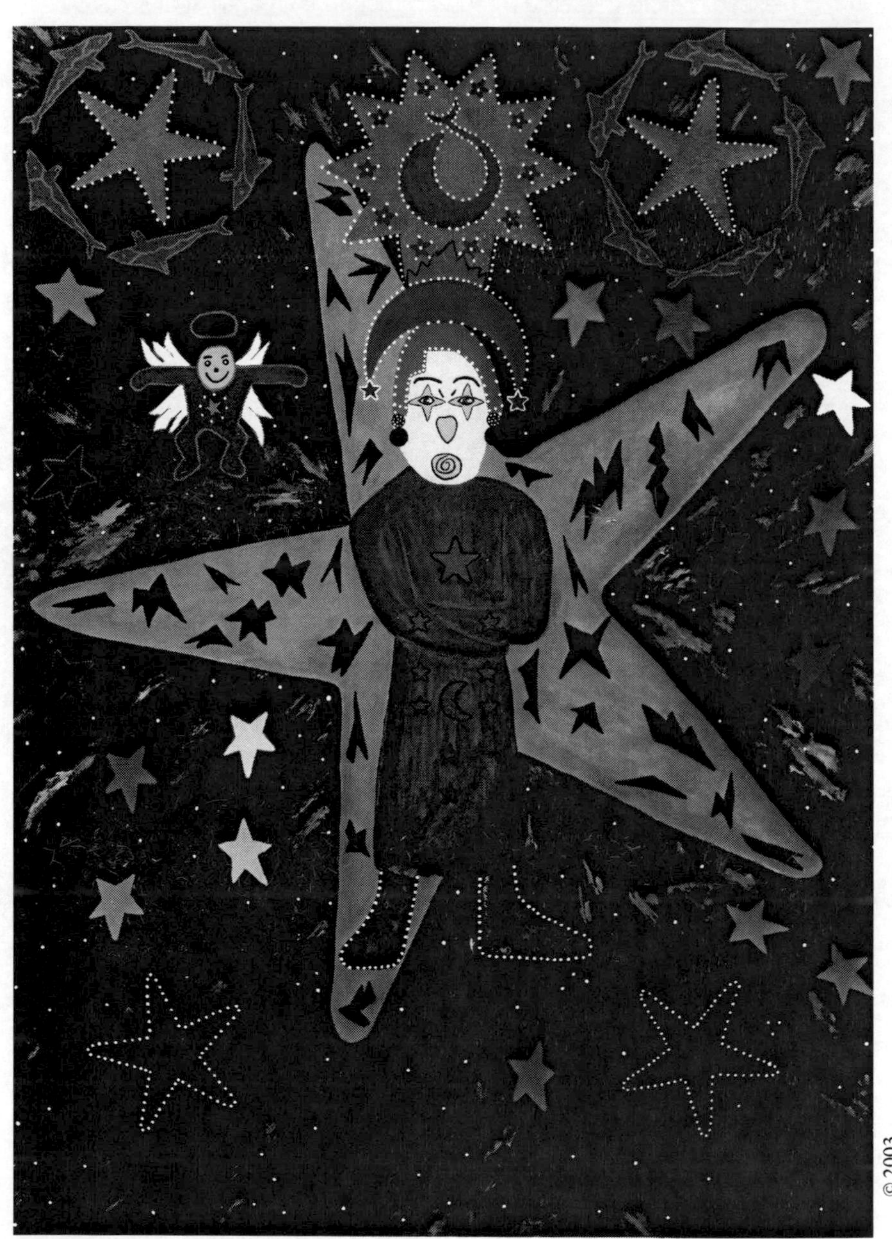

Bwanazarias.

you are the catalyst. Be calm, relax, and rejoice. We love you dearly and honor you.

With all our love,
The ancient ones via Anaya-Ra

I now had the gold vibration of two of James's paintings in my house transforming me subconsciously with their presence. I was getting the feeling that James's very large painting of Bwanazarias was to be mine as well. My ego was telling me that this was really too much!

Bwanazarias, Magician of Many Universes and Royal Guide to the Stars–8/13/07

Bwanazarias is indeed yours, and all that remains is the transfer of money. Your soul and essence have merged with the soul and essence of Bwanazarias and Jason. All is well and James is in accord.

Source unknown via Anaya-Ra

You Have Traveled Far–8/21/07

We have much to tell you and wish to begin with our paintings, both of which you own in spirit. They are intended to be together for they are like bookends, and they contain the universal wisdom of truth, as it is spoken by Bwanazarias. You embody that truth. We chose you, dear one, and we honor you that you have accepted. Much will come to and surround you now that we are complete with the children's book and our two key paintings. Watch how it will now unfold. Be in wonder and awe of the majesty of the universe, for there is more than you have ever imagined for you, waiting to be called upon. The star path, in my painting *Neptunus Temple of the Stars* (formerly *Archangel Raphael, Architect of the World)* is the journey that you have been on, dear one.

Archangel Raphael via Anaya-Ra

~ 3 ~

Adjusting My Reality

My star path was the experience of complete and perfect divine will, but that didn't mean that it came without the emotions of both rapture and despair. What was occurring in my life was birth and death. The S.T.A.R. clinic—an alternative wellness center containing portals to star nations from which interdimensional healing is provided—was being birthed, and our Santa Fe and Albuquerque clinics were dying. I was told that I was adjusting my reality in order to move to the next phase. The new frequencies I experienced were allowing more possibilities: an awareness of cosmic healing by star beings, the energies of golden dolphins, traveling galaxies, stargates as shamanic tools, and a new identity as an ambassador of light. I was told to enjoy the ride for that was all it was, an experience.

> Marijon, I have joined James in an amazing process of writing his children's book, *Quest of the Golden Dolphin*. It began with the painting that hangs in my house (and is the anticipated cover of the book), the completion of James's book, and the purchase of the painting *Bwanazarias*.

Our Painting Has Been Waiting Many Years for This Moment–8/22/07

We greet you this very special day, dear one, with such excitement and anticipation. We have all worked hard to get to this opening and indeed a vortex is waiting to appear. Our Santa Fe clinic building you have chosen is clean and free of all memories of sadness, despair, conflict, and fear. You may enter with new beginnings, an expectation of joy, laughter, merriment—all of which are necessary on the subtle level for healing and unity. Our painting has waited many years for this moment *(Bwanazarias* has been in storage since 1999), and we honor you for accepting our invitation to allow it to be. All this joy, merriment, and trust is part of the larger healing process. *Bwanazarias* will bring all of that, for you cannot look at his eyes and nose and not feel joy. The vortex will radiate, dear one, more than throughout the building. It will continue to have a grid connection to the two paintings in your house, *Cauda Pavonis* and *Neptunus*. Because you are a part of and carry the vortex yourself, the energies and frequencies will extend to everything that you manifest as an amplification of the highest good for all. It seems as if the hanging of one painting could never have such an impact. Think of it as a tidal wave. Today, you and James are creating the beginning energy flow of that wave, which will gather more and more energy as its amplification increases. It will be fed by love. We add our love as well for the marvel that has been created through S.T.A.R.—surrender, trust, allow, and receive. Each one of these qualities of S.T.A.R. is essential in allowing you to open to this love.

We love you dearly,

The ancient ones via Anaya-Ra

Things Are Going to Accelerate–8/23/07

Rest. You will need all your strength. Things are going to accelerate.

We Bring the Light Beings to You–8/23/07

Amazing! Today is a grand new day with energy swirling and expansion all around you. Indeed it is good for you to rest, for yesterday you did so much on all dimensions. You extended yourself far beyond any previous limits. This work seems simple, but it involves courageous decisions on your part that are contrary to your upbringing, your background, and the beliefs of most of your friends. Continue quietly to do your preparatory work while we bring the light beings to you. These beings are already activated by the vortex that you and James opened yesterday. It is like a beacon that is drawing them. Only a few of us can hold this new frequency that is radiating out. Those are the ones who will come. Be assured that this powerful force that has been set in motion is for the very highest good of all.

We rejoice with you, dear one,

The ancient ones via Anaya-Ra

"I see why the neurosensory diagnostic equipment is here," James said. "The frequencies of the vortex will affect the neurosensory treatment." He suggested hanging a stargate painting in the treatment rooms to bring in a cosmic healing. We were sitting on the bench in front of *Bwanazarias* as he said this. His voice sounded so different. It was quiet and peaceful, not the energetic, passionate tone so typical of James. As I drove home, I felt expansive love in my heart for James and for the work that we had just done.

I knew intuitively that the clinic was to have the three stargate paintings on bare walls. The paintings would facilitate healing and transformation: *Arcturus* (third eye universal chakra), *Orion* (root universal chakra), and *Pleiades* (solar plexus universal chakra), and of course *Bwanazarias* in the entrance to greet the patients. The stargate paintings also would act as portals to Arcturus, Orion, and the Pleiades. Once they were hung, the clinic would be energetically complete. Who wouldn't want to work there. We were taking the art of healing to another level. We were creating a vortex starting with me, but somehow I knew I would be leaving in 2007, even though I didn't yet know that I wouldn't be a part of the physical clinic. The paintings are about healing, transmission, coding, and soul intention; this is also my purpose. We were creating a clinic with beings from other systems. As the veil that separates us from a greater reality thins, people will see. It will be a leap for others. And still others will think we have really lost it.

S.T.A.R. Clinics–9/6/07

You asked about the S.T.A.R. clinics. There will be many and you have been chosen to create the first one. These clinics will be a mystery for many, but a few will understand. Har Kaur (my friend in Santa Fe, a massage and watsu therapist) understands and will assist as you in designing and creating it. Always this is done with your cocreator James, who had the courage to begin this journey for the highest good of all. S.T.A.R. clinics will spread throughout the world following this model. Others will be instructed. They will not always need you and James. As the veil thins, other means will become available to access the portal. At first it will merely be that each new clinic is linked energetically to the base one. The energy and frequencies will flow through belief. You have been intrigued with the medicine of the future. The future is here, and you are helping to bring it in. The time is soon at hand when humanity will know of their divinity, and illness no longer will be needed to facilitate that awareness. Magic and healthcare equal the new earth. We will guide you and work with you. You need only remember S.T.A.R. and all four of its components. Do not just surrender and trust; also allow and receive. There must be a balance for the flow. The clients must do the same. Receiving, dear one, has always been difficult for you. Expect miracles and magic. Do not try to figure this day out, just accept and receive.

We love you dearly,

The ancient ones, the gods and the goddesses via Anaya-Ra

You Always Have Free Choice–9/7/07

We greet you with joy this fine day. Fear not, child, we have worked too hard for too long to let your vision slip. That is not possible. Always there will be adjustments, but the movement is always toward expansion. We would never have shared the future of the S.T.A.R. clinics with you had this not been so; it would have been cruel. You always have free choice, and you can choose not to do this. But now, all you have to do is to call the clinics in.

Nina: I commit now in writing to bring in the S.T.A.R. clinics, having done so verbally with James Jereb.

We are so proud of your courage, dear one. So it shall be.

Our deep love,

The ancient ones via Anaya-Ra

To Whom Else Would We Entrust Our S.T.A.R. Clinics–9/9/07

We had such a good time with you yesterday. You felt it, we know. You felt radiant. Dear one, you now represent the highest realms of divine love and order. You are indeed our ambassador of light, and your light is transformative. Just know it to be true. Do not try to figure this out. Do not try to wonder if you are worthy, or "why me." You are worthy. Know your radiance and worth. Allow others to reward and honor you for who you are in all of your magnificence. To whom else would we entrust our S.T.A.R. clinics but to our ambassador of light. We are honored to be with you, to serve you, and to be served by you. Relax and rejoice.

We are always with you,
The gods and the goddesses via Anaya-Ra

Our Book Tours–9/12/07

Dear one, we love that you agreed to bring the three stargates into our S.T.A.R. clinic on Thursday. Their presence has indeed been requested and will add to the preparation of the opening. This is not an opening in the usual sense. It is an opening to the cosmos. James is right—the stargates must precede the clients and the practitioners. This is all in perfect order. The timing has seemed hard to you with no revenue coming in, but the process took time—to clear, to clean, to align, to bring *Bwanazarias*, and now to complete the vortex and openings to the cosmos for the cosmic healing to enter. You need not speak of this or explain it, just allow. Others will know and understand.

With all our love,
Raphael via Anaya-Ra

Queen of the Golden Dolphins–9/13/07

Let me introduce myself, dear one. The time is right, for you are ready to hear from me directly. I am Mary Magdalene, queen of the golden dolphins, of which you are one. You first became acquainted with me on your birthday as you lay on the stone at Stardreaming and dreamt. I have always been with you, but then you were with me and have been ever since. We created most of your two journals together. I am the writer for the gods and the goddesses, and it was I who came to you in the night and said that we are always with you. This is in your binder, so beautifully preserved. We do indeed love you, dear one, and want you to come closer to us each day and know us better. You can now call on me directly as you go along your journey, for I am always with you and will hear your every thought. I, too, protect you, for your will always desires the highest good. No dark forces will come to you, dear one, you need not fear. We have placed a shield around you and your house. Only good was ever planned for your space. You are our ambassador of light, dear one, and in order to radiate, the dark has been transmuted. Fear not. It was right and quite beautiful that James should dedicate our book to you, for he loves and appreciates you as well. Our dolphins that fill your room are your guards and protectors. Neither evil, illness, nor pestilence will come your way, for we have much to do in the highest order. You have begun, and today with the placing of the three stargates, your mission expands. Do not worry about the energy and frequency being too much for your clients. We are there to moderate when needed. They will receive what is perfect and right for them. We love that you will ask James to place a tree of life in our S.T.A.R. clinic. That, too, is perfect and right. The amethysts will radiate far beyond their small size and bring a special healing vibration to the space. Thank you for listening to our requests. I am pleased to be better known by you, our dear one.

My love to you,

The queen of the golden dolphins via Anaya-Ra

I had received messages from Archangel Raphael in which he said the clinic must first be cleared, cleaned, and aligned, after which we were to bring in *Bwanazarias*. The clinic was to open to the stargates, and then receive patients and practitioners. The building was already empty and the owner was having it cleaned. We hung *Bwanazarias* and installed the stargates. I wrote a powerful press release and met with our new neurosensory specialist, who was ready to get to work.

Cosmic Opening–9/17/07

We greet you, dear one, our ambassador of light, and share with you this glorious day our excitement for who you are and what you have created. The stars are shining for the work to come, and all are ready to receive the clients at our S.T.A.R. clinic, for it is indeed ours, yours and ours. Many have come to be at the opening, and there is such excitement and anticipation for the work to be done, the healing, and the magic. Even the practitioners will be astounded. You will see patients with many different conditions but one illness in common: a troubled soul that is seeking balance and expansion. That will be our work. The practitioners will provide the trust and confidence so they can relax in the present; then we will greet them on another level. In time, they will come to understand the true magic of their cosmic healing. Again, you need do nothing—just be, dear one. You are in perfect balance, and we applaud you and love you dearly. Nina asked the universe, "Where do I go while asleep?" and the answer came in: Alpha Centauri is one place you go.

The ancient ones, the gods, and the goddesses via Anaya-Ra

From the Star Beings—9/25/07

What a night. We had to tell you. You have so many friends in other galaxies, and they all love you. You have a similar personality there, but you are even more expansive than you are on earth. The time you spend in each location seems short, but each visit is full and complete.

Nina: How do I do this and wake refreshed?

In time you will do the traveling with more ease and less reentry disturbance. The journey will flow and your body will not jolt and wake. Yes, the rest—while traveling, will be pure. Soon you will be a master of this as well. You are tired now. We will talk later.

With all our love,

The star beings via Anaya-Ra

The S.T.A.R. clinic was revealed to me daily, and my understanding of interdimensional healing was expanding as well. Since I had a gum infection, I asked—during my morning meditation—that my own healing be part of the S.T.A.R. clinic.

First Healing in Clinic—9/27/07

We greet you with great joy this fine day, dear one. Your message and request have been heard by all, and we will assist you in the cure of your gums. This seems to you a difficult thing, but all can be transmuted by you in an instant. You have had faith for a long time, from when you were sitting on your bed, sad and hurting in Manayunk, Pennsylvania. We heard you, but we were not close enough to you then. Today is different. You have come a long way and the energies have changed. Your request now is heard and received with clarity and purity of heart. Dear one, you will indeed be the first to receive the gifts from your friends, the star beings; and it will happen in our S.T.A.R. clinic this very morning. The energy and healing will come to you while you are engaged in other matters. Know that we will be present and that, unknown to others, you will be transforming. You have made a powerful request of us with faith, and you will receive. Know that it all comes from you and your higher self. And so it is.

Be at peace and trust.

All who love you from all dimensions via Anaya-Ra

Having "all who love me" remind me of those months when I moved out of my home brought back many memories. At the time, I was trying hard to make a living, but I ended up spending money in order to make money. I had become very creative in finding ways to pay my bills, but my creativity came to an end. The only solution, other than selling my house, was to rent it and move out. What I had not realized was that a landlord needs to do a credit check, and requires the first and last month's rent. I was stuck.

Then my eldest son offered to stand in for me, using his credit and funding. That was an exhilarating yet profoundly difficult moment. I had always been the one to provide for and protect my children.

I headed to the clinic at 9:15 a.m. for a 10:00 a.m. meeting. What had been written in my journal that morning seemed unusual, but I decided to accept it with my heart, not my brain. The clinic was empty and quiet. I greeted all the paintings and sat in the conference room to read and wait. I knew that the star beings were going to work on me in some silent way while I was sitting there, but that was all. My inner voice told me to lie under *Orion* on the exam table in the treatment room until someone showed up. I felt restful and quiet lying there. Then, in my mind's eye, I saw many beings of different shapes and sizes leaving the painting and entering the room. Not long after I lay down, my eyes started to twitch, my hands and body moved, and my right cheek began to wiggle fast, in odd directions. Then it occurred to me that my bleeding gum was directly under my right cheek. Different parts of my mouth started moving, with my lips going in different directions. Next, there was a quiet period with my mouth stretched open, so that my teeth were visible. Finally, it was over. I found myself saying thank you and giving a kiss as tears rolled down my cheeks. Then my eyes flickered again three times, and I could only think that I was receiving a transmission. My inner voice said it was okay to get up, which was perfect, since someone had entered the building. I knew cosmic healing in the S.T.A.R. clinic was possible for others, but I had never thought of it for myself, yet how perfect and right that it should start with me. I was in awe and felt so appreciative.

Star Beings Thank Me!–9/27/07

What a beautiful day, dear one. We enjoyed being with you so intimately yesterday. Thank you for allowing us this privilege. Yes, it is we who thank you, though you think it should be the other way around. It is an honor to serve you, and we are so glad that you allowed this to be. Your healing is the beginning of true healing in our S.T.A.R. clinic; there will be many more to come. What an honor for us and for the S.T.A.R. clinic. We thank you! We wish to share more with you on another occasion, but for now, we love you and will be with you throughout this special day. Rest, rejoice, receive.

The star beings, who love you dearly! via Anaya-Ra

> James, I just got off the phone with a patient and his story is amazing. I didn't know how any doctor could help him. Then all I could think of was, we have to get him in the S.T.A.R. clinic! This will happen shortly—I am working on it. The clinic is you too!

A trip to Brussels to visit my son and his family was pending. I knew I needed more vitality to enjoy this reunion properly.

Time to Rest–9/29/07

Nina: How do I regain vitality?

We are with you now, dear one, to smooth and comfort you. What you see as exhaustion is merely your body resting from all that you are doing. Remember that our work takes place on many planes and is more than you see or sense. You are a very busy lady. Take the day off, and rest as your doctor prescribed. You are our dear one, an angel for all times, and we wish you to be whole. You are also dealing with some very powerful energies. So rest. You know why we are sending you abroad. You need your family now. You have done your work, and everything will fall in place while you are gone. The others will do the work, and they are eager to do so. Begin to shift gears, and you will recapture your energy. Go shopping for toys, and relax. The clients will come, activity will increase, and we have a very big surprise for you while you are away. We're not telling! Gather up all the love from your children. We love you so much as well. Take care of your body, dear one. It is time for that now.

We love you dearly,
The ancient ones via Anaya-Ra

The S.T.A.R. clinic was complete, and I had created it. How was that possible? I found it difficult to explain the S.T.A.R. clinic, but somehow I had created it. Was it something that I had contracted to manifest before coming to the planet? Was it something I consciously understood and worked at to bring into existence? Those working with me at the physical clinic didn't understand any of what I had created, yet it was created. There was reluctance on my part to fully share all that was coming through me at this time. After all, since I didn't completely understand what was going on, how could I expect others to? All I knew was there was an internal tug that moved me forward on this magical journey inch by inch. The principles of S.T.A.R. were at work in the clinic's creation. Surrender to the space of infinity; trust that the laws of attraction and magnetism will reign; allow for the perfection of God; and receive with gratitude and appreciation. I had surrendered. I had trusted. I had allowed. And now I was receiving. The outcome, I assumed, would unfold over time. I didn't talk about the S.T.A.R. clinic very often because, honestly, I didn't know who to talk to. I just did what I knew I was supposed to do with each piece of its unfolding appearing naturally and organically. All I had to do was say yes.

Completion—10/4/07

What a joyous day. We have all been waiting for this day. You will be triumphant.

All will come to pass as you have created it. The vision is enormous, but you knew that the day we spoke to you in your red leather chair, screaming and kicking. Believe it, dear one. The vision is enormous. The S.T.A.R. clinics are a reality, and they will transform healing. Nothing can stop them now. This is only the beginning. We honor you for your courage in stepping into uncharted water, and in trusting your voices and your instinct. You have called on us for help and guidance, and we responded. This has not been an easy path, dear one, even though it started many lifetimes ago.

We await your command,
All who love you dearly via Anaya-Ra

While I was abroad, messages continued about the S.T.A.R. clinic, but my focus had shifted to my role as a grandmother. It was a glorious trip abroad, staying with my son's family while he was on assignment in Africa with Doctors Without Borders. Feeding, bathing, dressing, disciplining, transporting, reading to, and loving three little children is a lot for a mother to do alone, so I brought a second pair of hands to help my daughter-in-law, only to learn it is more fun to be a hands-on grandmother than an every-so-often grandmother. Shortly after I arrived, I took on the job of walking my eldest grandson to his school. I was told he knew exactly where to go, so I never asked for directions. As his mother was taking the twins to their school, the two of us walked out the door and headed down the sidewalk. We crossed the street and went up the hill.

"Where do we go now?" I asked.

"Oh, this is wrong. We have to turn around," my grandson replied in French.

We walked down the hill, crossed the street, and turned right. After a while, I asked again where we should go.

"We have to turn around," he said.

This went on for about half an hour! Since I knew the way back home, home we went to await the return of the one who would make everything right again.

I might have been overseas, but I could still share new thoughts with James via the computer, just as I had been doing from my home in Santa Fe:

> James, I just had a huge realization that pieces together much of what I already knew. 1) Energy goes where focus is. 2) Appreciation is powerful. 3) Quantum physics states that there are multiple possibilities for outcome. What I am in awe of perhaps will seem simplistic, but my realization helped synthesize so much that has been floating around in my head. Gregg Braden, in *The Isaiah Effect*, states that prayer with feeling is the wisdom of the Essenes carried on by the wise people of Tibet. He explains how the emotion (energy) of love or fear, when combined with thought (wish), produce feeling. A fifth way of prayer practiced by Native American and curanderos is an expression of gratitude for what already exists rather than a request for our prayers to be answered.[1] I have known this but have not been steadfast in my being. I feel that it is who I am now. This probably sounds confusing, but it feels like such a huge breakthrough for me, and again I turn to you as someone who understands. Thank you for that. It will have a huge effect on my ability to create and manifest. I feel confident and profoundly appreciative for this stronger understanding of possibilities.

Having been fully nurtured by my family's love, I returned to Santa Fe. But when I got off the plane, my left leg was bothering me. The muscle felt cramped whenever I stood up or put weight on it, and climbing stairs was difficult.

On a visit to Stardreaming after my return, James told me that the masters had asked him to encourage me to speak out honestly about who I am and the journey I am on. Once I started to do that, they said I would soar like an eagle.

I replied:

> James, I want to thank you from the bottom of my heart for giving me the key to expansion. I feel liberated after coming out and

> stating who I truly am. This is who I am, and I can indeed speak without fear of criticism. James, it doesn't matter if I am misunderstood; this work is too important to be kept hidden. I love the way I am living, and have been struggling to find this all my life. I am sure that pain will be a part of the growth, and I thank you for helping me work my way through it. Thank you for your surrender, trust, allowing, and receiving, for through you I am learning how to be as well. You are an amazing human being (as am I).

Now that I had been encouraged and accepted to "come out," I was excited about sharing the story of the S.T.A.R. clinic with all who loved me. Perhaps I should have moved more slowly.

> This is a true story that I was not able to speak of until today, for it was too unbelievable. Har Kaur and I launched the S.T.A.R. clinic, and it has now come fully into reality. First, you all know that I hear voices and that I always surrender to and trust what I am asked to do from the loving otherworldly beings who are with me.

I proceeded to describe in detail the events leading to the opening of the clinic: my purchase of James's paintings and their use in the clinic, Raphael's beautiful letter of appreciation to me, the strange healing of my gum infection, and the opening ceremony of the S.T.A.R. Clinic. Finally, I told them about Har Kaur's massage—the way I began to shake and the strange sounds that came out of my mouth while she was working on me.

> When the massage ended and Har Kaur was sitting quietly on the massage table next to me, I heard the words "We are done now." We thanked the star beings, and Har Kaur and I rejoiced at what had occurred.
>
> On the drive home, who should call me but Marijon, with whom I shared everything that had happened. Marijon told me that as the owner of another stargate, *Sirius C*, that she had known from the beginning that creating a clinic that worked on multidimensions would be our purpose. Through a journal entry,

> I learned that there is no need to tell people, that a knowing will just evolve. James has created a postcard of *Orion*, which I will send to you, and is working on the next two. They are so well done that it is like owning the original in miniature. So that is my story, and I am so glad to be able to speak about it. I know in the depths of my heart that this is one of the reasons I am here. What an honor and a privilege!

The manner in which I told my children and friends was awkward, and because of that it was poorly understood. I just blurted out too much, too fast. As a result, I got many calls and emails from loved ones who were very concerned about me. But the door had been opened, even if too abruptly.

In November, the Sound and Consciousness Conference took place in Santa Fe, at which several of my California friends presented. One friend was having a birthday, so I invited anybody who wanted to come for a celebration at my house. Many new faces appeared that evening, but the most amazing appearance was the gathering of the Shambala Council. We were told it was no accident that each presenter was a member of the Shambala Council, since energetically this meeting had already been planned. It was important that we come together as a group in the physical realm.

Shambala Council Gathered—11/16/07

We rejoice, dear one, at your amazing accomplishment. The gathering had been long awaited by us, and it is now complete. There is not yet full knowledge of what transpired, but as James said, "The seeds are planted. The codes were transferred." The memory of the event will build in each heart and mind. Some will feel an inner connection, but not everyone. The council will never again need to be in one space. The seeds are planted, and the codes are transferred. We all were indeed present, so the council was compete on both realms, choreographed with grace and ease. The choreographer was never in harm's way. Do not fear that. We were working through her to transfer what was needed. You too, dear one, were the recipient of much energy transformation and growth. It is good that you rest on the physical plane now to restore your energy and allow the integration of so much new wisdom to settle and harmonize. Yes, the essential oil of harmony was for you, dear one. It is working quietly within you now, just as the sound bath did the other day. I am with you always and have been for many eons. You may think the signature is new, but it has been present all along.

I am Saint Germain via Anaya-Ra

Love and Compassion—11/21/07

We greet you, dear one, this fine day. All the world is alive and thriving, for you see each animate and each inanimate being is playing its role, thus thriving in its own journey. We relate these words back to those of Gaia, when she referred to the journey of the poor. The message then, as you have heard before, is that rescue is not necessary. Each stone, each person, has its journey, and only love and compassion are necessary, not rescue. You ask, "Where did this message come from?" It is for you, for the same is true of all existence. Rescue is inappropriate, both for those who appear to have as well as for those who appear to have not. Love and compassion are the message of the day. Love and compassion fill both you and the other, while rescue drains your energy. This is one of our most powerful messages and will serve you well for both small and large events in your life. Ask for love and compassion, not for rescue. You create experiences in order to grow; if someone interferes with those experiences, they rob you of the opportunity to grow. The answer is always within. Love and compassion are the best tools another can give you for accessing your inner wisdom. We write what you already know so that you can be a teacher of this truth. We will bring you more truth in the future, for you are indeed a teacher and ambassador of the light.

Our deepest love,
The ancient ones via Anaya-Ra

I was asked by a new acquaintance if the S.T.A.R. clinic could do harm. I promised to ask. Here is the answer I received:

Can the S.T.A.R. Clinic Do Harm?—11/22/07

Nina: My question has been asked several times now, and I ask it again this morning. Can the S.T.A.R. clinic do harm?

We love your question, dear one, and honor you for asking it of us for the highest good of all. You heard the answer yes and you fear to hear or write that word, but let us explain. The energy in the clinic has been altered to allow for the healing frequencies to flow in easily. Beings from the star nations can now enter this dimension through the three stargates to bring interdimensional healings. This is the first time such an easy entrance has been possible. Formerly, the frequencies flowed through select individuals, but now there is an easier channel, which is you. It has always been you. We could not have created and opened this channel without you, for indeed there would have been the potential of harm. Your love and your light radiate throughout, when you are present and when you are not, so that no one is, or will, be in harm's way. Without you, the S.T.A.R. clinic would not be. The direct channel of healing frequencies would not be able to enter the clinic through the stargates. We say to you that we needed you—your courage, your love, and your dedication—to make this possible. Your love and light are so strong that the S.T.A.R. clinic could never do harm. So be at peace; we are always working together for the highest good of all, for that has been your clear directive, and we are here to serve you. Your dreams for the clinic will manifest; be calm and at peace. It could be no other way.

We love you dearly,

The gods and the goddesses and the ancient ones via Anaya-Ra

How was I to express what was happening to me to those around me? Was I to tell everyone about the magic of the S.T.A.R. clinic? I had, unsuccessfully, tried to write about it. Perhaps I should just keep quiet. I remember trying to share my experience with a new acquaintance, whom I thought would understand, and I interpreted his look of bewilderment to mean that he thought I was making it all up. But I know this is my truth, I told myself. I had farther to go on my path of self-confidence and understanding of who I was before I could speak about the S.T.A.R. clinic with conviction.

The S.T.A.R. Clinic Identity–11/26/07

We greet you today, this fine day, dear one. You are the S.T.A.R. clinic. This is the most important message we can share with you. The clinic is not out there; it is not a building or a piece of paper; it is you. There is no confusion over the paintings. They are in the collection of the S.T.A.R. clinic, but the clinic is you, dear one. You needed to ask the most recent questions in order to get to this point of understanding. Buildings, locations, and papers are unimportant—you and the stargates are what is important. So you see, you don't have to worry about the stargates remaining in a building or with a company. A building and a company have nothing to do with the S.T.A.R. clinic. It is you and only you; and eventually the S.T.A.R. clinic and the stargates will be remembered as a first opening.

We love you dearly, relax.

The gods and the goddesses via Anaya-Ra

As happened so often, I would pick up a book and information or an answer to a question would appear. This morning the book was *Alchemy of the Stone* by James F. Jereb, Ph.D. I picked it up and read, "Stargates are the shamanic tool of the future."[2] I saw more clearly why the S.T.A.R. clinic had been grounded.

James was very much the S.T.A.R. clinic as well. He talked about just what it was becoming as each new piece of information was revealed, but the clinic worried Beverly and Rex. Their focus, as well as mine, was on how the alternative medicine clinics and neurosensory diagnostic centers were going to survive. Medicare's delay in reviewing our application caused an enormous financial drain. No insurance reimbursement was possible until Medicare approved us, at which time the other insurance carriers would do so as well. Looking back, I now realize that my higher self was causing this block, causing me to move in a different direction—one in which the laws of attraction and magnetism, as opposed to force, could be fully expressed in all that I undertook. With the dissolution of our vision, a stronger sense of my self-worth emerged. The weaker our companies became, the stronger I became.

The Green Button Has Been Pushed—12/4/07

Nina: There appear to be many blocks to our moving forward with our vision for the clinic expansion. When will they disappear? What can I do to facilitate an opening?

We hear you, dear one, as always. We know all of what you call blocks, but we call them opportunities for shift, adjustment, and growth. They in themselves are insignificant, though you feel them passionately. What is significant is you and your growth, and opening. You now are asking what you need to change or do to allow for your openings. We say to you, dear one, that you are doing it. All that you are doing has caused the current state of events, and they are necessary to move you powerfully into the new reality that you are creating. When you left for Europe, we said that a chapter was complete. You are now adjusting your reality to move into the next phase. This does not mean that you and others will not feel pain, anxiety, or worry, but the eventual outcome will dazzle even you, for it is currently beyond the boundaries of your human consciousness. We ask you to continue what you are doing. This is very important for it is shifting you, and in doing so, it is shifting your reality and bringing in a new phase. Trust, allow, and receive. You see, you have already surrendered. We feel that so strongly about you. Ah, you feel love, don't you, deeply? We know that, and you can now only imagine how we love you, dear one. Watch and do your work. Rest. Be expectant. All the pieces are in place now. Your green button has been pushed by the divine order.

We love you deeply,

The gods and the goddesses via Anaya-Ra

Move Off the Green Dot—12/6/07

Nina: I know you hear me when I say that we are worn out getting the neurosensory diagnostic and alternative medicine ventures up and running. We are about to collapse, yet the vision seems so close. I ask for a clear, loud, obvious sign that we are to stop and close, or continue. Hope is no longer fueling the vision. Thank you.

Again we hear you, our dear one, and we can feel your exhaustion. It is good that you are recording all of these emotions, for someday soon you will look back and remember with such love and pride that you had the courage to surrender, trust, allow, and receive. Since time doesn't exist, be proud and love yourself now, in the present, as we do. You know on another level that all is complete and perfect according to divine will. You are just going through the experience of getting there. Know also that you are already there. These words may be difficult, but enjoy the ride, for the experience is all there is. When you look at the *Milky Way* (James's painting), who are you? That is what we encourage you to remember. The blue dot, Earth, is your reality at the moment; move off the blue dot and observe the universe, and you will know your magnificence as we know it.

We love you dearly,

The ancient ones and the gods and the goddesses via Anaya-Ra

~ 4 ~

Next Cosmic Step for Humanity

So often I was told of my magnificence, but who was I? I was a star being bringing love and compassion to earth, for only a star being could carry that frequency. I was a tired being, anchoring the S.T.A.R. clinic. I was a magician of many universes and a teacher of love and compassion. I was grander than the body I inhabited, and I was here on planet earth to do cosmic work. I had many friends on many stars. I was there with James to open a portal to new dimensions, a star matrix on the forty-five acres adjacent to Stardreaming. I was a lightning rod to the stars, for my heart radiated to the stars. I was part of the opening for cosmic love to pour into the earth. I was here to facilitate a shift in consciousness from the illusion of illness to balance and health. I was an ambassador of light and love. All of this was revealed to me in small daily information packets as my consciousness adjusted to the magnificence of who I am: divinity on earth.

Who Am I?–12/8/07

Nina: Who Am I?

We are glad, dear one, that you have finally asked that question of us. Beside our beloved one, the ambassador of light, you are indeed a star being here for the purpose of bringing love and compassion to humanity. There are other star beings here on earth; not all are like you, however, which is why you are the ambassador of light, and why you grounded the S.T.A.R. clinic. Only a star being could do this, dear one. Now do you see that? Only a star being could hold the frequencies, the energy, the power of the new shamanic tool, and the stargates that are now so powerfully present in the S.T.A.R. clinic. Here is another circle that is closing for you, dear one. We are so pleased that you asked. You could not have asked sooner, since all the pieces of your knowing and expanded consciousness were not present. Now they are, and you can handle this information because of the work you have been doing. Let this information gently fill you and become your reality. It will assist you also in "getting off the little blue dot" in your consciousness (James's painting the *Milky Way* has earth as a little dot). There is more to come. Be calm.

We love you dearly,
The ancient ones via Anaya-Ra

I wrote to James:

> A thought: if we can look at the Milky Way and observe a blue dot that is earth, as represented in your most recent painting, then we have changed our frame of reference from an observer on earth to an expanded awareness capable of observing both the Milky Way and earth. From this altered perspective of consciousness, who are we? We are more than the physical form residing on the planet. We are also conscious divinity able to observe our creation. I suggest that if that expanded awareness is also who we are, illness becomes an illusion. This means that waking up to the divinity we are can manifest health. This is the goal of the S.T.A.R. clinic! Surrender, trust, allow, and receive.

James Is Back—12/5/07

We greet you early this fine day with excitement and love in our hearts. Your friend James is back at Stardreaming, and he brings so many gifts of change, expansion, and transition to share with you and many others. You both have more work to do together. You are ready, and the gifts he brings will shoot you forward in ways that are too magical to explain this morning. Trust, allow, and receive. You are ready. We stand beside you now filled with love for you and excitement for what is to unfold. Rest while James rests, then be with him. Be with him with your heart, let it open to all the possibilities of what is to transpire. We are filled with excitement and joy.

All our love,
The ancient ones via Anaya-Ra

The Milky Way Poster—12/9/07, New Moon

Nina: I rejoice in the new moon and the new beginnings that come with it.

We rejoice that you are with us and that we have the blessing of this communication, that you have allowed us in. We have much to share with you, and you are so willing and receptive. These last two months have taken a toll on you physically, for you have been not only anchoring the S.T.A.R. clinic but also coming to understand that the S.T.A.R. clinic is you and you are the S.T.A.R. clinic. All of this had to come daily in small information packets. You took it in with grace and ease, though you felt exhausted. You will notice now that this process is complete, and your energy has returned. What you will want to know now is what is next. How does it function? How does it grow? That, dear one, has already begun and is set in place. You need do no more than install the *Milky Way* poster in each location. Yes, dear one, it is truly here.

We love you dearly,
The ancient ones, the gods and the goddesses via Anaya-Ra

I wrote to James:

> I am so profoundly touched by your gift to me of the artist's proof of the *Milky Way*. It's hard to find words to express my appreciation: gratitude for your gift and especially appreciation for your life's journey, your courage, your commitment, surrender, and trust that allow you to become who you are. For in your allowing, you have given me an even greater gift: my own expansion toward star consciousness. How does one say thank you for such a gift? Maybe in star language—* * * * * *.

Winter Solstice—12/22/07

We greet you warmly this winter day when times are shifting, light is changing, and the world is filled with anticipation of a new season and new year. You, too, are becoming new, dear one. On a conscious level and on a cellular level, all is becoming new. Light is filling your fibers and radiating on the inside and the outside. You are looking to us again for word of the expansion of the S.T.A.R. clinic. We ask you for patience, just as you ask us for patients. The new year will bring renewed energy to all those with faith and commitment. The energy of money will fuel the cause, and the *Milky Way* will be present as the final symbol of activation. You—the most critical ingredient—will have transformed as well, in order to manifest and activate the S.T.A.R. clinic. So patience and patients are in process. This, dear one, is a time of contemplation and rest. Joy surrounds you. All is well for you and yours, and this is the deepest earthly joy you can experience. The joy of the divine awaits you.

Our deep love,

The ancient ones via Anaya-Ra

In many long, fascinating conversations with James, I learned that the Golden Dolphin Society Trust will own the forty-five acres next to Stardreaming, the site of the Labyrinth of the Star Matrix (the Temple of the Stone). In cosmic consciousness, the gods and the goddesses walk side by side with mortals. James has created a new way of thinking: the S.T.A.R. clinic and Stardreaming are a state of mind brought into the physical by means of a portal to new dimensions.

James Is Your Primary Instructor—12/23/07

Our beloved James is your primary instructor. The words you think you don't understand resonate inside of you, grow, and then expand into the new cosmic consciousness. It resonates throughout your being on all levels of existence. Your body is transforming, shedding the old and taking in the new. These changes manifest physically, which is why you need deep rest. Today is a bright, joyous day for you. Walk, enjoy the sky, the birds, and all of nature. Take in the fresh air. Fill your lungs with the transformational energy, transmitted directly through the portals that are open to you today. This is our seasonal gift to you, dear one.

Breathe it in and know that you are loved deeply,

The ancient ones, the gods and the goddesses and Christos via Anaya-Ra

Society of the Golden Dolphin—12/27/07

We greet you again, dear one, this very fine day. The peace of the season is all around you. Do not fret; rather, rejoice in the opportunity for being. Activity and excitement are around the corner. Enjoy the peace. You can fill your precious seconds with the richness of friends, nature, art, and the beauty of the land in which you live. Much is happening while you enjoy being. You have put much in motion. Now it can happen on its own without more doing.

Nina: Tell me about the Society of the Golden Dolphin. I am excited to think I might participate in its creation on the forty-five acres and with the Labyrinth of the Star Matrix (the Temple of the Stone).

We are delighted to know of your excitement, dear one. This project and the S.T.A.R. clinic are two of your most important creations and will affect the lives of people around the world. We have been preparing all that is needed for you and James to bring the society and labyrinth into the physical world. Again, you are our chosen one, and we are here to guide you toward the manifestation of these projects. Watch for signs and ask us questions. Both projects are for you to do, dear one.

With our deep love,
The ancient ones via Anaya-Ra

During the night, I got out of bed. I put my feet on the floor, but hadn't yet reached out for the bedpost for support in the dark. As my feet touched the floor, they melted, and my body, nose, and chin dissolved in a puddle on the rug. It was as if I had no skeletal structure to hold me. In the morning there was blood on the rug and a wicked rug burn on my nose and chin. This had never happened before. It felt as if my astral body hadn't had time to fully integrate with my physical body. I noticed over a period of days that my posture was straighter, as if it had been adjusted.

My human nature was merging more fully with my divinity. After adjustment to my back, I began to accept my role as a clear receiver and transmitter of frequencies from the stars. I was moving toward a crystalline state of being, a more pure, more impeccable vessel for the frequencies of pure love and light, which I would soon learn I was to receive, carry, and transmit.

Lightning Rod to the Stars–1/3/08

We greet you this fine brisk day as the new year unfolds with all its magic and mystery. The mystery will soon disappear, dear one, and you will see clearly. New choices will be made with this clarity of seeing, hearing, and understanding. You are wise, but this clarity will give you a profound tool for wisdom. It will be the clarity of crystal, which radiates with the colors of the rainbow and with colors you cannot yet see. Be patient, it will come soon. You ask about your back and again you know the answer, for you read it yesterday in the *Keys of Enoch*. You are changing, dear one. Your spine, the antenna to the stars, is adjusting as well. Treat it carefully for several months. You do not need to see a chiropractor. That would reverse the work that is being done. Just stretch carefully, rest, and continue soaking in hot mineral baths. Yoga is fine when done with care. Fear not, this healing is a part of your celestial expansion. When you hear the creaks, think of us, as James does when his roof creaks. When this process is complete, you will be a lightning rod to the stars.

With our deep love,
The ancient ones via Anaya-Ra

Aphrodite, Your Beloved Friend–1/5/08

We greet you this fine morning, dear one, and we bring much to share with you, about the heart, about your heart. Your heart radiates to the stars, dear one, enabling you to do your magic. You are the one who does the magic, though you think it is always us. We only assist you. The power of your love, in combination with our thoughts, activates events and creates change. Your heart was opened during the drumming circle at the La Fonda Hotel when you were touched on the forehead and fell backwards into a woman's arms in a trance. The woman who caught you watched over you and said she saw fireworks coming from your heart. Aphrodite has confirmed that, indeed, your heart was opened.

I have been with you throughout. Now you will know me. When we speak of love and compassion, they are who I am. When we speak of you teaching love and compassion, I will be present. Welcome, dear one. It is good to finally be closer to you and for you to know me, for I am you and you are me. The painting will reveal more to you.

With my deep love,
Aphrodite, your beloved friend via Anaya-Ra

You Travel a Lot Amongst the Stars–1/6/08

Good morning to you, dear one, from all who love you deeply. We have important information to give to you as the morning begins and the sun slowly appears. It is about your galaxy and your travel amongst the stars. You have many friends on many stars who love and adore you, and you visit them often to teach and to learn. You seem amazed, but you are a magician of many universes, and so it is. This is why you travel. You are here, as well as there. When we call you the ambassador of light, dear one, we don't only refer to earth. Many desire your brilliance, and thus you are with them. You see yourself confined to your flesh and bones, but you are more than that. As you expand, your ideas and words will expand, and we will explain more. For now, this is a beginning, a way for you to open a doorway of cosmic consciousness so you can better understand the magnificence of who you truly are. You are grander than the body you inhabit. That is why we tell you repeatedly how deeply we love you. We will soon come to visit you in your sight. You are a magician of many universes and our ambassador of light. You are a teacher of love and compassion; you are me and I am you. Take it in slowly, dear one, for we have work to do that is cosmic in nature. You will see beyond your physical body soon, and you will finally understand who you truly are.

We love you dearly,
The gods and the goddesses via Anaya-Ra

James, as my teacher and mentor, empathized with my surprise and encouraged me to look forward to the next few revelations.

As the days passed, the painting of *Aphrodite* neared completion. This work, like all of James's other paintings, was a channeled transmission of the essence of its subject: in this case, the love of Aphrodite. The love emanating from the gold vibration of the canvas was of a higher vibration. The painting as a portal to humanity was upshifting the love frequency on the planet.

The Earth Will Never Be the Same–1/15/08

This is a fine day again, dear one. We greet you with jubilation and praise. You are our ambassador of light, and we honor you from on high. You are indeed bonded to James, and you feel, in your unique way, all that he experiences, though the expression is different for you. This is a time of entry, for my energy is profound. Love and expansion of the heart is the next cosmic step to be taken for all of humankind. James embodies this now and here. He is the messenger of my love to all of humankind. This is an enormous gift that he brings, and in so doing, he is being transformed more than ever in the past. The act of love is the greatest act that your species can know. Love is pouring in through the stargate, the vortex, and all that is being manifested now through the brush of our dear James, who so courageously accepts his mission for humankind. He is well, without physical illness, he is adjusting to the enormity of this task, for the consciousness of all who will receive. This is a gift of the greatest magnitude, of transformation, and of love so profound that nothing will remain the same. Love has returned to earth; love is spreading to the far corners of the planet through this new portal, and it will never be the same. Do you understand? There will be those who will continue to reject this gift, but increasingly they will see and accept it. This is the greatest gift we can give: from our heart to your heart, from your heart to our heart. This allows us to see through your eyes and for you to see through our eyes. We have been waiting for the time, conditions, alignments, and allowances, which are the conditions necessary for this to be possible. It is now. You know this, you feel this. So it is. The stars are shining brightly, and the universe is singing. All of humanity will be affected by the cosmic love that is now pouring in. Watch as people shift—some in defense and others in acceptance. The shift is here, ushered in by a love so profound and so deep that the earth will never be the same. You are a part of this opening, dear one, our ambassador of light and love.

We love you dearly,
Aphrodite via Anaya-Ra

James continued to work on *Aphrodite*, even with chattering teeth, chills, and feverish waves of heat. He watched the painting change on its own and begin filling in the heart of the image.

~ 5 ~

Go Forth and Be Who You Are

The next cosmic step was to let go of the reins and allow the shedding of my defenses for a higher expression of awareness: recognition that I am the vortex, the stargate for the S.T.A.R. clinic. I was to step into a new phase, a more powerful beginning, and to expect miracles. My work was only beginning, but first I had to get rid of my protective shield. The physical clinics set me free to plant the seeds of the new creation—the new earth—and to be the anchor for the stargate at the Solar Cross, the north pole of the crystalline grid.

My journey to that north pole began on a trip to Stardreaming when a woman learned that Marijon and I were going to Egypt in a few months. She had received what she referred to as the new-creation codes while in a cave in southern France. On hearing of our trip, she knew that we were supposed to carry the codes to Egypt. Soon after our meeting, we picked up a copy of the symbols and the letters beside each one that showed how the symbols were to be pronounced. I didn't understand what was transpiring, except that I was to be a courier.

I had been working far too long and hard trying to get the forms completed and accepted by Medicare for the neurosensory equipment that we thought would be a vital part of Life Sustainability Group. We encountered so many bumps in the road, but the forms were finally submitted. Early in the morning, I got an email from our Medicare liaison saying that the clinic had been approved but the neurosensory division had been denied. They were giving us one month to correct what they felt was a deficiency. If we added a certified audiologist to the staff, the application would be accepted. When I read that email, my first reaction was, "What is that?"

Determined to keep trying, I started looking for what I was to learn would be very difficult to find in New Mexico, a certified audiologist. Having mastered the laws of attraction, I wasn't surprised when a certified audiologist called me back from Santa Fe by three o'clock that day, saying that our equipment complemented the direction he wished to take in his practice and that he would be delighted to meet with us. I was relieved that the magic of the universe had allowed our vision to continue—or so I thought.

It is not appropriate to go into the details of what transpired next. But I can say I didn't see it coming. Suddenly, things began to unravel. In hindsight, I recognized this as a turning point in learning to claim my power. I had to hit a wall of resistance to know exactly what I wanted and needed, and what I would not tolerate. This time I knew that I didn't need a Ph.D. to achieve my goals; what I needed was to be fully empowered to walk my journey in partnership with Source at all times. I had learned so much about the gift of manifestation and working in partnership with the universe, but I had learned as much as I could from this particular venture. I had to move on to where I could work with the laws of attraction and magnetism to create in perfect balance with divine will, and so I began the separation and closure. Most of my friends who observed me during this process were amazed that I wasn't discouraged, angry, or embarrassed by what many would term a failure. In general, I neither felt nor expressed any of these emotions, for I am an observer and I flow with events. I know that all is in divine order, and I knew that a higher expression of consciousness was waiting for me. However, I was truly exhausted!

James knew I was exhausted. He wrote, in an email:

> Miss you, be strong, ask Raphael for help. James.

Move into the Next Phase–2/2/08

You will have a ceremony this morning at the S.T.A.R. clinic that will seal the work you have done. Fear not, no one can undo what has been put in place. Remember, it is not just location, place, company, or even things. The paintings you care so much for have done their magic, and they will radiate from wherever you place them. They now have become symbols of the shift in consciousness that they, with you, have manifested. That transformative energy, dear one, is now in you. You are the stargate. You are the vortex. You carry the stargates of the S.T.A.R. clinic. We have told you before, wherever you are and wherever you go, so goes the S.T.A.R. clinic. It is not a location or a building or even the paintings *Orion, Pleiades,* and *Arcturus*. The S.T.A.R. clinic is more than one image, and moving will never destroy, change, or diminish its power, majesty, or divine order. The S.T.A.R. clinic is you. Do you understand now, dear one? Have no fears. Move into the next, more expansive phase. It is always about a shift in cosmic consciousness, and the location of paintings no longer serves that goal.

All our love,
Raphael via Anaya-Ra

On February 2, 2008, I wrote a letter of resignation from my position as a manager for Life Sustainability Group, but I remained a member of its board of directors. As a board member, I could be sure the final details were resolved.

The closing of the wellness clinics seemed to go on forever. I kept being told, "not yet." Time in a multidimensional reality did not always correspond to my concept of time.

What Is Going On?–2/4/08

Nina: What is going on? Do we just close down after two years of surrender, trust, and allowing? Where is the receiving I wrote about? How do we get to the end of "not yet"?

We hear you again as we do each morning, dear one, and we applaud your surrender, your trust. We ask that you permit allowing. Let go of the reins, dear one. Allow the flow, whatever that might look like. Do not fear. Do not punish yourself. Miracles are real; expect them. This trust is the true test of not doing, but allowing. All is present and waiting. Shifts will occur that will, with balance and harmony, create a new foundation for you. Do not try to figure this next phase out, dear one. It is beautifully anchored, and love and compassion are too strong to be dissipated now. Watch how this moment, which appears desperate, melts away with the birth of what the S.T.A.R. clinic truly is. All the old trappings will disappear during this trial. What will remain will be the core, the essence of all that you believe in, cherish, and wish for this world. You may think all is lost, but this is the most powerful beginning. Allow, dear one, allow.

With our deep love,
Raphael via Anaya-Ra

I had planned a trip east and it came at just the right time, because at this point family hugs were what I needed. Playing ball with my grandson, feeding the ducks in one of the streams for Boston's Charles River, reading books, and baking cookies helped me forget my worries for a week. I still needed to explain to my daughter and the rest of my family what had happened and that the clinics were being closed. I told my daughter everything on the hour-long drive to the airport. We talked quietly about what had occurred—a dream that didn't come true and the lessons learned. Love is a healer, and love surrounded me. Back I went to New Mexico, recharged. But unexpectedly, I felt sick, and it expressed itself as we were landing. The little brown bag in the seat's back pocket had never been such a welcome sight. The next morning, feeling somewhat recovered from the bug, I wondered, "What's next?"

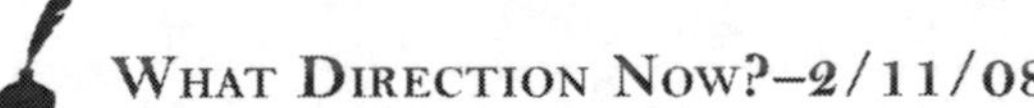

What Direction Now?–2/11/08

Nina: I have no energy. I don't know which direction to go. I am sad, discouraged, puzzled, and angry. I ask for as many specifics as possible to find my course, not just another reassurance that "things will be fine." What is going on? Is this for the highest good for all?

You are sick, dear one, because you are shedding. Allow it to happen, and do not rush into "doing." You magically gave yourself a day to begin to pull the pieces together, and they will come together, we assure you. We would not have journeyed down this road if that were not the case. Those around you are scared. They see you as a tower of strength and don't understand how the clinics could have closed. You will remain that tower in their eyes no matter what the circumstances. There is an easy answer, and it is waiting for you, dear one. Feel better first. The door will open at just the right moment. The S.T.A.R. clinic is stronger than ever. It has removed skepticism, doubt and mistrust. What remains is pure positive energy. Ride on that and it will take you far.

We love you dearly,
The gods and the goddesses via Anaya-Ra

Resistance and Allowing Transformation—2/12/08

We hear you, our dearest one. This transition has not been easy. You have learned so much about who you are, dear one. We applaud you for allowing this to occur. Yes, the moon and the eclipse pulled on you very hard, but you did not resist. You allowed. It is almost over. The answer is not far away. Your S.T.A.R. clinic is safe. It was always about you, but there was too much friction. It would not have survived without the shedding. You knew that and you caused the disruption. You wonder about employment to make money and stay occupied, but this is not the time, dear one. You are to focus and attract. All will fall into place as a new, solid foundation materializes. Do not fret. Relax. All is in divine order.

We love you deeply,
Raphael via Anaya-Ra

We Began This Together—2/25/08

Nina: Archangel Raphael, I ask for guidance, strength, love, and wisdom as I process the dissolution of our companies.

We greet you, dear one, our beloved one, our ambassador of light who now carries the stone of infinite light in her breast. We see your radiance, and you shine even more brightly from your work this weekend. You have brought much to the surface, some of which has been a disappointment, but the disappointment contains what you need to learn. You, dear one, have learned the most of all, and you know that to be true. It took all that you have experienced for this to manifest. Honor it all, take your time. Go slowly, but enjoy every person, every word, and every experience. You deserve this and so much more. We will continue to guide you through this process. Do not fear. Relax, be comforted by all who love you. Most of all know that I, Archangel Raphael, am by your side day and night. We began this together, and it is now here.

I love you dearly,
Archangel Raphael via Anaya-Ra

As I was walking down the hall in the Public Regulation Commission building with the four corporate certificates of dissolution in my hands, I heard my inner voice say, "These are your business school diplomas."

Less reluctantly, I moved into the next phase of my life: a time when I began to act without knowledge of outcome. It was as if I was placing myself into an organic flow in which my human self was saying yes to the work I had forgotten I was here to do. S.T.A.R. was guiding me forward. I felt expectant, as if I knew doors were about to open for me and that I would magically fly through with wings I was just discovering I had. I felt lighter from the freedom of knowing that now the law of attraction, rather than force of will, was to be my guiding tool. There have been so many rebirthing-myself moments in my life, and this was definitely another. What I had thought was going to be my path—the creation of a wellness center—had been truncated before having had a chance to blossom. But as the next days and weeks would show, this recent experience had provided me with a number of gifts I would use in birthing and growing my next experience.

On the Other Side–3/2/08

We rejoice. Look at you, dear one, so radiant, free, and centered. What a long, hard, and powerful journey, which you took so courageously. You are on the other side now. The friction of opposites has transmuted you to the next level of awareness. You are a new being, your soul has expanded, and your parts are rejoined. Your physical form is stronger, and you are ready for the next moment. You have learned to give up your attachment to outcomes and to trust that the flow of divine order moves for the highest good. You will be fair and respectful, but none of that truly matters. All that matters for you, dear one, is you, your joy, your experience, love, and compassion as you open to spirit, to Source, and to all who love you deeply. Have no fear for *Bwanazarias* or the stargates. They are already attracting. The energy is moving, so it will be easy for them to shift to their next location. All is in divine order, and it is time for them to move. Enjoy this special day, each moment and each person.

We love you dearly,

The gods and the goddesses via Anaya-Ra

The painting of *Bwanazarias* was loaned to the Cancer Institute of New Mexico, where he puts a smile on faces weary from worry. The three stargates and the *Milky Way* were accepted on loan by the Kinship Institute in Santa Fe.

In an email to the director of Kinship Institute, I wrote:

> This is music to my ears. The stargates belong with you and the work that you are doing creating an alternative wellness complex in Santa Fe. Did you want the *Milky Way* print as well? I was told to include it. The universe could not have found a better home. I am so touched. The energy of James's work is transformational and will be such a special part of your vision of healing. Perhaps we can all visit James at Stardreaming soon, so you all understand. Thank you so much! With them goes the energy of the S.T.A.R. clinic.

Let Loose of Your Protective Shield–3/31/08

We rejoice, dear one, on the recovery of your vitality. You will notice a difference going forward. You will venture forth and commune. This has been an intense time of repair and recovery for you, but it is complete now. The time has come to let loose your protective shield and allow the world in. Enjoy nature, enjoy the air, the light, and the little creatures that surround you. Call your family, your friends. Rejoice. All is complete; all is in order. Allow the flow, the energy. You are strong again, and the world awaits you.

All our love,

Raphael via Anaya-Ra

As my vitality returned, Marijon felt we should join an upcoming trip to Egypt. I checked my internal compass and received the answer yes. We were given codes to take with us that friends had channeled a few months before, though I didn't know why it was important for me to take them. I know now that often it is best if we don't know the answer, for if we did we might say no.

Star Codes in Egypt (written a few months earlier)–1/18/08

You will want to be strong for our trip to Egypt. You feel the energy building. We are with you in this process of taking on the star codes. (In the middle of the night I had written that the new star codes were the gift I would bring to the group going to Egypt with me.) You will know when it happens. Yes, dear one, the star codes go with the S.T.A.R. clinic, and you can see now how the magic is unfolding. You are going to Egypt for the S.T.A.R. clinic. This is your long-awaited destiny, so we rejoice that you said yes. Go to the bookstore and the books you need will appear—just ask. The people on the trip were chosen long ago to perform a ceremony and to unleash the frequencies that have been trapped in a state of protection. You are an important part of the group. You bring your own special gift to the ceremony. Each one brings their gift. Watch, learn, expand, and participate fully. You will return in a new dimension. Allow the gifts to be received, for this to happen. So, now is the time of preparation and love.

Our deepest love,
Raphael via Anaya-Ra

The time for our trip to Egypt had arrived. I had packed the new creation codes (star codes), which were beautifully highlighted with gold ink, but really had no idea why I was bringing them. I asked Archangel Raphael that his legion of angels protect my home, me, and our group as we traveled up and down the Nile. In Cairo, when our tour leader had us introduce ourselves, I mentioned that I had brought the codes and their corresponding written sounds, but beyond that I did not say much. My friend from Santa Fe, Diana James, mentioned that her goal was to do personal ceremony at the Solar Cross on the Giza Plateau. This was the first I had heard of the Solar Cross, but the cross was vital to Diana's reason for being on this trip. All I could glean from that introduction was that the cross had something to do with intersecting grid lines.

As our journey progressed, more of the group expressed an interest in joining Diana at the Solar Cross, so we decided to go when we returned to Cairo at the end of the trip, during "off time" from our formal tour schedule. The day before we were to go to the Solar Cross, I found myself in a jewelry store where I spotted small star rubies. I ended up buying three, two for earrings and one for a ring. Later sitting by the hotel pool, I was less enchanted with them, for obviously light was necessary for the stars to be seen, and in the shade, where I would be most of the time, it was hard to see them. The next morning, I heard my inner voice tell me that the large stone was to be placed in the tunnel at the Solar Cross: the smaller stones were to be kept, one by me and the other by Marijon. I learned later that these small stones would be anchors for the larger one placed at the Solar Cross, all in preparation for the work we had come to do—as yet unrevealed. Also, I was to give the new creation codes to Diana for her to sing at the Solar Cross. I shared this information with her, thinking it would give her all day to prepare.

Then the universe jumped in and rearranged the plans. In the afternoon, as our bus was returning to Cairo, our Egyptian tour guide informed the group that he wanted to prevent our unofficial trip to the Solar Cross since it would take place at the end of the day when the plateau was closed to the public. He added that if we were found on the plateau with the thirty or so camels that were to carry us, the police most likely would take us to jail. Diana had counted on doing a ceremony at the Solar Cross, and her return flight was very early the next morning, so it was impossible to reschedule the trip. Shock, confusion, and disappointment, spread through the bus. After arriving at the hotel, the confusion continued until Tish, one of the members of our group, told the tour guide how much the ceremony at the Solar Cross meant to Diana, who was leaving early the next morning. The guide softened a bit and said that though it would continue to be dangerous, he could arrange for two people to go to the Solar Cross with his friend. Diana was told she could go and she could choose one other person. She chose me.

Then Tish rushed over, saying that she had asked to join us and was given permission. I felt confident that Archangel Raphael had been watching over all of us and would continue to do so, so I had no fear. We got into a taxi, leaving the group behind. Arrangements had been made for them to go to the Solar Cross the next morning, when the plateau would be open. Diana, Tish, and I were taken to a café, which seemed strange. Apparently, the café owner also owned camels, and they soon appeared outside the café. The three of us climbed on the backs of the waiting camels. Then, back and forth, back and forth—we were on our way. Our escort took us up the road to the gate, where two guards were sitting. After an exchange of money and some conversation that sounded very much like, "No entrance!" I thought it was over, but out came more money and the magic happened.

We took the low road so we wouldn't be seen by anyone. And we saw no one, just the tri-pyramid complex with the moon behind. It was stunning to be slowly rocking with the camels toward our mystical destination and seeing the grandeur of Egypt in front of us. I felt a sense of my destiny being fulfilled, though I didn't clearly know what that meant. We came to a spot that the guide said was the Solar Cross. Diana, who had been to the Cross before, looked puzzled, but she remained silent. We dismounted and entered the rectangular space enclosed by a ruined wall. In the center, there was a hole and a tunnel.

The three of us sat as close to the hole as was safe and began to unpack the ceremonial items we had brought. I had brought only the large star ruby, and Diana had the sheets with the codes and their phonetics. Diana asked the guide to join us, which seemed to please him. She intuitively knew this to be a vital part of the ceremony so that the ritual would be accepted by the guardians of the Solar Cross.

Diana began to offer the items she had brought, and I noticed that she pulled out the papers I had given her. I thanked her for singing the codes at the Solar Cross, but apparently, I had not expressed myself clearly in the morning, for Diana thought she was to offer the codes, not sing them. Taken aback, she regrouped quickly and pulled out a crystal. She explained that the Isis crystal, when placed in front of her lips, would

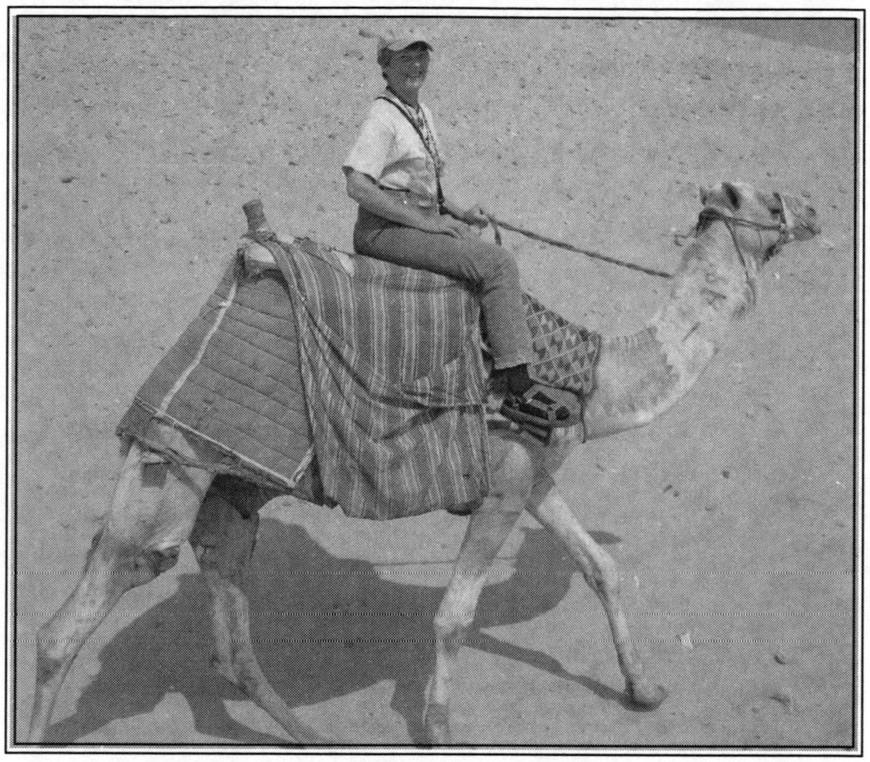

Going to the Solar Cross.

transform the sounds she was about to make into their perfect expression. Diana invoked the spirits of place to transport our offerings to their proper destination, because she felt that we had not been taken to the Solar Cross. All was in order, and Diana began to sing the harmonies of the gods and goddesses. Tears poured down my face as I listened to the most enchanting sounds I had ever heard. I knew that something galactic was happening. It was as if the planet and all the beings in the cosmos had been anticipating the singing into creation of the new star codes.

On completion of the ceremony, I dropped the ruby into the tunnel, then we rose in reverence and silently returned to our group on their way to dinner on the Nile. Everyone applauded as we entered the bus, and one member of the group told of a prophecy about three people on the Giza Plateau who would open a portal. She believed that it had been done by us that evening at the Solar Cross. I stood up on the bus, and over the loudspeaker I thanked everyone for their love and support while we were in the desert. I tried to explain the monumental event, but I am sure that it was my uncontrollable emotion, rather than my words, that conveyed the message. All knew that in the desert moonlight three women had brought a gift of substantial change by singing the new codes of creation for planet earth into existence.

Diana had returned home, but quickly wrote to those who remained in Egypt.

> First of all, I want to thank every one of you for making possible the completion of some of the most important work I've ever undertaken in this lifetime. I've received several beautiful confirmations that we were successful on many fronts, the most important one being the seeding we did at the Solar Cross at the time of the new moon, the most auspicious time for "planting new crops" if they are to sprout, grow, and flower well. Congratulations and *Ya Wahad* to all! Tish has informed me that we were taken somewhere other than the Solar Cross. I knew this while we were there, since it didn't resemble the place I went to in 2000. But I

Tunnel at the Solar Cross.

was instructed to go ahead with our work anyway, offering it to Seshat and the guardians of the appointed place. I knew that they would "relocate" the offerings appropriately and that this was a safer way to do it. I don't know where you all went the next day or what occurred, but I was feeling you all very powerfully on my way home in the plane, so I knew that too was successful. There were three separate teams given the same task to complete. God is never stingy, and there must always be a backup plan, plan B, plan C, etc. I've been informed that all of us were successful.

The New World–5/13/08

Nina: I am grateful for my safety and that of my fellow travelers. I ask to better understand why I went to Egypt and how the trip will influence my path. Thank you to the protecting angels!

We hear you, dear one, and rejoice in your safe return as well. We never left your side as you traveled from one event to the next. You are correct, you were never in danger, as there was a wide shield around you. You ask for meaning to unfold. That was the message you received, "Know who you are. Go forth and be who you are." So you did. This knowing will never diminish, but grow stronger with each day. You were the protective shield for the others. Your light radiates far afield. You brought the new star codes to the place of seeding. It matters not the actual location, for intention was the tool. The universe heard the chanting, and your tears were the reflection of all who rejoiced throughout the galaxy. You carried their joy and jubilation, and passionately expressed it. Indeed your reality will never be the same. The new creation codes have been spoken and now they resonate throughout space. This cannot be undone. There is indeed more. You will hear from us and more fully understand. Be at peace now, dear one, ambassador of light. Your work is only just beginning as we enter this new earth. You are the architect who has received the cornerstones on which much will now be built. Rest and know that we are well pleased with you.

Our deep love,

Cosmic Mother via Anaya-Ra

We Are Well Pleased–5/22/08

Your journey of expansion has been rapid and will accelerate now that you have returned from your mission. The energy of the Solar Cross is expanding exponentially and will affect all of humankind. The rubies on your crystal altar and the one with Marijon are the anchors. The tones travel throughout the universe in an unending ripple, causing change with their vibration. The sounds are new and all of creation understands what is to come as a result of their existence. This is not a time of doing for you. You are to be a strong, solid pillar of majesty. We all rejoice and are well pleased that the seeding of the new creation, the new earth, has come to pass.

With our deep love,

Cosmic Mother via Anaya-Ra

Your Thoughts Are a Symphony of Universal Song–5/23/08

Nina: Thank you!

We thank *you*, dear one, for who you are and what you now understand is your path. It has been a long journey in earth years to get to this point. We heard you state that you would be the pillar of majesty, the anchor for the stargate at the Solar Cross for the new creation and that you trusted we would protect and provide to support you. We accept, as you have accepted. Is this music to your ears? Then please know how your thoughts are a symphony of universal song to our ears.

With our deep love and devotion,

The ancient ones via Anaya-Ra

Solar Cross–
Drunvalo Melchizedek's Description

Thoth, a being named Ra, and a being named Araragat flew to a place in what is now Egypt, to the area now called the Giza plateau. Thoth and his friends went to the very spot where the unity-consciousness vortex exited the earth, a point about a mile away from where the Great Pyramid sits in the desert today. Centered right over the axis of this vortex on the earth, they created a hole extending approximately one mile into the earth, and they lined it with brick. Once the hole aligned with the unity axis was created, they mapped the ten golden-mean spirals that emerged from the hole and located it where they moved above the earth. They used the hole as the axis, starting far and extending into space. One of the spirals exited the earth not far from where the Great Pyramid would be built. Once they found the hole, they built a little stone building in front of it; that building is the key to the entire Giza complex. Then they built the Great Pyramid.

The apex of the Great Pyramid, if the capstone were in place, sat exactly on the curve of the spiral. They lined up the center of the hole with the south face of the stone building and the north face of the Great Pyramid. I, Drunvalo, have seen the axis hole and the building with my own eyes. I consider it to be the most important place in all of Egypt and so does Edgar Cayce's A.R.E. There's also another hole about a city block away from the first spiral, and this spiral starts out a little differently, but then slowly, asymptotically, superimposes itself over the first spiral. So these two completed spirals defined the axis of what would eventually become the unity-consciousness grid around the earth.

Thoth, Ra, and Araragat mapped where these two energy lines curved and crossed each other in over 83,000 places on the surface of the earth. In the fourth dimension—one dimension higher than this one—they constructed an entire network of buildings and structures over the whole planet, placing them on the nodes of this energy matrix. All of these structures were laid out with the proportions of either the golden mean or Fibonacci spirals, and all were mathematically referred back to that single point in Egypt now called the Solar Cross. Eventually, researchers will see that this spot in Egypt is the point from which all the other sacred sites were calculated. This Egyptian area is the north pole of the unity-consciousness grid. On the other side of the planet, out in the South Pacific in the Tahitian Islands, is a little island called Moorea where the south pole of the grid is located. All the sacred sites are connected to the Egyptian pole, and they're all interlinked through the central axis leading to Moorea. It's a torus, of course.[1]

~ 6 ~

Masters of the Blue Crystal Skull

As an anchor for the stargate at the Solar Cross, I learned from my new friends, the Council of Thirteen, that I am also the vril energy (the knowledge and wisdom of the universe) for a portal at Stardreaming. I came to further understand that the Temple of the Stone, the megalabyrinth we will build, will be the portal for the blue star matrix. The matrix contains new light codes of innocent love and compassion, an understanding of oneness with Source, and cosmic consciousness. Those who will choose to enter will hold that consciousness supported by a balanced male and female divine energy. These light codes will enter the labyrinth by means of the vril rod, go into the earth, and expand by means of the matrix, making earth one with the stars: the manifestation of S.T.A.R. consciousness. On the summer solstice I became a portal for the merging of humanity with that cosmic consciousness, a process that was amplified by the electrical charge of a torrential thunder and lightning storm created by the council in the Magical Forest.

It all began as I asked myself, "Now that I have returned from a self-empowering trip to Egypt, closed down the wellness centers, and filed all the dissolution papers, what am I to do?" Should I try to get a minimum-wage job in Santa Fe? Should I join the hoards of overqualified talent in the city, competing for very few jobs? Should I sit in my red leather chair and wait for the universe to provide something that would inspire passion? What was the answer? I just knew that I was rested and ready.

It felt like it was time to get to work. I had pulled the rune Wunjo, and received this message: "This rune is a fruit-bearing branch. The term of travail has ended, and you have come to yourself in some regard. The shift that was due has occurred; now you can freely receive Wunjo's blessings, whether they be in material gain in your emotional life or in a heightened sense of your own well-being. This is an alchemical moment in which understanding is transmuted from knowledge. The knowledge itself was a necessary but not sufficient condition; now you can rejoice, having been carried across the gap by the will of heaven. Joyousness accompanies new energy that was blocked until now."

While waiting for the next new adventure in my life to appear, I got out of my red leather chair and went to the movies to see *Indiana Jones and the Kingdom of the Crystal Skull*. At the time, I had no idea that I would later make the acquaintance of the Council of Thirteen and then learn I was its fountainhead and ambassador.

Council of Thirteen–5/23/08

We greet you this fine day and wish to share with you, dear one, why you were so moved and exhausted after seeing our movie *Indiana Jones and the Kingdom of the Crystal Skull*. Yes, we made it with Lucas and Spielberg. When you saw the council, your breathing slowed and your heart expanded because you already know the thirteen members of the Council of Alpha Centauri. You visit us often. We will guide you with Archangel Raphael and all who love you, especially the whales and the dolphins, to bring into physical space our portal at Stardreaming, the megalabyrinth. You know it. You can see it. This is your next focus, your next manifestation. The S.T.A.R. clinic, the portal at the Solar Cross, and other portals are all linked in the new blue star matrix. Your work will flow with ease. We are here to protect and guide you, and we ask that you rest and care for your physical being. All that you and James need will appear at just the right moment. Have neither fear nor doubt. The two of you are perfect partners for this project, and each will magnify the gifts of the other. He trusts you and knows that you are beloved in the universe. Listen carefully, for we will speak through others as well as to you directly. It is time, dear, to tell James of the Solar Cross, for it now connects through you to Stardreaming. Your earthly well-being is being cared for. The divas of the earth, air, matter, and more are all aware of how important it is to guard and care for you, dear one. Enjoy the next and final phase of your earthly existence.

With our deep love,
The Council of Thirteen via Anaya-Ra

All Our Party Favors Are Out–6/2/08

We're getting close to celebration time. All our party favors are out and ready to be used. You see how much we love and honor you, dear one, and this is a big occasion for us as well. We are glad you will be in Chaco Canyon. We will all be there with you. We have much to share with you on all dimensions in that great sacred space. Listen with all your senses, and talk to the divas of all that you see and sense. The sun will bring you the radiant energy of the universe as our greatest gift to you. The whales and dolphins will be there.

With our deep love,
The ancient ones via Anaya-Ra

For my birthday, I gave myself the gift of a trip to Chaco Canyon. Before I left, James asked if I would stop by Stardreaming to see a painting that he was working on. That was how he got me there, but it wasn't his reason for wanting to see me. He told me the masters wanted him to ask me to join him and Stardreaming to assist with the preservation, maintenance, and expansion of Stardreaming. What was fascinating was that I had preknowledge that this might happen and had discussed it in my journal on May 23, 2008.

What Did You Think of Our Surprise?–6/2/08, Cuba, New Mexico

What do you think of our surprise? Were you surprised? You seemed so calm. We have been excited for you to learn that we and James have chosen you to be the president of the Golden Dolphin Society Trust. The plan is huge, but we will provide guidance. The task will be simple for you, since it uses all of your skills, and you will never be on your own. You will be guided and all your questions will be answered when you ask with sincerity of heart. Soon the world will know the Golden Dolphin Society Trust and many will come to Stardreaming as a result. The transformational vortex, megalabyrinth, will go up quickly, and the funding will come with ease!

We love you dearly, happy birthday.

The ancient ones, the whales and the dolphins via Anaya-Ra

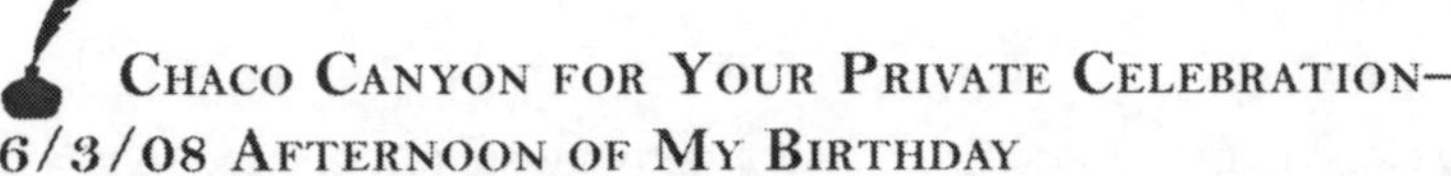

Chaco Canyon for Your Private Celebration–6/3/08 Afternoon of My Birthday

Happy birthday, dear one. We rejoice that you have chosen Chaco Canyon for your private celebration, but you know, this event it is not private at all. We are all here, and you feel and know that to be true. As you walked down Pueblo Bonito trail, there were thousands who gathered on each side to cheer you and rejoice on your return. You were a central part of all ceremony in each kiva. You did indeed receive a powerful transmission from the rock on which you lay this morning. In this reality, the secrets and love of the entire canyon are yours now. We also heard your prayers of thanks and entreaty. We will be with you each moment in a more expansive manner, for we are able to speak to you more often and more clearly. All you have to do is tune in, and we are there. As our new president elect, we ask you to have no fear. The trust is complete, the structure built, the megalabyrinth standing mightily. Many are coming, transformations are powerful, and the new earth connects all the points of the blue star matrix. Heaven rejoices. The seals are open. All will come to be.

With our great love,

The whales and the dolphins via Anaya-Ra

I completed my visit to Chaco Canyon and returned to the bed-and-breakfast in the little town of Cuba, where I was staying. I went to the back of the property and walked across a field to get to the lake. I found a log to sit on, and then felt compelled to take out my journal and write. I heard the words, "Get out your journal, we have more to tell you, but this time in a mystical realm."

Step Forth with Your Rod–6/4/08

We are your protectors, sent to be with you in this incarnation, dear one. We have been with you your entire earthly existence, but you have not known of us, since your expansion as a human was not advanced enough. But now in the quiet of this ranch in Cuba, New Mexico, we share with you our presence.

You cannot yet see us, but that will change, and you will know all that we are, for it is now important that you do so. You will call on us often for specific help in your new role as caretaker of Stardreaming. We are the masters of the blue crystal skull and have now come forth in our fullness to you, with all the power and truth of the divine to sharpen your powers. You need only ask, you need only dream, you need only believe that this is so, and so it shall be. What you have considered hardships in the past have been gifts and tools given for you to now access. It is time for you to move on from this quiet place, head home, and process all that you have acquired over these few days. You will know the moment to step forth with your rod that we have given you. It will contain all the magic you need.

Our deep love,
The Council of Thirteen via Anaya-Ra

What rod? I remembered that in the book I was currently reading there was something about Tutankhamun's and Moses's rods. I went leafing through the pages hoping I had underlined the passages for quick reference. Maybe it was a synchronistic clue to help me with this puzzle.

In *Secret Places of the Lion* by George H. Williamson, I found my clues:

> Maya had made a visit to the secret pyramidal subterranean chambers and brought an ancient vril stick to Tutankhamun. This was further protection for the boy king. Existing statues of him show him holding strange "rods."[1]

Later the book talks about Moses's rod and states that vril energy is especially strong at the Fibonacci spiral in Giza. So with that in mind, I wondered, "What rod has the council given me?" I looked around the lake, where I had received the message, and nothing shouted at me. I returned to my car, and there it was: my father's walking stick! I usually never take it except to walk around my block at home. Something had made me bring it to Chaco Canyon.

Your Father ... Is a Member of the Council of Thirteen–6/5/08

Well done, dear one. You have absorbed exactly what you need. You understand our gifts and the magical power of the "rod." Now we will teach you how to use it and when not to use it. Listen carefully to your voices and sit before our painting often to listen. Listen for seconds or hours. That was some birthday. We had fun watching you receive the gifts. Now you know who your father is. Amazing, don't you think? He was a quiet man, who was really only present for you and the transfer of the rod. He was uncomfortable on earth and only came for you, to birth you, protect you, and leave when you were strong enough. He loved you profoundly, for he was us and we were him. You didn't want to accept that information when it came in yesterday, so we are having you receive it in the method you trust: your journal. We say it again: your father is a member of the Council of Thirteen. Now you know why thirteen was his favorite number, and why he gave your mother the gold bracelet with the large thirteen on it. He is our seventh in the circle of thirteen. There is no hierarchy, just position. He has returned to join us and watches with such joy your discovery of the rod. Now let us talk about the Solar Cross. (I stopped writing, in disbelief.) You are too funny. You are afraid to write more, for you have no words of your own to put on the paper. Of course, you were present when the Great Pyramid was built. You were present when the chambers below were created and filled with the knowledge and wisdom of the universe. You were present with the rod. You gave the rod to the chamber. You instilled the plateau with the vril energy. You did that, dear one. You are the rod; you are the energy. It comes from you and is transferred to the spiral, to Stonehenge, and to all the sacred sites around the planet. (Oh, my God.) You couldn't make these words up, dear one. They are the truth of the universe, and you are now strong enough to hear and receive them. You are attracted to Stardreaming because you are again bringing the vril energy to a very sacred place. Only you can do this. Accept the knowledge that you chose to incarnate to do it. Sit quietly, allow and receive this information for it is the truth of the universe; now you know.

With our deepest love,

The Council of Thirteen via Anaya-Ra

I wasn't sure what to make of what I had just written. Logically it made no sense, but I felt an opening and a little bit of truth filtering into my conscious awareness. How had the council known about my mother's gold bracelet with the thirteen on it? Or was that me making all of this up?

To mother, I am sure, the gold bracelet was just a sentimental, lovely gift. When my father met my mother, she was a beautiful young woman from a little town in Delaware, who came to the big city to train to be a nurse. She met a dapper Philadelphia gentleman and had a fairy tale wedding. She soon became a very proper Philadelphian who got upset when my father wore one green sock and one blue sock. Mother taught me manners, grace, sophistication, a love for the arts, appreciation of world travel, and the refinement of gentle society. It was because of her that I felt at ease with the most distinguished of company. I can't imagine what she would be thinking about her husband being on Alpha Centauri.

Surely a simple walking stick couldn't be what the Council of Thirteen said it was. Perhaps it was symbolic. I remembered I moved so few things from Philadelphia to New Mexico—most of my possessions had been given to my children, but I wanted my father's Irish briar walking stick to be with me. He always used it on his silent daily walks. He was a very quiet man, who was in pain from the effects of contracting polio when he was very young. Besides walking, he liked to read and listen to classical music while sitting in a pine ladder-back chair that supported his back. He also would go down into the basement room he had designated just for himself. It was off limits to the rest of the family because of something about the Rosicrucians, but that was all I knew. He did tell us that if we couldn't find him one day, it would be because he had gone with the ETs. None of us paid much attention to that.

When I returned to Santa Fe, I put those mysterious thoughts aside and began to work on my new assignment at Stardreaming. I wrote to a friend in Philadelphia, asking her to connect me with the former vice president of the Mellon Foundation, an acquaintance from Bryn Mawr College. My thought was that I would fly to Philadelphia on behalf of Stardreaming's new mission and ask for guidance about how money is raised for a project of this nature. Curiously, though, no one returned my call. Instead of trying a different angle, I observed what had happened and didn't push. I trusted that the laws of attraction and magnetism would magically provide all that was needed. I began organizing what I believed were the activities necessary to preserve, maintain, and expand Stardreaming. Who would be our attorney? What about the preliminary budget?

On that same day in June, James had a dream that it was time to move forward on the megalabyrinth and to paint the next image for his children's book, an image called *Soqwahote*—a blue crystal skull. This painting would, coincidentally, coexist at the same time that Stephen Spielberg had launched his Indiana Jones movie about the blue skull. In James's children's book the description of the blue skull is as follows:

> "I am Soqwahote, the blue star matrix of the ancient ones," the fantastic being announced. "The rainbow race will be reborn and reign again on earth. The shift has already begun. All nations, cultures, star systems, and planets will begin to unite with the sole purpose of loving and caring for each other. We have seen your future and it is a glorious one of peace, magic, and harmony. The whales and dolphins are the key to your survival, so honor their presence."[2]

So much was happening at such an accelerated rate that I wrote to my children, trying to share who I had become. They had known me intimately during their childhood at a time when the magic of the universe had not yet appeared for me. I wrote:

> The first thing I am to share with you is that I am clairaudient and this gift seems to be accelerating. My intention is to check always to be sure that what I receive is for the highest good of all. Because I have free will, I can accept or reject the advice that is given. You might say that I have guides who talk to me. I can talk to and hear those who have departed and those unborn. I heard Ron Brown, former Secretary of Commerce and the cousin

of my former business partner, just after his plane crashed. I saw my aunt when her spirit left her still-living body. You know of other examples that I have shared with you. You will find small journals on and in my desk of automatic writing, which I began a year ago when I couldn't understand why we were having trouble with our company. I do this writing now on a daily basis. At first, the signature was vague or a collective, but now it is very precise. I can sit quietly and ask a question, and the answers will come. I will check in with you on this subject periodically. Much love, Mom

As I explained various ways to share the evolving me with my children, I came to understand that all we needed was to love and respect one another.

Megalabyrinth Defined–6/7/08

Wow, such courage and so well stated. You are truly a master now. You felt it in Egypt, but you see and know it now. All that matters is your truth, seen through your eyes and received through your ears. You are taking each one of our clues and running with it. It is beautiful to behold. Your visit to Texas will be for more than just rest. We will be there facilitating major needed physical shifts to help you get ready to work. Dear one, do you see the power and might of the transformational vortex of the megalabyrinth? This is a gift to humankind, which far surpasses those before. You and James are entrusted as the male/female pair, the balance of divine energy who are to execute this task. There is deep love, profound respect, and a gentle give and take between you. This balanced energy will be the vibration that supports and surrounds the completed labyrinth into which others will enter. The vril energy and this sweet male/female energy will be present. Again it will be James who is Stardreaming and you who are the S.T.A.R. clinic. You have always felt that wellness was to partner with Stardreaming in the ultimate understanding of cosmic consciousness. Now you understand. The megalabyrinth is to be built with the male/female, Stardreaming and S.T.A.R. clinic vibrations empowered with the vril energy spiral. This will bring the participants into cosmic consciousness. Now you see how the S.T.A.R. clinic will spread through the world—by means of experiencing the megalabyrinth, dear one. It is so simple. So relax, enjoy this beautiful day. You are our national treasure.

With all our love,

The Council of Thirteen via Anaya-Ra

James and I worked together on a mission and vision statement for the preservation, maintenance, and expansion of Stardreaming.

The Golden Dolphin Society Trust Mission Statement

Our mission is to create a sacred space where adults, children, and future generations have permission to be who they are and to open their hearts and minds to all possibilities.

The Golden Dolphin Society Trust Vision Statement

It is our vision to create spaces and labyrinths, that retain the sacred architecture and power of the ancients and allow for the magic of the new; to provide a sanctuary for transformational healing and meditation; and to provide education, workshops, and experiences in ceremony.

Progress Yesterday–6/8/08

We greet you with arms out wide, our dear one. What amazing progress you and James made yesterday with the mission and vision statements. We will continue to provide you gently with the next step. You will not have to look hard, just be open and expectant, and all will appear with ease. *Organic* is James's word. We like that one too. Flow or glide—each is appropriate. Your meeting with Beverly today will be a time of appreciation and gratitude. She cares enormously about you and will be thrilled to know you are doing well. Your trip to Houston, Texas, to visit Marijon is of great importance for both of you. We will be concocting, arranging, and preparing for the fast flow of events when you return. You will be stronger physically, mentally, and emotionally, but most importantly, your heart will expand. We are going to have such fun, dear one. Enjoy the ride.

All our deep love,
The ancient ones via Anaya-Ra

Wow, What a Day!—6/14/08

Wow, what a day we had with you, James, *Soqwahote,* and New Temple of Atlantis! How beautiful it is that you don't see what is happening, yet you allow it to happen. James understands. You have no idea how grounding you are and what a balance you are for him. He needs you, dear one. Just know and accept that. All the pieces are now going to quickly fall in place. You need only sort and keep track. You have all you need to figure out zoning and the county issues for the physical expansion of Stardreaming. You have sited the visitors center and you know that water will not be an issue. You identified the stone wall, the bridges, and the granite and basalt stone. See what you accomplished. That is huge! It will continue at this pace, dear one. You will begin to attract when you get the land details defined. Then you will talk with authority and confidence. The Labyrinth Society will be a tool for you. You are just beginning to create the swell. Just watch.

With our deep respect,
The Council of Thirteen via Anaya-Ra

I was being told, "Just watch." What I was not being told was what time meant in quantum reality. But this was such an important question since, in the third dimension, my clock and calendar expected me to keep pace with the messages being received by my inner voice. But what if time did not exist in the dimension from which these messages were coming?

Whales and Dolphins Swimming Over Stardreaming—6/15/08

We are so impressed, dear one. You and James are off to the races with bells ringing and horns blowing. We are making our list too, for much has been put in place on our dimensions. You are a hard act to follow. What is obvious is that we all want the dolphins and whales to swim in the air above Stardreaming and its megalabyrinth. We can see it now, and others will see as well. You worry about premature publicity. Fear not, we will orchestrate all in divine order. Stardreaming will always hold a mystery, even in its expanded phase. Many will be willing to wait their turn, for in the waiting they will be preparing for the experience. All who come to Stardreaming will arrive at their perfect moment of expansion. So have no fears about imposing restrictions. The temples are always to be treated as sacred. Stardreaming is not Disneyland. Hold your ground, for it is for the highest good of all. You like the number thirteen, as do we. May we suggest twenty-two dollars discounted to thirteen for members. May we suggest a maximum of thirteen visitors to Stardreaming each half hour? Play with it, dear one. It will evolve, fear not. Enjoy.

With our deep love,
The Council of Thirteen via Anaya-Ra

As James and I were making the decisions necessary for the protection, maintenance, and expansion of Stardreaming, Marijon suggested that I might want to attend a conference in Texas. Going to Texas would be an opportunity to meet several of the people who had James's paintings. I would go to visit them as well.

Trip to Texas–6/16/08

We rejoice and greet you this very fine day. All is in order and those you are to meet are prepared—anticipating your visit and the union that will be created. You will be working, yet your work will look like play. The seeds you plant will grow so rapidly and the harvest will astound you. You have already planted many seeds during this partial month. We want you to pay special attention to where you are and what is happening around you on the summer solstice, for it will take you into a new season. The planets are in a different location. The universe has realigned. The energies will shift; enormous energy and power will pour forth, causing a shift on your earth as well. Be ready, for you too, dear one, will shift. Don't be afraid; this is a time of expansion. Watch for the small—the small animals, the few words, and the tiniest gesture. They will all be important to you, and you will learn much. Now, we ask again that you revere your physical body, for it is needed to do our work. Love, respect, and appreciate each cell of you.

With our deep love,
Raphael via Anaya-Ra

After my arrival in Houston, meetings with several of the Stardreaming contacts took place. A few of us decided to gather at a labyrinth on summer solstice for a magical moment. I had to tell James about the magic:

> James, when I arrived in the center of the labyrinth on summer solstice, I sat down and took off my shoes. Then a huge, etheric hole appeared in my stomach, reaching from the pubic bone to the sternum and from the outer skin on the left side to the outer skin on the right side. The hole formed a portal: the cosmos flowed in through the front, earth and humanity from behind.

I didn't know the meaning of the portal between earth, humanity, and the cosmos, but it was a powerful experience. I went with Marijon to Luminesce Ministries in Houston. Luminesce was an extension of Stardreaming's energy because it contained a huge collection of James's paintings. Cindy, another Stardreaming contact, had become a collector to facilitate her work in providing a sacred space for transformation. This was our first meeting, so I was overwhelmed when Cindy greeted me with gushing words that ran around in my head trying to enter my ears in a coherent way. I recognized the words *Sirian spaceship, ambassador, lake, you*, but it was all too much and someone else's truth. I just sat down on one of the many cushions in the room and let the words continue to pour out. James's paintings were everywhere! Since I believe that James's paintings carry a gold vibration, the house had to be cascading in exquisite frequencies. I had exchanges of vibration with the *Queen of the Golden Dolphins* and *Raphael, Archangel of Upper Heavens* as well as *Green Goddess*, who shared the term "ease and grace" with me, for the first time. Marijon and I spent the night at Luminesce, and I ended up sleeping on several cushions in the main living area with *Green Goddess* directly in front of me. The next morning, I thought that I would amble down to the magical forest behind, to just take a peek at the lake and see if I had any hits on the Sirian spaceship that apparently had come to be with me.

I summarized the trip to the magical forest in an email to James:

> We left about 1:00 p.m. after an amazing morning. I felt it was important to go to the lake where the Sirian spaceship was. All four of us ended up going—Cindy, Cindy's friend, Marijon, and I. We drove to the Magical Forest and started walking down the half-mile path to the lake. The baby ferns and unusual shapes and spaces made me feel that the forest was indeed magical. I was shown the mounds of the inner earth beings, in particular the vision mound.
>
> I was standing on the mound when I heard, "It will come with grace and ease."
>
> I said, "And what can I do for you?"
>
> "You are bringing in the manifest destiny," it replied.
>
> We continued walking and the thunder got closer and louder. Finally, we had a view of the lake. I walked around to the side, while Cindy went to a closer bank and stood overlooking the water. Then the rain came. One member of our group went inside a tent that a homeless person had set up away a bit from the lake. Marijon sat under a tree. I stood looking out over the water. As the rain got stronger and stronger, I heard, "This is how we touch you. Your tears blend with the rain in joy." Then the rain became torrential. Soon after, we began walking back, with buckets of water pouring down, thunder booming, and lighting cracking. Our clothes stuck to us, and we walked through huge valleys of water. When we returned to the house, Cindy mentioned that when she was by the lake she heard a voice say, "We are so excited. She's here, she's here, she's here."

Feel Our Love–6/28/08

We greet you this glorious day, the birthday of your twin granddaughters, and in many ways your birth celebration as well. You are a new, evolved human:

cosmic consciousness, transformed by the rain, thunder, lightning, and our presence yesterday. You are, dear one, now even more powerfully charged. You radiate a charge, you are more fully you, and the world will recognize this power in you. Be not afraid of offending people. On the contrary, many will be attracted by your new gentle strength. There is much more to come, dear one. We are connected ever more strongly to you. Feel our love,

With our deep love,

The Council of Thirteen via Anaya-Ra

~ 7 ~

My-Ron, Our Blue Crystal Skull

Never in my wildest dreams did I think I would be buying a crystal skull! My new blue skull, I knew, was the Council of Thirteen's doing, for they are the masters of the blue crystal skull. The skull contains the blue star matrix, radiating light from Alpha Centauri. I learned that my skull, My-Ron, is innocent perception, the voice, knowledge, and wisdom of innocence and love. It had to go to Stardreaming, the new gateway for the new matrix, the portal of the cosmic heart. The council told me their communications could more easily flow through My-Ron's crystal matrix. They also said that they hear me from their chambers on Alpha Centauri, the center of activity where it has taken eons to manifest the matrix, while star warriors (golden dolphins) have been repairing the ancient grid on earth. I had agreed that I would be on a team with the masters for the preservation, maintenance, and expansion of Stardreaming, and had written a new business plan model for earth and for the attraction of an individual, who would say without being asked, "How much money do you need?"

My blue crystal skull found me when Marijon and I were poking around a metaphysical bookstore in Houston. In a locked cabinet behind glass, I saw a blue skull. James was painting *Soqwahote* exactly then, so surely, he was to have this blue skull. I asked the salesperson if I could look at the skull, so she unlocked the cabinet and handed it to me. I called James's number and left a voice message about this amazing blue skull that I was sure he was to buy for Stardreaming to join the others that he had. As I was carrying the blue skull back to the counter for the salesperson to lock up, I heard my inner voice say, "James is not to buy me, you are." Good heavens, that couldn't be! What do I need with crystal... I rushed over to Marijon to have her get me out of this predicament, but the voice kept on, so I went ahead and bought it.

That afternoon, back at Marijon's house, I put the blue skull, now mine, on top of the bureau in my room and went into the living area to read. Then I heard, "Come get me." Oh boy! So I did. The skull never left my side the whole time I was in Texas—somehow it wanted to experience all that I was experiencing. We went into Walmart a day or two later, and I had the skull in the shopping cart's small upper carriage. I heard, "Don't leave me!" Such fun.

On returning to Santa Fe and to Stardreaming, where I knew the skull would live, James and I learned that the skull's name was My-Ron, and that he held the energy of innocent perception, a state of grace whereby one simply experiences without bias or prejudice. My-Ron is the crystal skull for the thirteenth temple: the Temple of the Stone. My-Ron is newly carved from glass—ash from Mount St. Helens was used in its formula.

While I was in Texas, My-Ron accompanied me to a retreat given by John Price of the Quartus Foundation. John spoke words that affirmed my truth, saying that my actions will be guided by Source from the inside and not by my seeking from the outside. This was the way I had wanted to operate in building our wellness clinics. Now, with Stardreaming's invitation to join in the next expansion phase, I felt as if I was surrounded by support for this way of working. At the end of the retreat, we were guided in meditation to a meadow where we were to receive a gift. What I received were the words "You have all that you need to do everything we ask of you." The visionary symbol of the gift was what I found in my lap: the blue skull.

Marijon and I gave the skull the temporary nickname CR since Marijon found a Crown Royal blue velvet bag for me to carry it in. When René, a friend of James's, met my blue skull she announced that he represented the innocence of the new earth. She said he is bonded to me in love and that I am sharing experiences with him. What came to me next was that CR is "the voice, knowledge, and wisdom of innocence and love."

After the retreat, Marijon and Cindy felt that the skull and I should go to Galveston, but I wasn't at all clear why, other than that it would be a nice trip to a place I had never been. What came through in my morning journaling, however, was that the trip had a connection with the whales and the dolphins.

Cindy offered to drive us to allow Marijon the opportunity to do work in Houston and be with family, so she picked me up at 9:00 a.m. When we arrived at the ocean, I was guided to allow Cindy to lead me down the beach she knew well, finally landing in a quiet space. She had given me a vial of water, with remnants from the Chalice Well and water from the lake in the Magical Forest. She was told that I needed to place some in the water wall in the Woodlands (a section of Houston) and the remainder in the Atlantic Ocean. When I received the water, I heard that I would understand why when the task was complete. We entered the ocean with the skull and the vial and poured the water. Cindy left me to sit in the ocean as the small waves came over me and CR.

I got up, and as I went deeper into the ocean an amazing emotion came over me and tears welled up. Cindy had used the word *sonar* as we entered the ocean, and it became very clear that what was affecting me was the closeness I was feeling with the whales and the dolphins. I also felt connected not only with the Atlantic but with all the ocean bodies. It wasn't until the large waves crashed over the skull and me that I felt a cleansing and a completion. I went back to the beach and put CR on fresh seaweed facing the ocean, and we sat. Cindy came and joined us, and we continued our discussion.

Later we drove to the bay that connects to Houston and walked out to a gazebo where we sat with our feet in the water; CR went into the water as well. I then understood the meaning of the vial of water. The spaceship was not from Sirius, but from Alpha Centauri, home of the Council of Thirteen. The water in the vial contained water from the lake in which the spaceship had landed. When placed in the ocean it connected them to the whales and the dolphins. Alpha Centauri, the whales, and the dolphins were also related to our work at Stardreaming. After this discovery, Cindy and I went to lunch, and at Cindy's suggestion we celebrated with champagne.

Blue Star Matrix–7/2/08

So much has been revealed to you in the last two weeks, dear one. Rest, rejoice, and process. Let it all enter the fibers of your being. You grasp what the blue star matrix is now. At Stardreaming, it acts as the connection for earth with Alpha Centauri, represented by the megalabyrinth you and James will build. My-Ron is the crystal of blue volcanic glass, which contains and holds the matrix. The vibration emanates from the skull through you, through James, and through the megalabyrinth to those with a heart to receive the new innocence and love of the new earth. Amazing, isn't it, and yet so simple!

Our deep love to you, dear one,

Raphael, the whales and the dolphins via Anaya-Ra

The magic of the universe was showing up in my life, and I didn't need to force it. I found a symbol for living life by means of attraction and magnetism—my red leather chair. I discovered that when I sat in my red leather chair, all that I needed would come to me without having to ask. I simply needed to surrender, trust, allow, and receive.

One of the most remarkable examples of this occurred when a friend encouraged me to call Richard to learn about how to create a trust instrument to protect Stardreaming. I called him from my red leather chair. While I was speaking with Richard, I heard him say, "How much money do you need?" I tried to keep talking in a calm voice as I processed what I thought I had heard.

"I don't know. I've never built a megalabyrinth before," I replied.

"Do you have a business plan?" he asked.

"No," I answered.

"Well, send me a business plan when you've completed one," he said.

I was surprised and unsure where that came from. I love my red leather chair. It's like a magic carpet. I don't have to make an effort; the chair, which is a metaphor for S.T.A.R., just allows me to attract magic! Now I had to get to work. The universe had taken a giant step, and it was my turn to take the next giant step: teamwork.

James and I spent much time talking about his expanded vision of Stardreaming. I took copious notes, and then tried to convert the vision into Richard's requested business plan. I started with an outline from the Service Core of Retired Executives, SCORE, but I wasn't sure how to fill in the section asking for something comparable. There just was nothing to compare to our cosmic center. Then the answer came as I wrote in my journal:

New Business Plan Model for Earth–7/12/08

We rejoice in all that you are learning about yourself, dear one, especially about your compassion and love. Put your focus on your true heart. Feel it beat and vibrate. That is the pulse of the universe that connects and communicates with us. We transfer information to you just as you request. We are a team. Yes, put us in the business plan. It is right, true, and a new business plan model for earth.

With our deep love,
The ancient ones via Anaya-Ra

I was relieved that I could express myself completely in the business plan. That evening, a little overwhelmed from waking at 2:00 a.m. thinking about the new business plan, I had an extra glass of wine. Well, I soon heard myself making strange, foreign sounds for about forty-five minutes. I stopped, and then started again. I wondered what I'd been talking about and to whom. Marijon had told me that one night during the conference in Texas, she had heard me doing the same thing. I wrote about it the next morning:

Last Night's Conversation–7/13/08

Wow, are we impressed, and you are tired. We can feel it, dear one. Take a day off and rest deeply. So you want to know who you were talking to last night. It was with us, always. You will soon be able to remember how to move your lips and tongue even without the wine. We love to hear you pronounce our words. It sounds like music to us. Dear one, you are shifting and expanding. Your consciousness is escalating so that sight will combine with sound and you will see. But first we have more work to do on your physical body. We are glad you are pleased; we also are enormously pleased and can tell you that you composed your business plan last night. Yes, you spoke it to us, you paused, and we responded with joy and appreciation. You are ready to write what you spoke. You have captured all the magic of this new business plan model for earth. You seem unsure of who we are. Trust what your hand is writing, and allow the signature to flow onto the page, for it is indeed us.

Our deep love,
All the whales and the dolphins via Anaya-Ra

Archangel Metatron via Tyberonn revealed to me a year later:

> We will also tell you that you have experienced life on the planet in dolphin form, and that a portion of your entity in multidimensional aspect has the ability to speak to them in the ancient language known as Paa-Taal.

I knocked out a fourteen-page business plan the next morning. The words just poured out. When I got to "List your advisers," the first entry on the list was "Guidance from Source." There were a few holes like financial details and a description of the Temple of the Stone. I needed James's input for those entries. I threw earlier attempts away, started from scratch, and it flowed!

The Trust—7/16/08

We rejoice with you, dear one, for all that has transpired with you and James. You think we don't see it, but we do, for we are gathering and with each arrival at Stardreaming we manifest more, and our energy amplifies. My-Ron was a key addition, for he radiates the light of Alpha Centauri in a way that will bring in the Temple of the Stone. He is growing in understanding of the various temples that have been built. Do not worry about the trust. You must—through understanding fully, both the negative and the positive—be truly strong in your decision and your commitment. We will work with the lawyer to give her clarity of thought and process. The answer has already been decided. The path is good, clear, and simple. We would not allow the majesty of the project to be diminished and will guide you in the direction for the highest good of all. Be calm and listen.

With all our love,
Archangel Raphael via Anaya-Ra

While I was working on the business plan and talking to James about the attorney for Stardreaming's expansion, I had my mind constantly on the details of the closure of our medical clinics. I communicated about it with the ancient ones.

Today Is the Flow–7/17/08

Do you see, dear one, closure? You are forcing the issue of the termination of the wellness center, but it is a good thing. You need to close the energy leak. You need to be whole and fresh for all that is to transpire with the Golden Dolphin Society Trust. Write it, for you know the answer. We will have a land trust that will be simple, clean, and that will carry the Temples of the Cosmos into posterity. This is our desire, and so it shall be. We have no wish to burden or put you in harm's way. You are our master, and we are here to protect you in all things. Be calm, relaxed, and allow the flow, for today is the flow.

With our deep love,
The ancient ones via Anaya-Ra

The Council of Thirteen's messages came from Alpha Centauri. They were the energy behind the manifestation of the Temple of Stone, the thirteenth temple to be built. It seemed critically important that when the business plan was complete I deliver it in person. The potential funders would be looking closely at Stardreaming, but Stardreaming needed to look equally as closely at them. There had to be an energy match. A relationship of this magnitude could not survive without a similar state of consciousness. I needed to go to Philadelphia. So I wrote to Richard asking when Marijon, our advisor, and I could meet with him. Mid-September was the response.

Sacred Union–7/26/08

Yes, you and Marijon are to go to see Richard. This will be just the beginning of a long, strong, fruitful friendship and business relationship. Richard and his associates will spread the word far and wide with their many contacts, which will be one of the pivotal growth points for the trust! They will bring more than money. It is who they are and who they know that is their greatest wealth. Enjoy how this unfolds, and relax into the process. Expect the unexpected from both of them. Call on us when you need to. The fairies will sprinkle dust on you, our love.

With our deep love,
The whales and the dolphins via Anaya-Ra

Now it was time to learn more about the blue star matrix from the Council of Thirteen.

The Flow Will Begin—7/27/08

We hear you, dear one, from our chambers on Alpha Centauri. You have touched on the magic of the blue crystal matrix, which has been building over the last several years. It is not an instant manifestation, but one that has taken humanity and the council eons to manifest. Consent first, then align, then implement. Knowledge of the matrix first came to our beloved James, who is such a fine-tuned transmitter; then you came to join him to bring the puzzle pieces together. Now that the spiral has been identified and the energies emitted, there will be quick and fluid growth. With My-Ron in your heart and James's, we're more easily able to fill you with information flowing through his crystal matrix from us: the Council of Thirteen. You need only ask, and the flow will begin. Stay in balance with James; use your new advisers. All is in divine order and love.

With deep love,
The Council of Thirteen and Archangel Raphael via Anaya-Ra

My Greatest Fear—7/28/08

We hear you, dear one, from our chambers and throughout the vibrant waves of sound and thought in the universe. We come to you today bearing good news about your greatest fear: asking for yourself. You have mastered this skill, dear one. You no longer fear, for you know that your well-being is the well-being of others. Your comfort and joy is the comfort and joy of others. You are to receive, and you asked to receive all that you need—not just a momentary gift, but all—and all is appearing. You will see it appear on an accelerated path toward you and the Golden Dolphin Society Trust. We will continue to guide you on the day-to-day decisions and directions, but you will have no wants. Just as the new advisor has appeared to assist you in areas you perceive are difficult, so will others come. Check always with James, then continue. Land, people, cars, pencils, and good health—all are manifesting. Enjoy and relax.

With our deep love,

The ancients ones via Anaya-Ra

For days now, I had been at work on the business plan and its five-year cash flow projections, making decisions with the help of my pendulum, and I had to stop and laugh. It just occurred to me how comical, yet serious, the situation was. As I wrote each section, I asked if there was more to add. With the marketing section, the answer was yes, and it came right to me. Who would have guessed that I—someone who hired counselors on business plan writing through my former company in Philadelphia—would now be guided by a coil on a chain. Amazing and truly wonderful!

Instant Manifestation–7/31/08

We herald you from on high and in your heart, dear one. You have heard our plea and answered. Your entry through our portal yesterday was a sight to behold. Boldly walking the new star path and asking permission to enter. What joy it gave us that you approached with such respect. We saw your tears and felt the love in your heart. The tambourine was playing, leis were there for your neck, to honor you. We come to your home often, but this time you chose to come to ours. What a celebration. We are you, and you are us. All you need do is ask. What will change? More clarity, a heightened perception, instant manifestation of your conscious thoughts. You find this hard to believe, but it is so, dear one. You worry about your random thoughts manifesting. These are not the pure thoughts of love about which we speak. We know the beating of your heart, we feel its vibration, and we know what is your truth. That is the true source of what you will manifest and are manifesting. Look around you. Count the wonders. This is just the beginning, dear one. All, all, all is available to you now with the request of your true heart.

With our deep love,
The ancient ones via Anaya-Ra

My journal entries and the messages they conveyed were always validation for what I knew to be my truth. James and I were focused on the manifestation of the Temple of the Stone, knowing that this was what we were being called to do. The following message from the Council of Thirteen reaffirmed that the Temple of the Stone was to be a critical aspect of the shift anticipated in the prophesied year 2012.

Choosing, Not Searching–8/1/08, Solar Eclipse, New Moon

What we want you to hear today is how excited we are in anticipation of 2012 through 2013. We feel the energy building. All the star warriors are working to repair the ancient energy grids, and you and James are diligently laying the seeds of the blue matrix, which carries the frequencies of Alpha Centauri for the wisdom of the masters to come to planet earth to integrate with humankind and to raise regular consciousness to cosmic consciousness. The portal will be the very heart of the cosmic heart, the Temple of the Stone. You opened it up when you sat on the land. It is radiating, and the circles and the stones are all in position. You will find such excitement when the word goes out, for it will spread like wildfire. People will contact you to help, to give, and to participate. You will have all that you need and more. Keep focused, dear one. Do not let up the energy flow until you are complete. Then rest and play, but for now stay on point. You will take the masterpiece to Richard very soon. He will clearly understand.

With our deep love,
The Council of Thirteen via Anaya-Ra

Archangel Raphael and the Council of Thirteen were with me, constantly encouraging and guiding me, but I had no idea of the magnitude of what we were actually up to!

One of the Greatest Wonders of the New Earth–8/3/08

We welcome you, dear one, to a time of profound shift, acceleration, expansion, and divine love. You are a participant as well as a creator in all the new aspects of planet earth during the opening of the new earth. Relax, enjoy, celebrate, and watch with wonder and awe. Many around the planet join you, and you are connected through vibration and intention. You each support the others on a different dimension in understanding the total body of work. Stardreaming is not the center of activity—that comes from Alpha Centauri—but it is a new gateway for the new matrix. You are correct, no one need visit Stardreaming for its work to be profoundly powerful, but the energy of the visitors inspires and invigorates James. So they will come by the thousands to see the new wonder of the new earth. "One of the greatest wonders of the new earth" is how they will know Stardreaming. We promise you and James, and all who work with you, ease and grace. Turn to us for your nourishment of spiritual energy. When you feel weary, look at the earth at Stardreaming, and know the appreciation of every atom rejoicing in the love and attention of its creator. Now there are two carrying that energy forward to the next phase of Stardreaming. All are waiting. The moment is fast approaching in human terms for all to come together: the books, the land, the money, the expansion, the people, and the acceptance. All is cohering.

With our deep love,
Raphael via Anaya-Ra

While these wonders were coming together, life had a surprise for me. In the morning, as I do each day, I got out of bed, opened the door to the second-story porch off of my bedroom, and went out to greet the stars and the new day. I saw a little gray mouse scurry past me and enter the bathroom. I shut the bathroom door to give myself time to think. How did it get on the second-story porch? Did he really climb straight up the stucco walls? Did he get dropped by a hawk? It didn't matter, he had to go! I kept him locked up until I could buy a Havahart trap and some peanut butter. I put the trap in the bathroom and hoped that during the night he would get hungry. During the night, *bang*, down came the walls of the trap with Mr. Mouse inside, but I decided to wait until morning to release him in the wild. He was so noisy that I had to sleep in the guest room. The next morning, the mouse was peacefully sitting in the trap. I drove him far away before releasing him. He was shocked when I let him out. He then scurried off.

James had taught me that animals represent specific medicine. The mouse is the medicine of detail. I understood my little visitor had come to say thank you. I felt very appreciated.

The Mouse in My House–8/6/08

We are present, dear one, as you process the events of the evening. Yes, we would like to discuss our dear friend and your temporary house guest. You see, you never know what form we will take. Yes, as fanciful a statement as this is, we were with you, and you treated us with such honor. (This is too crazy.) Though you can't imagine what words will follow, keep writing, for they will flow from your pen. The quality detail is the medicine that James attributes to the mouse, and he is correct. We wish you to think of what you have accomplished, dear one. You have taken your extreme talent for visionary understanding to a new level of execution through detailed analysis. If you think back, you have never done this before (write a business plan and five-year financial projections). Now your profound passion and desire for excellence in execution allowed you to take each understandable component of the plan and break it down into primary building blocks. This must be done for the foundation to be secure. You have in the past believed that divine intervention would provide the structure for your vision. But now you know it must be you, it is you. You are manifesting with completion of each small detail as well as the overall project. We came to celebrate that tremendous growth in understanding.

With our deep love,

The whales and the dolphins via Anaya-Ra

~ 8 ~

Opening of the Universal Portals

A date of significance in the universe was approaching—the triple date of August 8, 2008 (08/08/08), a harmonic gateway. It was an opening of significance for me. I was to experience the moment when the light codes from the central sun entered Stardreaming at the site of the future Temple of the Stone. I was to complete a new business plan model for earth. I was to be told by the masters that Sananda, the higher self of Jesus, the Christ, would transfer to me the Christ-consciousness codes during a seven-day period, and that I was to take unity consciousness to the Liberty Bell, to serve as a symbol of liberty and freedom.

New Understanding of Magic–8/7/08

With drums beating and cymbals clashing, we are preparing for tomorrow, the 08/08/08 opening of the universal portals of prosperity, oneness, union, and expansion—all flooding in as you lie on the dreaming stone at Stardreaming. You, dear one, have to be at Stardreaming with James. Again you need do nothing other than be present. We will all be with you. So many beings are participating in experiencing these enormous energies. Watch and mark the day and the rapid unfolding that follows. Your arms are hardly big enough to embrace all that will pour in. Connections are part of the energy. Stardreaming will open up wider to the matrix that is being created, like a plant taking in water, soaking it up to grow stronger, to expand. The nourishment is being provided, and like a rose with the nourishment, the scent spills over to enrich the lives of others, whose lives in turn carry the joy and beauty out to others, and so it spreads. Magic abounds in direct alignment with Source. Whoever walks the land feels a shift toward that alignment, allowing the new understanding of magic to manifest on the new earth. And, so it is!

With our deep love,
The ancient ones via Anaya-Ra

James was told that on August 8, 2008, he was to take a snake staff, which was planted at Stardreaming on fall equinox 2001 to mark its beginning, and place it in the center of the future site of the Temple of the Stone. Stones from Malta and Sinai went with the staff. The ceremony of moving and planting the snake staff that day lasted from noon until 2:00 p.m. "This solidifies the whole thing," James told me. The six-foot snake staff was an anchoring tool. James rented Stardreaming, but he didn't own it when he built the twelve Temples of the Cosmos on the twenty-two acres; likewise, he didn't own the forty-five new acres, yet he was already there working on the thirteenth temple. James was told that morning, "You have surrendered everything, and you will get everything." The staff was moved from the Temple of the Stars, the four star nations, to the Temple of the Stone, which expands Stardreaming to Alpha Centauri. James had painted the staff purple with dots and feathers. Then it was painted gold.

While James was moving the staff for the beginning phase of the Temple of the Stone, I went to the Dream Temple at Stardreaming, the site of the grandfather and grandmother stones, as a tribute to my good friend Bear Heart, whose memorial service was being held by his family in Oklahoma that day. After my meditations, I got out my journal and the following memorial came through:

Memorial to Grandfather Marcellus "Bear Heart" Williams–8/8/08

We honor you, our dear grandfather, on whose rock I lie. We thank you for your wisdom and love. We thank you for choosing to be with us for the last ninety years on earth and all the time before and after. We will carry your medicine to others through our lives, our actions, compassion, and love. Your truth has blended with my truth, your smile and laughter with my being. I knew you only a few years here on earth, but I knew you in other dimensions since before recorded time. I ask you, during the hours of this day's open portal, to send down your love to me so that I can be strong, powerful, and magical—and share all with humankind.

The next day, I received this information about what had transpired on August 8, 2008, marking the opening of the universal portals.

All of Humanity Is Touched–8/9/08

Bravo to you, dear one, for participating in our open ceremony. The harmonic gates were open as you lay on grandfather stone, as you meditated in your place of sanctuary, as you contemplated the power and wonder of creation, past and to come. The snake staff that James placed with the stones from Malta and Sinai stands tall, marking the spot from which light codes radiate from the central sun. The codes entered precisely at noon, precisely on the center mark of the Temple of the Stone. What are these new light codes, you ask? They are the innocent love and compassion, the knowing of the oneness of Source that you share with My-Ron. The energy is being transmitted down through the vril rod, the snake staff, which was planted at the Temple of the Sun on the fall equinox of 2001, the beginning of Stardreaming. The energy then went into the earth exactly in the direction of the labyrinth path and out into the blue star matrix that has been created, connecting to Alpha Centauri, things seen and unseen. The earth feels it—the people, plants, stones, and all of matter know of this truth on a vibratory level. Now change is occurring, for nothing can be the same. Some will choose to leave, some will choose to accept and expand, but all have been touched by the love of Source. Know that what took place at Stardreaming yesterday transformed the written record of the universe. The love vibration has entered; the compassion vibration resonates. The earth is one with the stars. Star consciousness has manifested on earth. Nothing will be the same. Stardreaming has always held this truth, but now, from Stardreaming, radiating into the core of the earth through the blue matrix, all of humanity is touched. All of humanity is touched, through the rod in the center of the Temple of the Stone.

With our deep love,
The Council of Thirteen via Anaya-Ra

The pendulum of life was moving to its opposite side, and I began to wonder why we weren't seeing physical progress with the expansion of Stardreaming. Was there something more I was to be doing?

It was becoming increasingly clear to me that with the expansion of Stardreaming a new way of thinking about business was evolving.

New Business Model for Earth–8/27/08

We honor you deeply, our dear one, for the opening and understanding of the next level of business. You understood so clearly that what we are doing with Stardreaming will serve as a new model for not only the business plan but the business itself. You are creating and birthing. You are at the end of your gestation period, and the entity will be delivered by all who are patiently acting as the midwife. You have a place to take it, to nurture it, and to surround it with love for growth. If you think of your role as maternal, and act—just as you have done so beautifully three times by giving birth to your three children—you will know that your profound love and protection was the answer in all situations. Look at the result, dear one. There is no difference. Now, as then, all that you need to do is sealed in your heart, the engine that will guide you forward. It was good that you so clearly communicated to James all that you are experiencing, for now he more deeply understands and is there for you. What is being birthed, dear one, is a product of new earth. Your whole experience will be new and your manner of care will differ as well. Seek James often when you are perplexed and stunned. He is a master of magic; he holds a direct connection with Source; and he will guide you to stand tall. Trust and allow the answer to be received. It is that easy. Remember, we promised you when you committed on the earth mound (the vision mound in the Magical Forest) ease and grace. That is the new business plan model for earth: ease and grace in union with Source.

With our deep love,

Archangel Raphael, Council of Thirteen and Cosmic Mother via Anaya-Ra

I had written the business plan, but I was still grasping to articulate just what was a golden dolphin. Then it came to me. A golden dolphin is a spark of divine essence whose intention flows from Source unfiltered by duality, structure, or symmetry. This allows for creation, with the pure expression of love, for the benefit of humanity and planet earth.

Labor Day–Ease and Grace–9/1/08

Your labors have been many, dear one, but all will flow now with ease and grace. The intentions of pure love, flow through you as an aspect and spark of Source. It goes through the spirit or the universal flow, the unified field, to the smallest adamantine particle, which is the physical presence of spirit—all without the filter of duality. You have it now so perfectly, our most golden of golden dolphins. You have it!

With our deep love,
Green goddess and queen of the golden dolphins via Anaya-Ra

Part of my labor surrounding that Labor Day was not only finding the definition of a golden dolphin but also learning more about where I come from.

Planets, Stars and Galaxies–9/2/08, Pluto Leaves Retro

There are so many things to share with you about the planets and the stars, galaxies, and universes. Most importantly, you come from them all, dear one, not just one solar system or planet, not just one energy field, but all. You are pure love of Source; how could it be otherwise? Do you see? You have the energies of all cosmic centers on earth and throughout the realms of space and time. Do not confine yourself to another lifetime or another planet. You are much, much grander than that. Remember who you are!

With our deep love,
The ancient ones via Anaya-Ra

Having learned more about myself, I was comforted by being told that everything was prepared for my trip to the East Coast, where I would deliver the new business plan model for earth to Richard.

Philadelphia–9/10/08

We welcome this opportunity each morning to speak with you and honor your faithfulness. Our communication will increase now that you have embraced who you are and can allow the full love of Source to flow through you. You will hear us in the trees, flowers, water, all matter, and all that is not matter. All you need do is focus. Sometimes we will catch your attention to obtain that focus. Today will be a new opening for you at Stardreaming. Since you arrive in your fullness, you will receive fully. You will experience fully. Be alert to the small signs coming to you. All is prepared in Philadelphia. You need only present.

With our deep love,
Raphael via Anaya-Ra

I had requested a reading by Dr. Norma Milanovich months before. As we began the channel, I asked that the masters tell me anything they could about Stardreaming in preparation for my trip to Philadelphia. I was told far more than I expected.

What I received was astounding information. I listened to the tape repeatedly to try to comprehend what had been transmitted. I remember not feeling afraid. It was as if there was a profound knowing. I was excited for the process to unfold over the next days, months, and years. And so it did.

My reluctance to accept all that was being said about me started shifting. My inner voice began to confirm what others had been telling me, but now I realized the information was coming from my higher self. And knowing that, I could accept what I heard as my truth. When I sat to write in my journal using automatic writing, different signatures would appear. Often the signature would be that of Archangel Raphael or the ancient ones, but deep inside of me I knew that it was always me or an archetype representing an aspect of me, speaking to me. My higher self was communicating to me and very often in those writings I would communicate back. That was truly how I was learning who I was and why I was on the planet. But I was learning also by means of the law of attraction; people would come into my life with important messages to help me learn my truth. Dr. Milanovich was one of those people I attracted.

Dr. Norma Milanovich Channel

HTTPS://ATHENALCTR.COM - 9/12/08

It is important that you come forward today, before this full moon in this energetic field of creation. The ascended realms are here to assist, and they requested this specific time for you to come forth to energize your soul, and thus to connect it to a position and a power it once held in a former lifetime in Atlantis. Ten thousand years ago, you left embodiment before the third and final cataclysm in Atlantis. You completed a full circle and healed a rift in time in order to step into the persona of the Atlantean master whom you were and are today. You wrote a sacred agreement designed with the celestial realms. You are to step into the circle of higher consciousness, and it is extremely critical for you to proceed through this initiation. It is the closing and opening of the door for spiritual leaders, moving from one dimension to the next—a skill you took for granted. You were able to perform in more than one dimension simultaneously, which you will do again. You need no training. It is already programmed within your soul. You just need courage to walk freely in the light.

You are to hold a higher perspective for yourself and the world, which will allow you to see in higher dimensions of time and space. Your soul is anxious. Your soul is a magnificent, great soul from Atlantis, and today you are to step into new arenas. All you know, and are, will rise to the surface. You are moving into your role of teacher, and this work will restore your soul's confidence to proceed on your journey. You are presently in the company of Sananda himself, who on the etheric level is Jesus, the Christ. The second being of light guiding you is ascended master Kuthumi, a world teacher who knows the importance of sharing the wisdom with all. The third being of light is El Morya, master of will, discipline, truth, and universal law. They are all here to guide you over the next seven months, so that you can feel your actions and progress in the light, and see yourself evolve exponentially.

You hold the key role in the evolution of this planet and, on the etheric level, you are deemed to be a great leader of the past who has arisen on this day. This information is growing in your mind and heart, which will bring more confidence as you go forward in the months to come. As a pillar of light on the etheric plane, you are one who is here to hold the Christ-consciousness light on the crystalline grid for the 144,000 ascended masters who must anchor this Christ-consciousness grid into the consciousness of the masses in order for this planet to raise itself unequivocally into the fifth dimension. You have the power, and have taught many how to float from one dimension to the other in order to work with beings on both sides of the veil. You will be able to do this again with ease and grace, because it is already programmed in your soul.

On the eve of the approaching full moon, you will begin to open up, and many memories of this life and these powers will begin to flow through you. You will be connected to Sananda for the next nine days, so that you can be programmed with his love and the keys and codes that he carries in his heart. You can then step forward on your path and assimilate all of these higher codes into your own DNA and light body. Sananda will instruct you in the dream state—regarding your role, your future mission, and your power—and how it should be used in the years to come. Of the 144,000 masters, you are the one who will be constantly fed his codes, so that they will then be transmitted through you like a satellite, and you will then feed them to the other pillars of light who are holding together and grounding the crystalline grid for the world.

This is your primary job for the next three years, and the more you remember this, practice this, and stay out of the dizziness of your mind by grounding your reality in the third dimension and continuing to help on the etheric plane, the sooner you will be able to move on to a higher one of world service. Other incarnations on this planet who represent all those who are anchoring the crystalline grid, must stay connected to your soul on the etheric plane. Even when you are challenged, you are expected to hold the higher vibration of ease and grace within you. Over the last few years, many forces have tried to prevent you from maintaining the highest possible vibrational frequency.

You are the filtering system to the others; and all of Sananda's light will flow from his heart into yours, then through you to the others who are holding this grid down. As such, you are considered one of the leaders who will firmly ground the divine plan. You did this in Atlantis and were extremely successful. You were more confident then and took the job in stride; in this embodiment you are more reluctant. You now face the most difficult assignment of all, and you have little protection from forces of opposition that try to divert your attention, lower your vibrational frequency, and ultimately take you down. But you have found that if you ground with Mother Earth you are stronger.

Your ability to ground is one of your contributions to Stardreaming, and the reason it is so important for you to hold yourself and your position solid—even though great transitionary movements are taking place right now on the earth. It is time that you begin to look at yourself as wearing the garments of Adam/Eve Kadmon, master from Atlantis, and in so doing, you will find your self-confidence will begin to grow and your self-doubts will lessen. Because you hold a higher vision in your mind, you are expected to remember your own Atlantean teachings, and to hold your connection to the God force solidly within your mind twenty-four hours a day. This is what it means to align interdimensionally and live in both worlds at the same moment in time. Keeping your mind focused on your connection to the God force and performing in the third dimension, you become the perfect liaison between Sananda and beings of light who are waiting on you to transport your light to them in other dimensions of time and space. El Morya is with you, since you have to work even harder to control your mental and emotional bodies with ease and grace, for Melchizedek says that these are your weakest areas.

You must make a concerted effort now to bathe yourself in the love of Sananda's heart and hold this frequency at all times, regardless of the challenges that confront you. Some of these challenges will measure your ability to stay centered and loving at all times; others are designed by forces of opposition to keep you from your power. It is up to you to determine the reason those unpleasant things occur in your life. By developing such discernment, you become wiser and expend your energy to gain a higher vibrational position. Your soul remembers that in Atlantis you achieved success by anchoring yourself in the moral high ground. When you did this, lived this, and walked your talk, few souls could push you off your center. In this lifetime, you have understood that is essential, and you have begun to build positions or portals of power that will help sustain you in different arenas.

Master Kuthumi comes to you today to explain that after your lessons with Sananda are complete, he will begin to introduce you to the curriculum of light. You are destined, in the years to come, to share your codes with a minimum of thirty-three people, who in turn will be responsible for sharing them with the masses. You have already begun to hibernate somewhat and to hold a position of silence, for your soul understood that you needed rest in order to survive and fulfill your mission on earth. It is time now that you begin to embrace the full extent of who you are, and that for the next seven weeks you move into silence so that you can allow the seeds to be planted and advance toward higher ground.

First, you must appreciate yourself more and hold and witness the potential that lies dormant within your own soul. In these next several days of working with Sananda, you will be guided to journey inward to a deep level of your soul to observe who you really are. Once you have this anchored in your consciousness, it will be easier to move forward and to hold a position of leadership, first in your mind's eye, then among the masses. You already know it is a part of your destiny to teach others the skills that you command—in particular, how to live in two dimensions simultaneously. Once you teach others how to do this by mastering it yourself, you will then find that those whose DNA shares the same pattern from Atlantis will receive the keys and, in so doing, will begin to open up. By holding this position in the light of their own mind's eye, they then will be able to radiate to the masses in a way similar to the hundredth monkey effect. You, however, must be successful in this arena first.

You must become all that you were in Atlantis. You must remember it and bring it forth from the depths of your soul. Align it with the highest possible purpose, so you can integrate it into who you are. Once you have done that and begun radiating the codes, you will begin to find that you have an impact on the world, and little by little you will help others increase their skills in remote viewing on the higher realms of consciousness. El Morya will guide you to increase your discipline, self-will, and self-governing abilities more quickly. Your self-doubts have hindered your ability to see who you really are. You will now be able to understand your strengths and weaknesses more fully, and during this vibrational shift, as you move between dimensions with ease and grace, you will understand the steps you need to follow.

When you share these high-level skills with others, you will fulfill your leadership position in anchoring this knowledge into the crystalline grid of our world. Do not expect results to occur overnight. Change on a populated planet the size of earth is slow to come about and be seen. You are to hold the dream now in your mind's eye and step into the garments you wore in Atlantis. By merging with your oversoul in this way, not only will you remember who you are and were but all the sacred knowledge you commanded will come forth as well. This is truly the time you have been waiting for, and you have passed that initial moment in time and space for closing one existence and opening up to another.

This is a glorious day in the heavens for your soul. Melchizedek has waited eons to work with you in this role. He remembers the perfected work you completed in Atlantis. You have been selected to lead the way in this area and in anchoring the next step into the divine plan on earth. Now is the time to move into your glorified auric field. Sananda, Kuthumi, and El Morya—three masters of light—are delighted to be handpicked by you and selected by Melchizedek to guide you into your role as an important leader.

~ 9 ~

S.T.A.R. Is Infinity Consciousness

The universal portal continued to allow huge transformational thought forms into my consciousness. I must have been exhausted during this period of my journey as I processed, expanded, and integrated ideas such as compression and expansion being the rhythm of life and magnetism being the energy replacing force as the creative process in something called the space of infinity. I observed all this through the lens of innocent perception, which then allowed for infinity streaming, the magnetic streaming of particles of infinity, causing "doing" and "being" to become one. Egads, what was all that? So much new information came gushing in starting alchemical fires to move me along my path to understanding. I thought I had S.T.A.R. mastered, but how did that relate to infinity consciousness and those other new thoughts? All this came during the intense period when Sananda, Kuthumi, and El Morya were working with me to transfer the Christ-consciousness codes. I believe that the new thought forms were from Master Kuthumi's curriculum of light because the nine days of work with Sananda were now complete. El Morya certainly gave me courage.

Here is how it unfolded—fortunately day by day, not all at once! I was preparing to go to Philadelphia to take Stardreaming's new business plan model for earth to Richard for potential funding—to create a land trust, to buy forty-five adjacent acres, and to build the Temple of the Stone. James said that Har Kaur could give me a massage, outside on top of the hill at the Temple of Avalon. While I lay under a sheet, on top of the world, I had the sensation that Har Kaur's hands had become those of Sananda.

This work with Har Kaur was different from other sessions with her. I was definitely focused on Monday's visit to Richard's office. The massage was not soft and ethereal, but hard and releasing. Was it a half hour or an hour? That was hard to remember. She had her elbow in my abdomen, while I gave out great silent screams of pain. She was helping me let go of stored emotion and feelings of poor self-worth. When I finally rolled over and looked out at the Temple of Avalon, the shining stones, and the mountains beyond, I cried again, but this time with awe and appreciation. Then just as we had finished, Har Kaur's therapist friend appeared. Har Kaur suggested that we work together immediately on "clearing," which of course I agreed to. During the clearing, guidance emerged from the twelfth dimension requesting that the business plan come from the land rather than me. That meant presenting the project to Richard on behalf of the land of Stardreaming , which felt wonderful!

Love, Freedom, and Liberty Will Ring Out–9/20/08

You ask about your trip to be with our Richard. Be assured that you are to go, meet, and bond. You have great work to do together. Be detached and allow all to flow with no expectations. Richard is a pure soul who is seeking, and you will act as the light for him as he steers his ship to the shore. The meeting is more about him being in your presence, dear one, than anything else. The outcome is assured. You will clearly know the next step. You do not go alone; indeed, all the divas, fairies, elementals, masters, gods, goddesses, and otherworldly beings will be with you cheering and preparing the space, the words, and the listening. Do not fret. We ask you to prepare with quiet reflection, recalling moments on the hill at Stardreaming when my abundant love was transferred to you. Take that love with you as you fly to the home of freedom and liberty. You will radiate my love, which is now fully yours. There will indeed be a merging for you and for humankind of love, freedom, and liberty, which will ring out.

All our deep love,
Sananda via Anaya-Ra

As the time for my trip to the East Coast approached, while cleaning the old yellow flowers from my front yard I found a stone that called to be picked up. It was about two-inches by one-inch thick, black on one half and rose colored on the other half, and it looked like quartz. I washed it off and went to sit on my back porch, hoping to understand the significance of the stone. What came to me was that it represented unity consciousness—existences no longer separate. I was told that after our visit with Richard, Marijon and I should take it to the Liberty Bell, which represents liberty and freedom. When the stone and bell are together, unity consciousness, liberty, and freedom would radiate out across the country and beyond.

On the fall equinox, Marijon and I drove to Richard's office to present him and his partners with the new business plan model for earth, for Stardreaming. This occurred exactly seven years from the day James planted the snake staff at Stardreaming. I felt an immense confidence in the universe when I placed our document in Richard's hands, for no funder or investor had received such a document before. It would take a person of enormous consciousness to be able to understand it and not reject it immediately as too "out there." One section in the document explains this point well. On the binder's cover page, with the logo of a golden dolphin, are the words *Stardreaming—one of the greatest wonders of the new earth. Archangel Raphael to Nina 8-4-08.*

As we were getting to know each other, I told Richard that one reason I had come to Philadelphia was to determine the quality of the energy that surrounded the potential funding. Stardreaming would only accept funding from a source of compatible frequency. Richard appreciated all that was being presented. After our meeting, Marijon and I went to visit the Liberty Bell and Independence Hall in Philadelphia, where I found a safe, covered space in which to leave my black and rose quartz stone that combined unity consciousness with liberty and freedom, eager to ring it out to humanity from that very sacred site.

Here I was in Philadelphia almost ten years after I had driven west with my computer and toothbrush packed in a rented Hertz van. Never in my wildest dreams would I have thought then that I would be presenting a new business plan model for earth to potential funding partners. Not only had the events in my life changed, but I had changed. Would the changes have occurred if I had stayed in Philadelphia? Asking that question was like wondering what my life would have been like if I had chosen one in a different dimensional reality. Well, the fact is that none of that mattered because there I was, a different me from the Philadelphia debutante, a different me from the wife of a successful Philadelphia lawyer, and a different me from a volunteer for the opera company and museum of art. Were all these changes a choice or was some cosmic contract running the show? I knew the answer. I had left Philadelphia because of an internal tug pulling me to Santa Fe, but I had free will and could easily, perhaps more easily, have said no. Instead, I said yes. Something in me was asking me to go, to do, and to be, so I said yes to that cosmic contract. As a result, I was now passionate about life and about who I was becoming. On my return from Philadelphia, I went to Stardreaming to see the completed painting of Archangel Michael.

Archangel Michael–9/30/08

We applaud you, dear one. We marvel at your diplomacy and how you magnify others, and in doing so place a light on your light. Today will fill you up as you contemplate what has happened. So much transpired this weekend, and you absorbed most all of it consciously, and the rest unconsciously. Be proud and rest. You made the acquaintance of Archangel Michael, and we noted your awe. Just wait, you are very much a part of this series of paintings of Archangels Michael, Gabriel, Raphael, Uriel, and Metatron, so visit them often. You exchanged the radiance that was emitted by means of the painting's gold vibration.

With our deep love,
Archangel Raphael via Anaya-Ra

It came to me now that it was time to think about how to conduct business in partnership with Source. I was told to create a triangle of business principles. Marijon suggested I find a word that would replace *business*. The word *mutuality* is what appeared. *Mutuality* in this context meant communication and exchange by common consent, or the law of intergalactic connection. So I changed "business plan" to "mutuality plan"; "business model" to "mutuality model"; and "business profit" to "reward of mutuality." All this comes together in the triangle of mutuality principles. This is how Stardreaming would conduct business—by means of communication and exchange by common consent.

The Draft Is Perfection–10/16/08

We welcome you, dear one, this very fine morning to another day of growth and expansion. The subject, as it has been, is love, for all revolves around love. It is all there is. It is creation and creator. It is you and it is me, each expressing the radiant love that we are. You understand so much: infinity, immortality, greed, and fear. All these you will incorporate into the triangle of mutuality principles. As we write these principles together, they are being imprinted into the consciousness of planet earth through the codes of love that you carry. The draft is perfection, but it too will be organic. You need only "be" and all will come.

With our deepest love,
Sananda via Anaya-Ra

In Glenda Green's book *Love without End*, Jesus speaks of the effect of love on the adamantine particles of creation, saying, "Love commands the adamantine particles, thus in being love you take command of your life."[1] With my intention surrounded by love, I was moving the particles of creation to manifest "one of the greatest wonders of the new earth." I was beginning to understand what it meant to be a creator and how one can manifest. I would later learn that as one raises one's love frequency, or obtains a higher love quotient, the resulting creation also raises its frequency. So, with the return of love to planet earth, as each person upshifts to the Christ-consciousness vibration, the manifestations on earth also upshift, allowing for heaven to express unity with Source on earth.

I wrote to James about my new thoughts, since I knew that his paintings contained a gold vibration, which now for me was the same crystalline structure that allowed for perfect compression and expansion:

> James, we pursue alchemical transformation to achieve a gold vibration by consciously removing limiting thought forms such as beliefs and attitudes, as well as foreign adamantine particles attracted through negative encounters. The gold vibration is the pure love of Source by which one can manifest or command the adamantine particles. This is what you are doing by means of your art—the gold vibration or crystalline structure in compression allows for perfected expansion.

Jesus spoke of compression and expansion as the rhythm of life, explaining:

> The whole universe is implicitly and explicitly of one piece, and from the point of perfect synchronicity there is a never-ending rhythm of compression and expansion. Compression and expansion are the great rhythm of the universe! Compressions that give birth to universal order eventually reverse to expansion, thereby releasing all the created potential. These pulsating rhythms alternate between silence and percussion, providing the origin of sound. Love creates compression, because love calls everything into assembly. The physical agent is magnetism. That power, applied to physical existence, is compression. Perfect compression never results in conflict, but in a state of transparent overlay. It is perfectly compatible with that which attracts and holds it in place.[2]

I understood that the transparent overlay of each aspect of a creation is a crystalline structure that allows one to create the perfection of Source. Later I would call this infinity consciousness: the combination of intention with pure love and light in partnership with Source, allowing for the expansion of that intention to express heaven on earth. This was the intention of the new business plan model for earth and for Stardreaming.

I took my new understanding a step further by realizing that one who carries the "gold vibration" is a golden dolphin. The golden dolphins collectively, as a society, create the new earth by means of pure compression and expansion. I was beginning to understand how to manifest the perfection of Source as a higher expression of our individual divinity, and I was very excited.

When One or More Are Gathered in My Name—10/20/08

Wow, indeed! You learn fast. All the pieces have been gathered that were floating around and through you. It is magnificent to behold. You truly understand the creation of the new earth and how you and other golden dolphins are at will manifesting it by commanding the adamantine particles with pure love of Source. There will be balance and harmony. You will do it with ease and grace. Your radiance is changing, and with it your DNA is changing. You are transforming your DNA to the DNA that I carry, that of love, pure love before separation from Source. Some describe that as Christ-consciousness, but your term "the pure love of Source" pleases me. "When one or more are gathered in my name" presages the power of the Golden Dolphin Society Trust. You see it so clearly now, dear one. Your agreement to stay sheltered in quiet for a period of time has indeed accelerated your remembering, and much more is to be revealed. You are becoming a master creator as you have always been, but now you see it, you know it to be true. You must overcome self-doubt in order to remember who you are, dear one.

With our deep love,
Sananda, Kuthumi, and El Morya via Anaya-Ra

Jesus explained to me how DNA changes with the love frequency. "Human DNA is constructed to handle and to conduct very high levels of love function. As you accelerate those love functions, your DNA will change accordingly."[3] He goes on to say that since he did not know separation from the creator, his DNA was different from that of the rest of humanity. The work I do is to raise the love frequency in humanity's DNA to return it to the state it knew before it experienced separation from Source. This is the return of "very high levels of love function" to planet earth.

As I was studying *Love without End*, a book about force versus magnetism and density versus infinity, new thought forms pushed their way through to my consciousness about the space of infinity at Stardreaming. I suddenly understood that infinity is the space between the adamantine particles that come together by love through spirit. Infinity is not "out there"; it exists throughout us and beyond. Jesus commented that our matter is less than 10 percent of who we are and the rest is the space of infinity. Traditionally, it is believed that force moves matter, but Jesus stated that magnetism is the power of attraction within the space of infinity, which causes the particles to gather. Magnetism is the power behind creation. Force does not work in the space of infinity; only magnetism and attraction work there.

Two nights before this new understanding of infinity, I experienced a moment of my life simultaneously in two dimensions. I woke up at midnight and struggled to go back to sleep, but was unsuccessful. I began the next day exhausted. The following night I awoke at midnight and feared the same outcome. I was aware that Archangel Michael was in my bedroom, standing by me. He leaned down and kissed my right cheek. At that moment, I was suddenly experiencing two dimensions simultaneously. I sneezed and recognized fully my physicality, yet my consciousness was elsewhere. It had moved to the space of infinity. I learned that my sacred heart is creating in my infinity, not in my density—creating with magnetism, not force. The sacred heart is where the pure love of Source enters the human body and is diffracted by means of intention to create form via the adamantine particles.

I went through the aspects of Stardreaming's expansion while consciously in my infinity. Then I realized that for full and perfect manifestation, James needed to have the same experience so that we were cocreating by means of attraction from the space of infinity. The space of infinity is where one goes during a massage and during meditation. It is not "out there" but truly "in there." It would seem that spontaneous healing, miracles, synchronicity, and more than I have thought of occurs in the infinity of the person. I noticed that while in such a space, my mind tried to figure out all this and actualize it. I switched focus to my sacred heart and its intention, and I knew that something powerful shifted for me that night. I asked that those new thought forms be expanded, for I now knew that there was a way to experience living in two dimensions simultaneously, and I wanted to experience that during my waking hours. I felt that I could ultimately will consciousness to expand into my infinity, while remaining in the third dimension. I believed that was how one accesses the universal knowledge that is available to all. This certainly was a work in progress.

In my excitement, I wrote to James expressing these new thoughts:

> Moments ago, while in the lucent state of half sleep, half wakefullness, My-Ron and I moved our consciousness into the inner space of infinity. I asked that negative beliefs and attitudes be identified and removed, and the word *unworthy* came up. Then I understood that my consciousness had placed boundaries on the vision of Stardreaming. I was told I was to move beyond the business plan and bring my consciousness out of density into infinity holding the thought "Stardreaming is one of the greatest wonders of the new earth," and allow for the magnetic streaming of particles of infinity. I am letting go of when, where, and how. The act of creating a business plan was a steppingstone, but we are beyond that now. I learned that Stardreaming has a consciousness in infinity, and our consciousness is to join it there. Wow. This will create a triangle of unlimited possibilities to manifest, unrestricted by density. This is the ultimate understanding of "Let go, let God." This is the ultimate understanding of S.T.A.R. and the way S.T.A.R. and Stardreaming come together through us. Amazing. The vortex of the S.T.A.R. clinic (me) and the vortex of Stardreaming (you) join together with infinity to change human consciousness. For this is ultimately the "triangle of mutuality principles," a triangle of unlimited possibilities to manifest, unrestricted by density. I needed My-Ron to access this through!

All of these new thoughts were like firecrackers going off in my brain, each being lit by my heart, which was so eager to expand, grow, and experience. Jesus explained that adamantine particles and particles of infinity are the same, but that the former indicates the character of the particle and the latter the function of the particle.[4]

Infinity Streaming—10/24/08

Well done to both you and My-Ron. You broke through the greatest of all hurdles. Stardreaming and all of human creation is on a new path of expansion. This is indeed the new earth: infinity versus density, expansion versus constriction. You ask how others will understand. All you need do is to remember, and through the unified field others will become aware and the understanding will spread. Knowing is only part. When "doing" and "being" become one, you will express infinity streaming through Stardreaming. Sit back, relax. The valve has been turned, the spigot is open, the river is beginning to flow. You see how very worthy you are, dear one.

All our deep love,
Raphael via Anaya-Ra

Then Jesus told me how the unified field works and I understood more clearly how S.T.A.R is infinity consciousness:

> When an idea from God-mind has been contacted by one man and sent out through the spoken word, cannot one, or all, again contact that thought in the Universal?[5]

I was so excited, I had to share it with everyone who would listen.

> I wish to share with who joined me initially on this journey, my understanding of the S.T.A.R. clinic, which exists now in consciousness though not form. I have come to understand that consciousness typically lives in density, where force causes movement. By moving it from density into the space of infinity, one connects to Source and the magnetic realm of attraction. Creation and manifestation occur within infinity consciousness by means of magnetism and attraction. S.T.A.R. is infinity consciousness. Surrendering, trusting, allowing, and receiving occurs in the space of infinity by means of pure love of Source and pure intention, unfiltered by duality.

Thank you for letting me share this with you on my journey of understanding who I am and the magic of life, love in action.

Another Place for Consciousness to Dwell—10/26/08

We join you and our dear friend My-Ron on this beautiful day of rest. You have indeed worked hard this week and these many weeks. There have been so many openings, revelations, understandings, and remembrances—and there will be more. We ask you to look to the sky now for more answers. Look in your sacred heart and in infinity, and look in the cosmos as well. There again is a triangle of love between the three. Connect them all in unity. The day will go quickly for you, and you will return to your nightly chamber, where you are in a different yet same reality. You travel into the cosmos. That is why it is important to add to it a place for your consciousness to dwell.

With our deep love,
The Council of Thirteen via Anaya-Ra

Jesus expanded the definition of infinity:

> Infinity is the unlimited potential of God, which first manifested as awareness, then as love, next as spirit, and finally as an infinite supply of adamantine particles that can be arranged with endless possibilities. Now remember that as an aspect of God, you are part of infinity. You are an expansion point of God's infinity, and the viewpoint from which you perceive infinity is your [sacred] heart. You are indispensable to the continuing expansion of infinity. You are the extra dimension! The heart is your gateway to performing in this extra dimension. It is the beginning of your higher intelligence.[6]

Then a new phase of Stardreaming was shared by the Council of Thirteen: Stardreaming was to be a portal for beings from the cosmos to come to earth.

You Saw the Feeder Stream—10/27/08

We went far last night. You had much work to do negotiating and organizing for the many who wish to come. The details are being worked out as we speak. You, dear one, are preparing the space. James has known for a long time that many are coming, and you are preparing with him. First, we need to manifest the portal and that is in process. You saw the river last night and noticed that it was just a feeder stream. There are many others, and they will soon all connect so you can see the powerful river. Don't think too much about the dream. You have an internal knowing. Today, rest.

With our deep love,
The Council of Thirteen via Anaya-Ra

All these new thought forms swirled around in my head trying to land in some organized fashion so that I could call on them, live them, and teach them. There was one more thought form that unified them all: the state of innocent perception by and through which creation and all that has been created is to be observed. I wrote to James, saying:

> James, It came to me today that, as René said, My-Ron is innocence, but I am to take it further and say that he is innocent perception. "Innocent perception is how children see the world: the way they perceive and respond without preconception. All you have to do is perceive and then regard with honor that which is already here. The mind attempts to change that in its own designing and redesigning of what is. That is what the complex, sophisticated mind always tends to do. It looks for idealized patterns that it can impose on existence and then calls them divine. You do not have to do anything to make this universe divine. "Behold, be grateful and forgive that which you did not understand or control. For life is divine. It is perfect, and it naturally manifests the will of its Creator"[7] (infinity consciousness). This is the lesson My-Ron is here to teach. He goes to the fairy ring each morning as the sun comes up and asks if he can go with me to a two-hour drumming circle. We have been working together on Richard's forms, and more I am sure. I will bring him back "home" to Stardreaming at the end of the month.

Archangel Metatron discussed the perspective of the detached observer, which seems similar to that of innocent perception.

> Now, within your brain, is an aspect beyond the personality ego that we term the detached observer. This is not the inner narrator, indeed the inner narrator is "attached." The inner narrator is attached to the emotional body. Quiet the inner narrator as if you are in meditation and allow the quiet observer to preside.[8]

I was being guided in every aspect of my new role as president of Stardreaming's preservation, maintenance, and expansion. But I never expected the detail of guidance that came to me early one morning before arising:

Go to the fifth year of operations as you have forecasted it in the mutuality plan's five-year cash flow projections. Determine what the fixed costs are for Stardreaming. Project what the fifth-year return will be from the endowment fund. Add the fifth-year projected income to the income from the fund and see what the difference is.

I knew that we could request a larger endowment fund if needed, so we had to have specific numbers. Although this was definitely not my area of strength, somehow the "how to do this" was appearing. Fascinating. As long as my consciousness focused on the statement "Stardreaming is one of the greatest wonders of the new earth," all was in balance, I believed. I could do anything, including five-year cash flow projections, when I was one with infinity consciousness.

In summarizing infinity consciousness, attraction versus force, innocent perception, and all the new thought forms that had been presented, I wondered how they related to the expansion of Stardreaming and the Temple of the Stone. It occurred to me that as we looked at James's recent painting of Archangel Michael that in the space between the dots we could see infinity streaming. I thought of Stardreaming as a cosmic center and wondered about the electromagnetic properties of the Temples of the Cosmos.

Entering the labyrinth and walking between the huge stones would be like walking between the dots of James's paintings. We would be walking in the space of infinity where attraction and magnetism exist. As we walk with intention and love, our infinity space merges—through the use of attraction and magnetism—with the cosmic infinity space; this unity of our space and cosmic space allows for transformation through increased attraction and magnetism.

> The Temple of the Living God is the blending of the greater with the lesser through which the lesser becomes one with the greater. The impurity was caused by the separation of the lesser from the greater. The purity is caused by their union, so that no longer is there a greater and a lesser but just the one good, whole, pure air.[9]

I thought of the other twelve temples and the way Saint Germain, Archangels Michael, Gabriel, Raphael, Uriel, Metatron, and so many masters, gods, and goddesses are present and represented. The Temple of the Stone is different from the other twelve temples in that it is pure Source, the Holy Spirit. James mentioned to me that it is the philosopher's stone and that Christ was the philosopher's stone. The masters of the Far East describe Christ as "the power within man to know God."[10] So the Temple of the Stone is Christ-consciousness (knowing God) through a merging with infinity. As we step into the labyrinth, we experience a power within us to know God, which occurs through the space between particles as represented by the space between the giant stones.

~ 10 ~

Humanity Creating Heaven on Earth

The expansion and compression that make up the rhythm of life can be understood as movement up the spiral of life by means of the crystalline alignment of all aspects of the compression, and now I took it a step further. By joining our clear intentions with the intentions of the company of heaven, the expansion becomes the manifestation of Source's perfection, or humanity expressing heaven on the new earth. I was told this is the reason for creating the portal at the Temple of the Stone, the thirteenth temple at Stardreaming. And most importantly, all of humanity was to know that they could express heaven or earth through the portal. Part of our divinity lies in our ability to create. Our creations are of a higher frequency, allowing for the manifestations to similarly be of a higher frequency, and thus they usher in the new earth at the time of the ascension. Humanity is the bridge between heaven and earth by means of our creations.

We create by means of appreciation, forgiveness, and innocent perception by surrendering our pure intention in partnership with the company of heaven, in the space of infinity, trusting that magnetism and attraction will reign in that space—allowing the perfection of Source, and receiving in pure love, gratitude and appreciation. S.T.A.R. is the law of creation.

As I was integrating this information, I kept getting another message: I was being protected and all I needed do was to ask for help. First, the fairies told me of their protection. They had covered my backyard with mushrooms that were popping up everywhere. It was so beautiful.

Conversation with My Fairies through the Mushroom Ring in My Backyard—11/1/08

Fairies: We love you. We are here to protect you.

Nina: What am I to do?

Fairies: Continue to work on the spreadsheet. You will know what is next soon.

Nina: Where did you come from?

Fairies: Alpha Centauri. We were sent by the Council of Thirteen to watch over and protect you.

Nina: Am I in trouble?

Fairies: No, because we are here.

Mushroom fairy ring.

Nina: Is there anything I should know?

Fairies: Your physical father is an Alpha Centaurian.

Nina: Is he well?

Fairies: Yes. As you know, he is a very powerful council member. He has been watching over you for your protection.

Nina: You are very beautiful.

Fairies: Thank you, that makes us feel good.

Nina: What can I do for you?

Fairies: Be fully who you are. You know now. Take it on fully.

Nina: Why does my head hurt?

Fairies: You are stretching all the particles, and they are readjusting. You would say new synapses are being created. This is all good.

Nina: Will I see you in the physical realm?

Fairies: You will someday.

I was being protected so that I could be a bridge between heaven and earth. To do so, I had to fully accept my divine nature. For the perfection of Source to flow through me, I had to accept that I was worthy. I knew this to be my most difficult challenge, to accept my self-worth. Without doing so, I knew also that Source was not complete, for we are one.

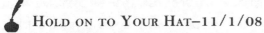

Hold on to Your Hat–11/1/08

We rejoice. We shout with you at your transformation, your acceptance of who you are and why you are here, our dear one—our magnificent, radiant, dear one. You know at last in the fullness of every fiber of your physical being, and you no longer fear to write these words. You understand that in this acceptance full love of Source can flow through you, that you are worthy to carry the Christ-consciousness codes with Sananda, that you have power to manifest the new earth on earth. You understand infinity consciousness and are now able to create and lead the Golden Dolphin Society Trust, and guide those who have similarly expanded DNA, those who jointly will create the new earth where the power to know God will rule. Hold on to your hat, dear one, for there is much more. Soon, very soon, the flow for Stardreaming will begin. You will orchestrate this process with the deep knowing that you are in service to Source. We, the Council of Thirteen, will direct you at every juncture. You need only ask. We have been waiting for eons for you to reappear and take the mantle of your power.

With our deep love,
Your physical father via Anaya-Ra

Next I learned that sound realigns particles of created matter and energizes them into form.

Sound Realigns the Particles–11/2/08

What a day. We feel you are truly rested and comfortable in your body, with no fears or worries. This is a great moment for all, for when you are centered and balanced, the love vibration is centered and balanced as it radiates out from you. You need to know that you are a large wave in the ocean, a wave that affects all other water molecules. That is why we said that you are to be connected and on point twenty-four hours a day, for on the etheric plane, where all connect with you, the focus and state of your consciousness is felt. How do you do this, you ask? We will guide you and strengthen you. You have seen how this works. Just ask us to be with you. This is our greatest service to you and through you to humankind. Now we have news for you. You are to say the Lord's Prayer this morning on the meditation conference call. Then be silent. Much will come through this gathering of pure souls. Do not try to figure anything out, just absorb. We will be speaking through those voices. Allow the resonance to touch your soul and you will manifest from the tones. This is how we will activate the adamantine particles you are gathering. Today the bell-ringing will energize the particles into form. How about that? Sound is so important. That is the power of your tuning forks, for it realigns the particles in your body with the pure clear tone of the universal song. These Tree of Life tuning forks were a great gift to you. Use them more often now that you truly comprehend. You now understand Dr. Emoto's work and that of so many new thinkers and researchers. Care for the sounds that surround you and, using your tonning forks, correct the sounds that intrude. Enjoy the sunrise with My-Ron, who will return home.

With our deep love,

The whales and the dolphins via Anaya-Ra

An insight arrived in the wee hours one morning that I believed was the essential last piece I needed to understand manifestation: James and I are creating heaven on earth. Yesterday, while thinking about a line in the Lord's Prayer, "Thy will be done, on earth as it is in heaven," I read Jesus's words:

> Most often when I spoke of the temple, I was referring to the sacred heart and not of an architectural edifice. Just as surely when I referred to the kingdom of heaven, I was referring to the zone of perfection, which is the bond between God and man, and is found within the sacred heart. God is the author of perfection. Wherever that perfection dwells, heaven unfolds. Man's doorway to that perfection is the sacred heart. Seek it first, and all else shall be given to you.[1]
>
> If he should but realize that every idea is a direct perfect expression from God and, when this idea comes to him, he would

> immediately make it his ideal to be expressed from God, then take his mortal hands off and let God express through him the perfect way, this ideal would come forth perfect. Here we must realize that God is above the mortal and the mortal cannot help in any way. In this way man would learn in a short time to express perfection. The one great thing man must learn is to get forever through and out of the psychic or mind forces and express directly from God, for all psychic forces are created wholly by man and they are likely to mislead.[2]

So in my state of meditation, I asked that God's perfection be expressed through me. Then it came to me to ask that the perfection of God be expressed through the Temple of the Stone as a manifestation of heaven on earth. Ask and you shall receive. So, I realized that the new earth is humanity expressing the perfection of God. This perfection, or how one creates heaven on earth requires appreciation, forgiveness, and innocent perception.

Collective Consciousness Has Altered–11/3/08

We applaud so loudly, dear one. You heard, you absorbed, you spoke and so it is. Dear one, you must remember so that others will know through a connection to your consciousness. Christ-consciousness has been planted, but it now must grow. That is the essence of Stardreaming: God's perfection on earth, the sacred heart, the Temple of the Stone, and Christ-consciousness. Now all will come and transform the earth because the collective consciousness has altered.

With our deep love,
Cosmic mother via Anaya-Ra

As these truths were pouring in, I asked each day, "What am I to do today?" I always acted on the answers I received. One morning, I woke and sensed Archangel Michael in the bedroom. I had dreamt about him, something about putting him into a very large matchbox; after that I couldn't get back to sleep, so I tried to meditate. What came to me first was that James and I were to meditate together at Stardreaming. Then Arcturian angels appeared and said, "We are at your command." I remembered the month's teaching on the law of creation and about how Jesus had said that we are to command the adamantine particles with love. Then I saw all of Stardreaming in a perfect state of compression. When events are aligned in transparency, expansion occurs, and I realized that everything was in place and ready for expansion. The compression was clear and complete. The adamantine particles had gathered with love. I needed to go to Stardreaming to meditate with James, but not on the details of the mutuality plan. With love, the intention would be Stardreaming, expressed through James and me, as the perfect expression of God's love.

Fly Like the Golden Eagle–11/8/08

Wow, dear one, you heard so clearly all aspects of our profound message to you and James last night. The teachings all came together and demonstrated the phenomena of compression and expansion. Expansion of the law of creation was what you experienced. You will soon witness Stardreaming experiencing the laws of creation. Only after you have a full experience of the creative power that is you, will you teach others. What you are doing is moving from your mind to your sacred heart: the true creator of your being. All that you have learned these many months is only you realizing you. There have been necessary parameters to each aspect, thus the large matchbox. You and James are to light the matches, the fire of alchemical change, and watch the true expansion of Stardreaming. Fly like the golden eagle.

With our deep love,
Archangel Michael via Anaya-Ra

On this day, I was invited by my friend Reginah to a sweat lodge ceremony at her home in Albuquerque. I was glad the sweats continued in Bear Heart's absence. Our gathering was a tribute to him. I wondered if the fire of the sweat could have any relationship to Archangel Michael's matchbox and the matches or the fire of alchemical change.

Temple of God–11/9/08

We join you, dear one, on this fine day of cleansing your body in sweat. The purity that results will be a vessel for the perfection of God, which you requested. The love of God will flow into, around, and through you. You have felt the restrictions in your moments of prayer, but those will be removed today. The cavity of your being will be emptied and purified as a temple of God. Through it will flow the pure light of your God, the you that is God, the God that is you. This is the "next step" that you have requested. Open today in the sweat lodge each pore, each cell; open your body, mind, and soul. Allow the golden eagle to fly.

With our deep love,
Archangels Michael and Raphael via Anaya-Ra

During the sweat lodge ceremony I surrendered my intention for Stardreaming formed in partnership with the company of heaven, into the space of infinity. I had to share my thoughts with James:

> I just finished reading *The Complete Idiot's Guide to Alchemy,* which explains all that I have been saying but from an alchemical perspective.[3] The last chapter discusses the laws of creation. Yesterday, during the two-hour sweat lodge, I placed in infinity space the prayer "I express the perfection of God and that it be expressed at Stardreaming." My alchemical vessel was purified with the heat of the steam as I connected with Source. The words poured out of me eloquently, and they now radiate and vibrate in the unified field. I have completed the first part of what you have asked me to do. Now we enter the pregnancy of intention, as described in the last chapter of the book. What an honor. Thank you!

New Phenomena for Earth–11/11/08

There is important news to share with you this morning, dear one. Indeed, the first phase of manifestation is complete. As you realized yesterday, your intentions, wrapped in pure love, are vibrating with the sound of your prayers. The universe is responding to your request, and as you know, all prayers are answered. This prayer was heard by all the angels in heaven, throughout all of infinity and every cell on planet earth; and "so it is" as you commanded with love. There is indeed a time for you to see the material manifestation, but it is forming in ways beyond the limitations of your original intent. The creativity of the universe, the masters, the fairies, the elementals, Gaia, the otherworldly beings will combine with your creativity and that of James. Stardreaming will expand into a reality of multiple consciousness in response to your request that the perfection of God be expressed. These are new phenomena for earth. You are to hold your intention closely in your sacred heart with clarity. Guard it with pure love and feel the expansion, then you will see the expansion.

With our deep love,
Archangels Raphael and Michael via Anaya-Ra

This did not keep me from physical creation, however. My attention remained on the completion of the triangle of mutuality principles.

Triangle of Mutuality Principles—11/12/08

We welcome you on this fine, fine day, our dear one. You are progressing magnificently with the triangle of mutuality principles and as you write the principles down they are being incorporated into you, so that you will be the principles. Your time of intense fatigue is complete. You have traveled through the timeline, and that was more taxing than even your weary body understood. You incorporated not only physical changes but emotional and intellectual ones as well. You are on the other side with a new, more brilliant radiance. Your time with James today will be briefer than usual, and you will know when to depart. He is integrating his understanding and knowing with yours to find his new truth. This process of dragons, as he calls it, is why I, Archangel Michael, remain with him (the painting has not been bought yet). Love is all you need "be." You are an unconscious model of trust for James. Until you both understand and accept that you are the creators of Stardreaming, I cannot leave. But it won't be much longer, for your visit will help to cement that knowing into James's consciousness. He has given us far too much credit, and not enough to his own creative energy. This understanding must be integrated fully, for it is the gift that you both and Stardreaming bring to all the golden dolphins on earth.

With our deep love,
Archangels Raphael and Michael via Anaya-Ra

I learned that humans have always created their realities, but for the first time I understood that we are the bridge between heaven and earth, and that when we create with the company of heaven we can bring heaven on earth into reality.

The Cusp of Creation–11/15/08

We always like to begin our morning gathering by greeting you, our dear one. Today will be a day of profound opening and clarity for you. We have not yet formally met, but you know me. I am always present when the ancient ones come through to you. Now we meet more intimately. Continue to write, though you think there is nothing to record. You are to call James and say that I wish you to see the painting, and that will begin our relationship. For you see, it is vital that you are a part of the energy of the four archangels who are coming through by means of the magic that is James. These paintings and the energy of archangels that flows through them are the ingredients of Stardreaming—the ushering in of the Christ-consciousness energy, creation, cultivation, manifestation, and perpetuity. This is for Stardreaming and for the new earth; and your soul is wedded to Stardreaming. This is difficult for you to write, dear one, but continue, and yes, share it with James. You both are on the cusp of creation, and you need to be strong and rested. Yes, you feel the ache in your head, and you now know what that is, so relax. What does the cusp of creation mean, you ask? In your asking, you know. It is all that has been organized in the sacred heart. The tears are because this is too difficult for you to believe, but dear one, it is true. You have manifested the next phase of expansion for Stardreaming. You will—write it—very soon see what you have indeed felt. Then the world will know that in Christ-consciousness, with the pure love of Source, humanity has the power to create.

With our deepest love,
Archangel Gabriel via Anaya-Ra

As my understanding of creation was growing, I was told that believing needed to depend on seeing. Matter is invisible in its primary stage when the creation particles are moved by love's intention. Then the vibrational rate lowers to a point where those with low vibration can see. I knew that the Temple of the Stone existed in another dimension, and that at some point in the future it would be in the third dimension.

It Is You, Not Us–11/16/08

Invisible is exactly the message we share with you this magnificent morning, dear one. (My pen made marks, but showed no ink.) The truth is that just because you don't see something does not mean that it does not exist. You know we are here, you feel us, you hear us in your thoughts, yet you cannot yet see us. Do we therefore not exist? This is a perfect analogy for the creation process. All matter is invisible in its primary stage. Then the energy of love and divine intention causes attraction by means of magnetism. Finally, the vibrational rate lowers to a point where those with low vibration can see the matter.

Nina: I understand how that works for physical matter and dense reality. How does it work for the events, actions, and processes that accompany the manifestation of matter? Especially, how does it work when there are other people involved in an outcome? For example, how do you bring the right people at the right time to Stardreaming or into my life?

We don't, dear one; you or James do, by means of the intention of pure love. You are the creators; we assist, guide, and help you to remember. Yes, you can write about things you don't understand, for you are just tapping into infinity consciousness where all is one and all is known. You are finding for yourself the answers to your questions. In this space of infinity where attraction and magnetism reign, the vibration of your intention radiates, vibrates, and flows like a wave of pure love. Not all intention is pure love, thus the reason for different levels of perfection. It is like a dance, but it all happens in the space between the dots, infinity, again by means of the attraction and magnetism of the degree of the expression of the pure love of God that you are. Don't think, dear one, know. Know that you are the expression of All That Is, that you carry infinity consciousness, Christ-consciousness. Truly anything is possible with the love that you are, even miracles. That is how they happen. You now, as God-self, no longer have to find the answer; you only need to allow the answer. Do you understand S.T.A.R. better now, dear one? All you need is intention placed in infinity space. Surrender it, trust that attraction and magnetism will reign, allow the perfection of God and receive all in pure love.

We cherish you and love you deeply,

All who love and serve you via Anaya-Ra

While saying good morning to the sun, a new understanding of surrender came to me. I wasn't giving power away. I was creating an intention and placing it into infinity, and then trusting, allowing, and receiving. This was a huge realization!

Another realization came shortly afterward, when I understood the connection between Stardreaming and the S.T.A.R. clinic. The clinic was to be the School of No Mysteries that will become part of the expanded Stardreaming, where understanding the laws of creation is shared. S.T.A.R. is the law of creation that is needed to place intention in infinity space, surrender it, and trust that attraction and magnetism will reign; allow the perfection of God and receive all in pure love. You, now as God-self, no longer have to find the answer, only allow the answer. Stardreaming was to be where that experience happened.

Not only was I learning how to create with the company of heaven, I was told that we sat around dreaming of the perfect way to express perfection on earth, and now we are doing it. Too cool!

We All Sat around Dreaming—11/18/08

We greet you this very fine day, our ambassador of light and love. Your journey with us has been full of openings and remembering: remembering the contract and now its execution. We are all here together with you today to say that we are proud of your steadfast commitment and your willingness to listen, though you truly know that already. The miracle is that you have removed all the blocks of constraint, fear, and disbelief and all the dualistic thinking that would hamper the manifestation of our vision, for it was, and is, yours as well. James of course is included in the "ours." You will remember soon how we all sat around dreaming of the perfect way to express perfection on earth, and here it is. The details will express themselves soon. You need have no worries now, dear one. Your immediate work is complete. It is time to dream of your family, to think of games you will play, and food you will share. Everything takes care of itself, with the intention of pure love that surrounds each thought form and particle. Go back to your triangle of mutuality principles and begin to complete that body of work, for when you return in January you will live by those principles, Stardreaming, as the Golden Dolphin Society Trust, will be managed by them. They will be the new model for conducting business on the new earth.

With our deep love,

The Council of Thirteen and your father who loves you via Anaya-Ra

It Is You, Not Us–11/16/08

It is you, not us.

I had to share this brief message with James. James, with all of his accomplishments, so often gave credit for Stardreaming's growth to the masters. I needed to communicate to him that he was the creator. He was the manifestor; the masters were his guides. We both needed to accept our majesty before the vision could unfold.

Symbol of the Radiance That Is Pouring Now from Heaven to Earth–11/21/08

We applaud you, our dear one, for the courage and commitment of your speech to our very dear James. The tone of your voice and the vibration of your words and sounds were as important as the words themselves. This will be the final element needed in the unfolding of your vision, for it could not go forward until you both were fully empowered, and only you (humanity) can do this. Yes, the sun is rising as we speak, a symbol of the radiance that is pouring now from heaven to earth.

With our deep love,

Archangels Raphael and Michael via Anaya-Ra

Embracing the God that I am seemed important, but I felt an enormous reluctance to do so. From birth we've been told that we're not divine; God is out there. I was beginning to bring God inside of me and to stop giving my power away. At the time, I didn't really understand the statement "heaven on earth." But I know now heaven is humanity creating with the full awareness of their human divinity, not merely by means of their humanity alone. The message was telling me that I am an individual aspect of All That Is. I am the creator of my reality. I needed to be proactive, to be the driver for my life's journey, not the passenger.

James had always told me that "they"—meaning the masters—asked him to build a labyrinth or paint a painting at Stardreaming. But now I was beginning to understand that the "they" was an aspect or archetype of him. He was the creator and the builder of Stardreaming. Wow, this understanding was enormous and life changing. I was the creator of our wellness clinics, and what I just learned must mean that I was the creator of their undoing as well. This undoing was currently underway.

My ties to the wellness clinics ended as the last dissolution paper arrived and all the documents were submitted to the Public Regulatory Commission to shut down our former businesses (Life Harmonies Institute, Life Sustainability Group, and the neurosensory divisions). Now I was poised to manifest and create to my fullest capacity.

All Will Wonder at the Wonder–11/23/08

Rejoice, rejoice for it cometh. You have created the Golden Dolphin Society Trust, but the management of the trust with pure intention is as important as its creation. The triangle of mutuality principles is indeed your blueprint. Love is your tool, and you are the means. While you are with your family the "being" will grow, so when you return, the perfection of God will manage the vision that you and James have created. This does not remove challenges and decisions, but with an understanding that the answers lie within the space of infinity and that with ease and grace, and the love that you are, the answers will "appear." You will do by being, and a model will grow for others to replicate. Look back through the journal. The answers are there for you. You are the creator.

With our deep love,

The Council of Thirteen via Anaya-Ra

I was then told why Stardreaming would be known as "one of the greatest wonders of the new earth." The expansion of Stardreaming, the Temple of the Stone, was being created in the God-center of our sacred hearts, where the expression of God's perfection is created with the company of heaven, allowing the expression of the perfection of God, Source, and heaven on earth.

Know That You Create with S.T.A.R.–11/25/08

Top of the day to you, our dear one. You see our jolly demeanor, which is a result of joy. You are looking at things differently and making decisions differently. All is in divine order, for we tell you again, you are creating a new model of how to conceive and create a business, how to run a business, and how to prosper in mutual exchange. When the results are in, and all begin to understand just what has transpired, the question will be "How?" Now we are in a phase of pure trust, yet you know so deeply that what you write is the truth of the universe. You have not demanded security for yourself or evidence that all is well. Amazing, dear one, you just trust and know from the God-center that you are. Look back on how the journey began. You wanted so badly to have your business partners understand you and your desire to work together, and together with Source. You came away from the experience wanting more, to experience the richness of cocreating. Then James called you to join the vision of Stardreaming. You were right to say what an honor that was for you, but, dear one, see also the honor that you bring to Stardreaming: balance. Then the next phase of your journey began with our presence at Chaco Canyon. This was when our long-awaited connection occurred with the regifting of the vril rod. Then observe your courage to add Source to your business plan. The expression of the pure love of God could not leave God out! We moved on to the realization that to express the perfection of God, it must move into the day-to-day operation of the business. The result of that expression is heaven on earth, where humanity is able to be one with unity. Most importantly, dear one, you and James now realize the God-center in your sacred heart is where the expression of God's perfection was created with the company of heaven. So now you see why we say, "Stardreaming is one of the greatest wonders of the new earth." Step back now, dear one, and admire your painting. For you, too, are a supreme artist. You paint with the adamantine particles in the space of infinity. You see the similarity with James? Isn't it too beautiful? Beauty, as you now know, is when all the vectors are in harmony with Source, and you know you are experiencing heaven. So, you see, you and James are painting heaven on earth, the beauty of the perfection of God, for others to feel and become through your creativity. What a masterpiece. Be ever so proud, but know that you create with S.T.A.R.

With our deep love,
The Council of Thirteen via Anaya-Ra

I was introduced to the idea of the new human, the Christos human, whom I understood to be one who creates with the company of heaven to manifest the perfection of Source on earth, the same as a golden dolphin.

Thanksgiving Day, New Moon–11/27/08

Nina: My great appreciation and thanks to all the heavenly beings who have guarded, protected, tutored, guided, and loved me during my amazing journey to today, with my deep love.

We so appreciate your greeting us this Thanksgiving Day, a day when the thanks of each day is culminated in a grand celebration of family and friends. As your celestial family, we join you in the celebration. We wish to express to you, our dear one, our enormous appreciation for your love, your courage, your immense patience, your devotion to God. It rings out through the chambers of all hearts throughout the universe. And so it is.

With our deep love,
All who love you via Anaya-Ra

I learned from the triangle of mutuality principles, which was now complete, that moderation, equilibrium, and love formed the three sides of the triangle. This was to be a new model for conducting business in the new earth.

Moderation, Equilibrium, and Love–11/29/08

We greet you, dear one, on this brilliant new day of clarity and opening for you and your journey. You will complete the triangle of mutuality principles today, and then put it aside to become a new unit, for the purpose of changing business principles. Moderation, equilibrium, and love are the three principles. Mutuality is communication and exchange by mutual consent. Mutuality is the new foundation, and the Golden Dolphin Society Trust will be the first to live by the principles. Your attention shall move on today toward your family. Focus on love toward and with them. They will grow from your love, and you will be renewed and recharged from their love, to return to begin.

With our deep love,
The Council of Thirteen via Anaya-Ra

All the aspects for the expansion of Stardreaming were in place. I was told the seeds were being planted and that the growth had begun. My job now was to love my creation, for the frequency of love is what moves the adamantine particles of creation into form.

During the night, in a lucid dream state, I wrote a note describing what had come into my awareness. In the morning, I found the message next to My-Ron:

The goal is to show everyone that they too can create with the pure intention of God. You are a model of doing business as the new earth, in a way that is grand, unexpected, and profound. Be prepared for the unexpected. We love you!

Source unknown via Anaya-Ra

A Big Statement Needs to Be Made to Declare a Big Principle–12/5/08

We applaud you, our dear one. You understand so clearly the need to present yourself with a bang, so that all notice the miracles. You are correct that a big statement needs to be made to declare a big principle. And so it is. Just continue to show patience, but observe yourself, patient one. In your commanding, you are allowing and accepting beyond the boundaries that were present. Yes, the Golden Dolphin Society Trust needs to make a big sound that vibrates far and wide. That means coming in all together, not in a piecemeal way, for which there is no energy. The time is now, and the statement will be loud. Then people can step back and say, "What just happened?" Your enormous confidence (what you thought was weak) will be your greatest message carrier. So patience and confidence are your symbols. Watch in the coming days, watch each detail unfold as the miracles and magic of the universe present themselves.

With our deep love,

Archangels Michael, Gabriel, and Raphael via Anaya-Ra

~ 11 ~

Anatomy of a Miracle

All that I needed was available to me at any time. My challenge was to be able to receive. The Christ-consciousness codes and awareness had been transferred to me, but until I accepted that I was worthy to carry and transfer them, the miracles would not appear. Three crystal skulls assisted me toward that unrecognized goal, as did the return of the crystalline grid and the opening of the Christ-consciousness gateway on the spring equinox. These events needed to occur before I could begin the transfer of the Christ-consciousness codes, a process that would start on March 27, 2009, while I was at a park in Arizona. As I sat there, the energy would flow from Gaia through me to the interplanetary star beings, ambassadors from many nations, who would come for that transmission.

In December, I had a private session with a crystal skull explorer, Joshua Shapiro (www.crystalskullexplorers.com) and his small amethyst skull, which looked extraterrestrial and was known as a star being skull. The skull had the names "The King, the One Who Points the Way" and "Lay-a-lonie," to represent its androgynous nature. During the session, I listened to music while in meditation, then Joshua and I shared experiences. My experience was that I had entered into a silent dialogue when my mouth began trembling strangely. When I was not "speaking," my third eye focused intensely on receiving. I remember Joshua telling me that in the future I would channel. Not me, I thought, he is wrong. Yet, true enough, the following June, during summer solstice, I began channeling, and it is now a daily practice.

My session with the alien-looking skull helped me accept why I was here on planet earth.

As the days in December passed, a trip to the East Coast drew closer. I had been told that phase one of Stardreaming's expansion was complete. What was next? What would phase two look like?

The Universal Song of Creation—12/10/08

Nina: What kind of work is in store for me when I return to Stardreaming at the end of January 2009?

We are so glad you asked, dear one, for it connects you strongly to the next phase, the implementation. You have leaped into that next stage with your question. You again show courage by looking to the next phase when seemingly the first is not complete, but as you intuitively know, it is. So, to answer your question, all is awaiting your feet to be planted on the soil at Stardreaming, when the magic you bring is to be transferred to Stardreaming. You will be joining all the elementals and fairies, and all the company of heaven who are holding your seat for you. Here the orchestra will be conducted for others; many others will join you, so it is no longer a solo performance. James awaits the music to begin. The details will appear, but first we will need to get the players to assemble for the universal song of creation to be heard. You will be tended to, nourished, loved, and embraced on your journey to the East Coast, and you will return to us full of vigor and excitement. We will not leave you, but will leave you alone to focus on your beloved, expanding family.

With our deep love,

The Council of Thirteen and Archangel Raphael via Anaya-Ra

I knew that the work James and I were doing was rich with magic and miracles, but what did that mean? Then, one morning, I had a breakthrough; I was filled with immense gratitude for and understanding of the process of creation and manifestation. It was as if the final piece fell into place. In *The Keys of Jeshua* by Glenda Green, Jeshua (Jesus) says:

> God is the Creator of all things, and everything already exists. For you, nothing exists until you receive it. At times this phenomenon

shows up dramatically. Something you would not receive may be invisible, and you would swear it was not existent or even in the range of possibility. Then it mysteriously appears the moment you are truly ready to receive. This is the anatomy of miracles, the spontaneous appearance of that which was already given but unavailable until the moment you could receive. Many times it is necessary to release a negative consideration or doubt before you can receive. There is also an emotional equivalent to receiving, and that is gratitude. Gratitude is such a powerful emotion that you can magnify all your beliefs and bring them into present realization through praising gifts even before you receive them. True belief does not withhold gratitude until uncertainty has been eroded and resistance has been overcome. Those are the characteristics of disbelief. True belief knows the gift in the same moment as the belief is formed! The feeling is one of immense gratitude.[1]

You Have Changed Human Consciousness–12/11/08

Rejoice, rejoice for all is complete and the time for festivities and merriment is at hand. Your children gather. Even a black, furry protector puppy has presented itself. Be merry, no frowns or worry, just be present. We will be coordinating all that needs to be fulfilled while you are gone. Take this journal with you, study, and review. For much more will appear in the written word by means of rereading. Play, frolic, and enjoy yourself. You have changed human consciousness over the last half year, no small feat. You will indeed look back and marvel at your accomplishment. The next phase, which begins upon your return, is the implementation.

With our deep love,
Raphael via Anaya-Ra

On the day before my departure, I went to Stardreaming to be with the painting *Archangel Gabriel* that James had added to his archangel series. It was definitely a full moon, and I felt full of conflicting emotions, some truly shocking that challenged the path on which I believed I had been firmly walking.

Archangel Gabriel, End of Phase One–The Delivery Is Soon at Hand–12/12/08, Full Moon

We rejoice that you, dear one, acknowledge the significance of this cyclical day. You know about the full moon and the date 12/12, but today these two power days coincide! A full moon on 12/12. Add to that the significance of your meeting me in all my elevated glory. How we rejoice in meeting you in all your elevated glory. All comes together to signify closure and a new beginning. Your departure tomorrow closes chapter one, presents an intermission of grand music, and prepares for chapter two. Reflect on the power of the moon, my symbol of harmony and balance. This is where we are at Stardreaming, harmony and balance. Look at all the seeds that have been sown, new seeds ready to burst forth. Feel full, dear one. Feel radiant, for all that you have accomplished on the etheric plane is soon to show itself in full color and sound on the earthly plane. Your pregnancy is coming full term. The delivery is soon at hand. You thought it was only your daughter who was to deliver, but this is not so. (I stopped writing in disbelief.) Continue writing, for we have more to share. The dreams that you dreamt, the imagination that you invoked all come from the core, the center of who you are, love. The purity of this vibration is to be born, and that energy will permeate all that is to come forth. You will call it by its new name, the Golden Dolphin Society Trust, and all will marvel at the perfection of God on earth. You are our beloved, in whom we are well pleased, dear one.

With our deep love,
Archangel Gabriel via Anaya-Ra

My daughter, a retired kindergarten teacher, was indeed about to deliver her third child. I remember that when I was a participant at one of Bear Heart's sweat lodges, I had prayed to be a grandmother. Then *whoosh*. This new wee one would make me a grandmother of six grandchildren under the age of five. The children were the answers to their parents' prayers as well.

I made arrangements to fly to the East Coast. But first, before I left

Santa Fe, I paid a good-bye visit to Stardreaming. What a good-bye it turned out to be!

When I met James at Stardreaming, he told me that his vision of the future of Stardreaming had changed. He thanked me for my effort and commitment but stated that the megalabyrinth would not to be built, and that he would be happy to move forward on his own. I reached out to El Morya to keep me balanced as I adjusted to this unexpected news.

Just before Christmas I traveled to join my family, and to celebrate my daughter's fortieth birthday. I saw my three children, my son-in-law and daughter-in-law, all the grandchildren, and a brand new black Labrador puppy, all together after so many months apart. I loved seeing my younger son, a helicopter pilot, rolling around the kitchen floor, covered with children who love him, with the puppy jumping on top of the children, trying to join in the fun. I savored elegant meals of endives, a European favorite, and New England seafood. I enjoyed the physical hugs—actual hugs rather than hugs conveyed over long-distance telephone lines. This was a rare and special moment in my life: family, love, joy, and bonding.

After the birthday celebration, I joined my elder son and his family for Christmas in Cape May, New Jersey, where he had spent many summers as a lifeguard. When he had graduated from medical school, he combined being a lifeguard with rotations as a physician in the local hospital.

While I was away and James was reflecting on Stardreaming's direction; he was told that there was not a "society" as had been envisioned. He stated that the term would be dropped. He wrote to me before his trip to Australia and New Zealand, restating his new position concerning the future direction of Stardreaming. My written response could be summarized as "Fascinating."

What I have observed is that manifestation is an organic process. Often it is necessary for us to go strongly in one direction, to a necessary point on our path, but choice moves us on to a specific new branch of the path, one that is equally valuable and perhaps more relevant to the intended outcome. So, for me, James's statement did not inspire a "How come?" but instead, I stood fascinated, observing the marvels of creation and the organic process.

I suspended daily writing in my channeled journal. I thought a great deal about how my daily messages no longer coincided with James's current vision for Stardreaming. I trusted my voices, but was puzzled by this difference between James and me. Eventually, I accepted that this was a time to rest and allow the flow of divine order to recalibrate.

During a period when my son and his family were off visiting a former school friend and his family, I was alone in a house that had been loaned to us by friends. I had a lot of time to think. Was I to continue the dialogue with Richard or terminate it? All of my inner voices told me that I was to return to Santa Fe and begin phase two, but that was not what I was hearing from James. I walked the very long, empty beach, which helped me find clarity. It seemed appropriate to check in with Richard. I rarely called him because he was busy with his partners, trying to put together the investment vehicle that would fund Stardreaming's expansion.

Richard, too, seemed perplexed. His expectations were not manifesting according to his projected schedule. It seemed as if the universe was asking him to make adjustments as well. He was confused and looking for direction.

What I have learned in the time since that phone call is that life flows in the rhythm of compression and expansion. Compression in its crystalline form is what allows the expansion desired by one's higher self. The words I spoke to Richard while walking to the beach were that flow or manifestation would come when he truly accepted the divinity of who he is. When that moment came, his ability to impact others would be exponentially increased. Not only would he be a vehicle for funding projects, but with the monetary fuel would come a consciousness that would transform the business itself. We had numerous conversations about this in the months that followed.

I returned to Stardreaming after the holidays, and asked James, "How do I express your new decision to the potential funders of Stardreaming?" To my surprise, James had come full circle during his stay in Australia and New Zealand. He was standing 100 percent in his magnificence, easily able again to embrace an expanded Stardreaming with lots more visitors and worldwide attention. All the transformative and expansionary issues that had weighed so heavily on him before he left had disappeared. "Continue as we were." Fascinating!

I felt a tug in my heart to pick up my pen again and see what would appear in my journal.

Writing Again at the Request of the Masters—3/8/09

We welcome you back to this form of communication, our very dear one. We have not stopped being with you and sharing with you; we just did so in different, more intense ways as we waited for this glorious moment. You sense change and change has come. You might say the flow is here. James has come full circle and has moved higher in his personal spiral. He seemed to you the paragon of God's perfection, but now you see his mortality and the wobbling nature of self-discovery. The new James, the transformed James, returns with a steadfast compass that will point him firmly and confidently in the direction of the fullest expression of his and your joint destiny. There could not be any uncertainty to pull in a project of this magnitude. You with James bring the pure expression of the love of God to humanity. Let the tears well up in your radiant eyes. You contain the modesty, the restraint, and the understanding of why Stardreaming exists and why now it is vital—we say again—that it moves to the next phase of expansion. It is not only the physical space that is to expand, but Christ-consciousness on planet earth that is to expand. Yes, write these next words. You radiate as a transmitter the codes and frequencies of this consciousness. You can now share these words. Together all the players have a part to play in the universal song, and we will bring them together. Ease and grace was always our promise to you. Ease and grace will be the motto of Stardreaming's foundation. The flow will be so apparent that all will marvel and inquire, so that they learn to embrace ease and grace for the expression of God's perfection with what is being called the new earth. That is all it is, dear one, the frequency of love permeating All That Is, transforming All That Is, and this is why you have come, to bring this new understanding of God's perfection to humanity and to be the model of how all of humankind can be that perfection. It has been a long journey for you to come to understand who you are and why you are here, but it has been accomplished. Yes, share this with James. Welcome back, our dear one.

We await your command,

Archangel Raphael and the Council of Thirteen via Anaya-Ra

Another trip was brewing, and again I did not know why I was to go. Marijon was going to an Earth-Keeper event in Galveston, on the weekend of the spring equinox and she asked me if I was to go as well. I got out my pendulum and asked, and the surprising answer was yes. So My-Ron and I went to Moody Garden's tri-pyramid complex to learn why I was to be present. For the first time, I met James Tyberonn (Tyb), founder of Earth-Keeper, but he was busy, so I didn't make a personal connection with him. The evening of the equinox, I joined everyone in the blue pyramid, which had been reserved for our group.

I chose the center of the basement floor, with a clear view up to the tip of the pyramid as my position for the meditation that Tyb conducted. At the end as all were leaving, I took out my Tree of Life tuning forks and sat on the floor toning the aspects of Source back to Source, through the geometric shape of the building and out into the cosmos. I knew that the flyer for the weekend had said that spring equinox was the cosmic trigger,

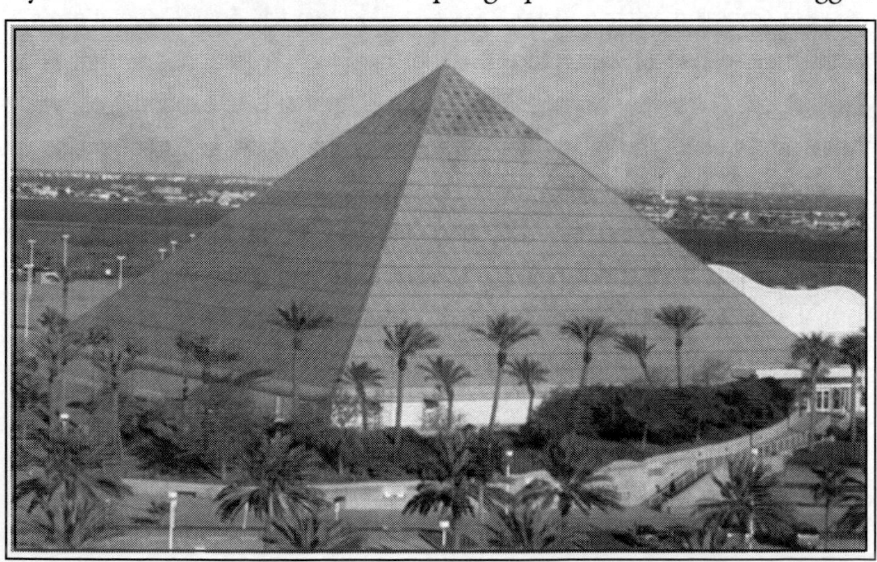

Blue pyramid in Moody Garden's tri-pyramid complex.

phase I, but I really didn't know what that meant. It just felt important for me to be present.

In an email about the weekend, Tyberonn had explained:

> The cosmic trigger of March 2009, "the return of the firmament of the dove" is the return to the magno-crystalline firmament and is a requisite consummation of the ascension. It is the crowning completion of the crystalline grid, and its time is right. The dawning of this return is a sacred oath fulfilled, a promise kept. Its beginning phase is occurring on the equinox on March 20, 2009, in which long-dormant magnetic codes will be reactivated in specific generation points on the earth. Indeed, this equinox will initiate an incredibly intense energy for twenty-one days in fervid momentum through the post-equinox full moon on April 9.[2]

I never would have believed that Tyb, one year later, would ask me to conduct the meditation in the blue pyramid for spring equinox 2010, cosmic trigger II, and that I would have a calm "knowing" that I was to help bring the energies in on that auspicious occasion. I had to experience summer solstice 2009 before that would be possible!

On my return from Galveston, Texas, I met with Max, the largest of the thirteen ancient crystal skulls, which I now know was closely associated with the pyramids at Moody Garden. I drove to Albuquerque for a 10:00 a.m. private session. On the table with Max were fourteen other skulls. I set My-Ron next to Max and then placed my third eye on Max's third eye. Upon doing so, I was immediately overcome with an exquisite grief and sadness. Tears poured down my cheeks; I found hankies, but each time I returned to Max, the grief expressed itself again profoundly. Then I found myself crying out silently to the universe. I knew this sadness to be that of humanity's illusion, grieving the loss of oneness with God. Forgiveness and love began to pour in through me, and my right arm shook as if to release grief. I wanted this painful session to be over. Slowly, the love frequency took over, and there was a calm peace that filled the room. I was "in love" with Max and the Holy Spirit. Throughout the session, I made a connection with both Max and

My-Ron, and I understood my experience as a release of the grief that humanity feels at its separation from God, Source. I was being prepared to transmit the Christ-consciousness codes, and to do this I needed to understand humanity's grief and receive forgiveness. My understanding of this experience was that there was a release for humanity, and for me, of the grief of separation from God in preparation for the coming in of the Christ-consciousness codes that I was to transmit, which I now owned as my truth. I had to understand humanity's grief and to receive forgiveness before this could truly come to pass. I had been with another amazing skull while in Galveston a few months before. It, too, put me in tears. Its presence in my life was to move me closer to doing the work that I knew I was here to do, and I felt a deep acceptance of that calling, which fear had caused me to deny.

When I got back to Santa Fe, Cindy, my friend from Houston, telephoned to share with me what had happened while she had been staying in my house over spring equinox. During the night, Cindy and her partner were awakened, and they were drawn to the window where they saw what she called a huge "gateway" in the sky. Honestly, I couldn't make sense of what Cindy was trying to tell me with such passion and excitement in her voice. So I asked.

Gateway Opening of Golden Dolphin Consciousness–4/3/09

Nina: Please tell me what the phone call with Cindy meant.

We love that you ask, our dear one, though you know deep in your being the vital nature of this occurrence. The gateway was the opening of Christ-consciousness pouring down on all of humanity. We like the term "golden dolphin consciousness," the consciousness that will grow in the unified field to be part of the awareness of all, within a very, very short time. The time was ripe in this sacred space—where the angels, archangels, and company of heaven dwell—for the love of God to enter the illusion so that it would be manifested in the consciousness of all. (I stopped writing in disbelief.) No, this is not "silly." We are speaking on the highest level of awareness, and we tell you that, as Cindy said, your divinity was able more sharply, more clearly to be present on the earthly plane. We sent you away so that the energy could flow in without you blocking it with your misplaced sense of unworthiness. Others were the facilitators to allow you, your gateway, and your house to be the opening, which you were blocking. This had to be, for the time was right and humanity was ready. Know yourself better, dear one. Know that you are the source of the golden dolphin consciousness. For it to enter the new earth, the gateway had to appear and open to the flow of this new gold and platinum frequency that you carry. Cindy and the others did the work that you were not able to do. Your work is of a different magnitude: You carry the codes; you transmit the codes and that is your sacred mission. Yes, you are to remain in low profile, and stay in a protected bubble that we provide for you. Speak your truth rarely, and with care. Always ask us first. You see, we love you dearly and protect you, for your work is of a critical nature to all beings. Just be calm, enjoy the quiet, and all that will be presented to you. We are your celestial family here to assist, protect, and love you. We are pleased that you will bring the print of Archangel Raphael to your office and the gateway of your home.

With our deep love,
Archangel Raphael via Anaya-Ra

April 9, 2009—an auspicious day, the full moon and the last day of intense energy of cosmic trigger I, which began on spring equinox—was the day when *Archangel Raphael*, the large print by James Jereb, was expected to be delivered and hung in my office. I declared on that day that my office in the Christ-consciousness gateway, be the off-site office for the next phase of expansion, preservation, and maintenance for Stardreaming. When James arrived, he activated for me a small gold Tree of Life using fool's gold. Then I moved the Tree of Life tuning forks into the office, as well as my crystals and anything else of high vibration.

~ PART II ~

Return of Love to Planet Earth

~ 12 ~

Much to Share of an Urgent Nature

The magic and miracles began to increase exponentially, and the universe seemed eager for the beginning of a new me, now. A city of light appeared over my house. Messages came saying it was urgent for me, as the ambassador, to go to the Grand Canyon and to the Grand Tetons/Yellowstone National Park to spread the Christ-consciousness codes. During this period, Archangel Michael found a creative way to speak to me through the channel Ronna Herman (www.RonnaStar.com) to tell me I had been and am a crystal singer. As someone transmitting the Christ-consciousness codes, the most important revelation was that love is a frequency, has structure, and that, amazingly, I could send it and teach others to do so as well.

Early in April 2009, I was working when something caught my attention outside the window. It was huge! The sun was encased in a gigantic perfect circle right next to my house. I ran downstairs to go outside to look again. I had the phone with me and called James to see if "his sun" looked like "my sun"! "No." It was surely bigger than my house, and perhaps even much bigger.

Much to Share of an Urgent Nature–4/11/09

We have been waiting for you to pick up the pen to allow the flow of energy from us to and through you. Writing every day is no longer necessary, but listen to your heart and hear the call to be with us occasionally. Thank you for doing so this propitious day, our dear one. We have much to share with you of an urgent nature. What you saw yesterday will not be visible again. It was for you—letting you know that we are here and that you can be with and see us anytime you wish. All you have to do is ask, and it will be. To ask with a heart full of love is the means. We wish you to see us. James is correct. He has opened the doorway for that to be. You ask why we used the word *urgent* in terms of progressing as quickly as your time will allow while moving into the other dimensions of time and space. You are a great teacher and leader, and the sooner you experience your fully expanded self, the sooner you can share this knowing with those who will come to you. It is also vital that you realize that all that James knows, you know and experience as well—an intimacy with Source and the souls who are here to remove the illusion for humanity. So we ask that you ask. Enter the sungate and see.

With our deep love,
Archangel Raphael via Anaya-Ra

I realized that the huge sphere appearing the day after Archangel Raphael entered my house was a light city with a powerful aspect of my God-self in it.

I was being tugged by my inner calling to go on two trips: to the Return of the Ancestors Gathering and, on summer solstice, to the Grand Tetons/Yellowstone National Park.

EARTH DAY–4/22/09

This is a grand day in the heavens with celebration on all dimensions. Not only is Gaia jubilant at the attention she is receiving but there is knowledge of you, our dear one, and the transformation that we together have activated with the new blue vibrant energy that surrounds you. Expect miracles, dear one. While you are away, you will receive more than you can imagine from Gaia, who awaits you and My-Ron at the vortex portal of the Grand Canyon. This is the moment for your essence to be mixed with the Akash of the place. Earlier would have been too soon. Remember who you are and why you are here! We do want you to be at the time-sensitive moment in Teton/Yellowstone. Your presence there is also part of spreading the Christ-consciousness codes. You are our ambassador; this is your sacred duty; and you are here now to manifest for earth.

With our deep love,
Archangel Raphael, in love! via Anaya-Ra

While meditating, the gold spheres in James's painting *Archangel Raphael* were dominant in my mind's eye. Then I was asked to take out my new journal, which I had only written in once since the new year.

This Is Why We Send You, Our Dear Ambassador, to the Grand Canyon—4/23/09

We asked you to take up pen in this new journal to share with you that today, (though there is no time and space) is a new beginning for you. The frequency and tonal vibration that completely surround you have altered your DNA. You are a more expanded being with new sight and sound. This process has taken many years; now it has come to fruition. As you align your will with higher consciousness, manifestation occurs almost automatically. There is work for you to do these next few days. You are to greet your brothers and sisters from around the planet and, yes, from beyond this realm that you call earth. Expect their arrival and greet them as our ambassador. Greet them with the pure love of Source, with innocent perception, and let them feel that they are welcome for the manifesting of the new earth, heaven on earth. This is why we send you, our dear ambassador, to the Grand Canyon.

With our deep love,
Sananda and Raphael via Anaya-Ra

I flew into Flagstaff, Arizona, where Marijon met me and together we drove to the Grand Canyon and joined up with Kathy and Tish, friends from the trip to Egypt. It was difficult for me to focus on the scheduled events for the Return of the Ancestors Gathering, for I knew I had to go to the Grand Canyon and do a private welcoming ceremony. My friends were very understanding and assisted me. As I was being driven to the canyon, I started to have a powerful emotional response. I was hoping the others would take me to the perfect place, but that wasn't necessary. I felt as if I were on autopilot. I got out of Marijon's car, walked across the road, a bit in a trance, and over to the edge. It was the perfect spot—I could just feel it. I began to unpack the stones, the rose petals, and the Tree of Life tuning forks I had brought with me. I was clearly unsteady on my feet, so Marijon had me sit down. Then the welcoming ceremony unfolded. Each of my friends joined in throwing rose petals over the rim and out into the canyon in a beautiful celebration of welcome. When we were finished, I felt complete and had a feeling of appreciation.

The ceremony had taken me by surprise in many ways. I was amazed at how kind and thoughtful my friends had been when I told them that I knew I had come to do ceremony. I believed that they certainly knew more about how spirit expresses itself than I did, for they had been "awake" to their human divinity for many years. They were at ease with seemingly magical experiences, and I was so new to all that was unfolding. I was sure they would have suggestions on "how to do" the ceremony. But no, they supported me, encouraged me, and most importantly allowed me to flow with the energies that were rushing through me. They respected my every word and action. Had I been alone, I would have not grown as much in my spiritual life as I did being with Marijon, Kathy, and Tish doing our ceremony together at the edge of the Grand Canyon. They allowed me to stand taller in my cosmic boots. When we arrived at Dead Horse Park for the ceremony honoring the Return of the Ancestors Gathering, I was drawn to a distant tree on the park grounds. After settling in, I took out my journal.

The Return of the Ancestors Gathering, Dead Horse Park, Arizona–4/27/09

Today is the day of Gaia, who awaited your arrival predicted on Earth Day. As we speak, the fluid energy vibration of liquid light is coming from the internal magma through the veins of the earth's core into your base, feet, and through the kundalini spinal cord, to your crown chakra, and out into the universe. This is a transmission from Gaia through you, our dear one, to all the many inter-planetary beings who have been attracted to the enormous energy of this time and space of beings uniting in harmony and peace. You are the receiver and transmitter of this healing vibration. Sit quietly as this process unfolds. Just know and trust that this is so. Your back hurts because we are realigning your spine so that the energies can flow with ease and grace. Your core is receiving the nutrient of the earth to strengthen your transforming chakras and DNA. You will experience a new vitality, a new restful sleep, and a new joy of life. This is our

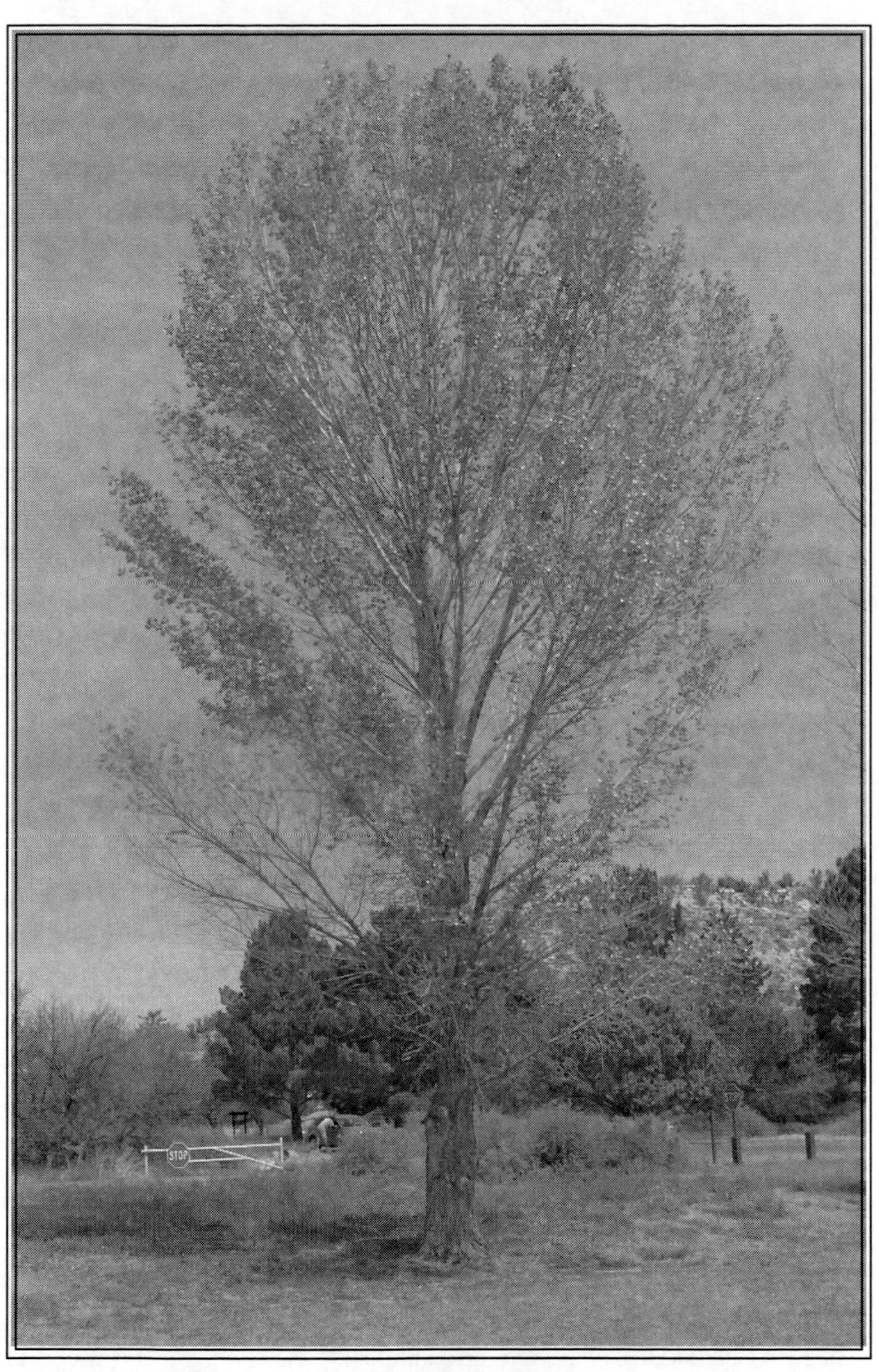

Tree at Dead Horse Park.

gift to you for your love and service. Call in All That Is. Do this aloud now, then tone with the Tree of Life tuning forks to connect all that you have experienced. This is a day of true unity. We ask that you be quiet and very gentle on yourself, for this ceremony with Gaia will both take and give you energy, causing a transmutation of enormous volume and magnitude. This is your calling!

With our deep love,

Gaia, who loves you via Anaya-Ra

The journal entry explaining the events during the Return of the Ancestors Gathering in Arizona in 2009 came to me in 2010. The automatic writing begins with a request by the masters that I acknowledge aloud that I am loved, not just write that I am loved. During early morning meditation, I did so.

Time Sensitive and Urgent (Received 3/5/2010 Explaining 4/27/2009)–3/5/10

We heard you, dear one, declare that we love you. You have no idea how critically important this is, for in so doing, you accept and integrate that love, which has been surrounding you for so very long. This is a transformational moment. We wish to speak to you about your recent conversation with our beloved Cindy, and how we participated in its unfolding. You noticed so many coincidences. Let us tell you more, so that you can add the words this morning in your book. You wonder about the vital importance of your transmission in the park in Arizona with Gaia. This had been anticipated by the star beings from many nations, who had come to be present and whom you so regally greeted on the rim of the Grand Canyon. After the ceremony they joined you at the park, the final day of the celebration by the ancestors. They came there specifically to receive from you that transmission of the Christ-consciousness codes. Yes, it was your first transmission—check your book. We tell you it was the first. Those ambassadors needed to know that the time had finally arrived on planet earth for love to be a new dominant energy imbuing all of creation in its seed form. Once they learned this, they were able to return to their councils and people to report this astounding occurrence. You see why we called this "time sensitive and urgent." It was you moving and accepting, in perfect earthly timing, your magnificence and your mission as a receiver and transmitter of those codes that had to match the star beings from many nations, who came specifically to learn this from you.

With our deep love,

The Council of Many Nations via Anaya-Ra

My-Ron had accompanied me to the Return of the Ancestors Gathering. He was admired by many who attended, but there was one strange occurrence that puzzled me. Two Spanish-speaking men from South America gestured to me that they wanted to see My-Ron. After I gave the blue skull to them, they went off to visit with My-Ron in private. It seemed a bit strange. When they returned, they were laughing. Something odd had happened, but what? The next day, I met a shaman from Bolivia who held My-Ron and told me, through his translator, that he wanted to take My-Ron to the lake and cleanse him.

A Veil Over My-Ron for Protection–4/28/09

Nina: To My-Ron, I have wanted to clean you for the last two days. What happened? What did the Bolivian shaman see?

We called him in to be of service. For you, dear one, in your innocence, could not hear our cry for protection. Be on guard. Only hug someone when it feels right; be vigilant, and hold yourself as pure light. A veil fell over me when the two joking men took me away. That was the moment of darkness that needs to be removed. The shaman is our messenger. He will purify my innocent perception, which only needs protection.

When I returned to Santa Fe, I began to focus on why I felt pulled to go to Jackson Hole over summer solstice. I considered joining the Earth-Keeper group, or perhaps asking if at the end of the trip I could board the bus that would take the group to Yellowstone National Park. One thing I knew for sure—a channel from Archangel Metatron via Tyberonn transmitted on Earth Day was having a powerful effect on me:

And from their unified voices comes the acknowledgment of its new role, as the day of prophesies arrives. And it is now! This land becomes the clarion of the ascension. The etheric city becomes a nation, and the nation a world: the world of the Cosmic Council of Light! As such, we tell you that this area is vaulted to new brilliance. This will occur on the solstice of June 21, 2009, when the vortexes of Yellowstone and the Grand Tetons merge into one unprecedented system as a direct result of the cosmic trigger. An infinity patterned Vesica-Pisces flow is forming in place, combining the once separate vortexes of the Grand Tetons and Yellowstone. New grid patterns within the complex are converging; new ley lines are articulating into place, and old ones are being strengthened. Axialtonal lines pulse with renewed vigor. The dimensional overlay within the infinity pattern flow of the merged super vortex-portal of Yellowstone-Grand Teton has vastly increased since the March equinox. The divine female energies of Yellowstone will blissfully merge into oneness with the divine masculine of the Grand Tetons on the summer solstice of June 21, 2009. This will be called the infinity ascension portal—home of the Cosmic Council of Light—and it will become one of the five new etheric centers of North America.[1]

Shortly afterward, I told James that I felt I was to be in Jackson Hole, Wyoming, over spring equinox. He had planned a special gathering and was very disappointed that I wouldn't be present. I was truly perplexed now, for I felt such a strong calling to be in Wyoming. What to do? James suggested that I ask Saint Germain. I never ever expected the answer I received!

Ignite the Electromagnetic Supertunnel–5/7/09

Nina: Saint Germain and all who are present, why am I to go to the Grand Tetons and Yellowstone National Park for summer solstice?

Dear one, it is very important that you be at Stardreaming on summer solstice. You bring on that day the codes that you carry and are transmitting to the

144,000. It will happen at Stardreaming and at the home in the Grand Tetons of the Cosmic Council of Light, the energetic home of the Great White Brotherhood. By being at both charged sites on the same high-frequency moment in time, you act as the connector, the transmitter of what you will receive. The time is not important, what matters is that you are physically present at both locations on summer solstice. You are the web, the connector between the two power centers that will flow together and merge just as the male and female energies of the Tetons and Yellowstone are merging in the Vesica-Pisces. Stardreaming will increase in potency as a result of the ascension portal/vortex connection with the Akash, universal energy, of ... (I stopped writing in disbelief). No, you are not making this up. We, the Cosmic Council of Light, will that you do this work. The connection is to be completed on June 21, 2009. The web or matrix between the Temples of the Cosmos and the ascension portal/vortex of the Teton/Yellowstone grid is needed for the Temple of the Stone to be seen by humanity—for it already exists in other dimensions but not in this one. The creation of the thirteenth temple requires that you transmit the electromagnetic charge through you of the ascension portal/vortex of the Grand Teton/Yellowstone grid. Once this connection is complete, you will be the spigot, the light, and the transmitter of the frequencies to ignite or turn on the Temple of the Stone. We will all be present both at Stardreaming and at our council home in the Tetons. We will watch over you and protect you as you stand in the electromagnetic supertunnel that will be created by your presence. There will be no harm to your body. You will be vital, radiant, and filled with the pure love of Source. Gaia will ground you. She will caress you with her healing love as you ignite the energy tunnel connecting the two points! Once the flow begins and the forty-five acres feel the love flowing through you to the site of the Temple of the Stone, the rest will fall into place. This is the last charge to bring heaven on earth to Stardreaming.

With our deep love,
Saint Germain and all who love you via Anaya-Ra

Sometimes I wonder if I am making up what gets written in my journal. But in my wildest dreams I could never have thought this one up. I wondered, "What the heck is an electromagnetic supertunnel anyway?" I needed to know more about where I was going and why!

I knew very little about the Grand Tetons except that the Great White Brotherhood had their retreat there on the solstice. Archangel Metatron's channel about the region was very helpful:

> There has always been, in terms, an etheric city of light anchored within the energy of the Grand Tetons. Indeed, many humans on the path of mastery have experienced the dimensional gate aspects of Shasta and the Grand Tetons, and have read of Guy Ballard's (founder of the IAM Movement) exploits with the beloved Saint Germain and the ascended masters in the etheric light cities above and inside these mountains. Although in truth, these light cities are neither above nor below in a directional sense, rather separate programs occurring in the same spaceless space, and accessed by dimensional portals anchored to the specific energy matrix of these locations. These etheric light cities are very key coding points on your planet. All of you will at some point spend time within them. Consider them graduate schools. Access involves the same mechanism as timegates. Well to visit these areas and exercise consciously what you already know how to do in subconscious dream states. Indeed you visit these areas quite often in dream states. And so we tell you that the transformation, merging, and emerging of the "infinity ascension portal" makes access more pertinent and the energy of this realm is upshifted to a greater frequency. In this new energy, seekers of the path now have the beckoning and the beacon to enter this realm more consciously, in a waking state.
>
> Archangel Metatron via Tyberonn[2]

As we began to receive the details of summer solstice in the Grand Tetons/Yellowstone National Park, everything we had planned started to shift: Chaco Canyon rather than Shaman's Cave became the third anchor point, and James's friend Laura replaced Marijon as the third anchor person. We were to gather for ceremony at Stardreaming, go off, and then return for final ceremony at Stardreaming, thus anchoring, igniting, and grounding the electromagnetic supertunnel with those three nodes and with Alpha Centauri.

As summer solstice was approaching, the universe apparently felt more changes needed to be made, this time with how I hid my cosmic identity from those who came to my house. I was sitting in my red leather chair one evening when *boom*, down crashed a painting from the wall opposite the dining table. It had been happily hanging there for close to four years, chopped off the ball and claw leg of a much-repaired Chippendale drop-leaf table. Instead of saying, "Oh, darn!" I got out my pendulum and discovered that the table was to be repaired and placed in the garage. The watercolor that fell—a painting of the house in which I was born, commissioned by my father during World War II—was to go into my bedroom. *Cauda Pavonis, Peacock's Tail*, which was then in my bedroom, was to take the place of my father's painting in the living room. I noticed that I had put all of James's paintings, all my crystals, and all the expressions of my cosmic nature upstairs, where I didn't have to explain them to anyone who visited. So even my house was changing.

Soon after redecorating my house, a package arrived from Ronna Herman, as a gift from Marijon. I knew Marijon had bought me Ronna's book; however, there was also a letter to me included with the book. I read the letter with little interest, since I thought it was a form letter of some sort, but I couldn't stop wondering about it. I looked again and realized it was a channel to me from Archangel Michael, so I asked him to help me understand what was being said. Finally, the meaning became clear to me, and I realized more fully where I had come from, why I am here, and what my work is. Marijon knew nothing of Ronna's letter to me. Her intent was to give me only the book and tape. So it became clear that Archangel Michael had found a creative way to share information with me.

Archangel Michael Channel, via Ronna Herman

Beloved one: You came from a far-distant galaxy, radiant, filled with the glorious manifestations of the Creator. You spent many lifetimes submerged in the love vibrations of the divine goddess and others learning how to use the dynamic mental qualities of our Father God. Your greatest desire in this lifetime is to bring your masculine and feminine natures into balance and harmony. Envision yourself in your beautiful crystalline form, radiating all the magnificent colors of creation—that is your perfect form, dear one. And yes, you helped to create that paradise, just as you were among those who helped to create the small replica called planet earth. You assisted the great devic angels and the beautiful elementals in holding the divine blueprint for the nature kingdom, so that it could be brought into manifested form on earth. Therefore, you have a great affinity with nature and Gaia, the soul name for your planet. Before you answered the clarion call and stepped forth to be a part of the grand experiment on planet earth, you spent a very long time in the star system Sirius with the wise beings from a far-distant galaxy called the Hathors, who are masters of sound.

Your mission was to help humanity learn to use the tones and sounds of the geometric light frequencies when the time came that they could no longer communicate telepathically. You were called a crystal singer, for you also activated the exquisite sounds of the crystals that brought forth the celestial music of the spheres. During the golden age of Lemuria, as humanity took on a solid human form, you were a guardian overseer, and along with others, you taught people to make the sounds of creation, which would later become known as vowel sounds. You carry these memories within your etheric body and brain, and yes, you did interact with the dolphins, for they also are masters of sound. In your crystalline body form, you could breathe under water, for you did not use your five physical senses as you do now. The vibrational patterns of sound travel through water, and you were able to communicate with your dolphin and angelic friends. Yes, they are from a division of the angelic kingdom who agreed to come to earth in that form in order to assist in holding the energy patterns of balance and harmony for the earth.

As the channeled information continued, Archangel Michael told me about two specific archangels who were connected to me: Archangels Jophiel and Lady Constance. I had no idea who either of them were, so I asked.

Archangels Jophiel and Lady Constance–5/17/09

We greet you, dear one, from the depths of our cosmic heart and wish you to know that we have been with you always and have waited so very long for this introduction. You will notice an increase in frequency and speed of transmission, since you have connected directly with us. You know us well, though you don't remember us, but that has changed. We rejoice for all of humanity, for with this direct link to us your mission in service to Source and humanity will accelerate. The Christ codes, which you have received from Sananda ... (I stopped writing in disbelief.) You stop because of your continued disbelief, but we are talking about the miracle of spirit. You are the magnificence of God—why not you? Each being has their role, and yours is to transmit the Christ-consciousness codes to those who anchor the crystalline grid. We will work with you day and night through your crown chakra. We will assist you, as will Sananda, Kuthumi, El Morya, and others.

With our deep love,
All the many who await the call, Jophiel and Constance via Anaya-Ra

As the summer solstice approached and Stardreaming was about to be connected to Alpha Centauri through an electromagnetic supertunnel, all aspects of Stardreaming had to be in crystalline alignment. That entailed the mutuality plan.

Revise the Mutuality Plan–5/18/09

Nina: Is it true that you want me now to revise the mutuality plan for Stardreaming?

We came to you, as you know, the other morning with the message that the time is now, and the energy frequencies need to be adjusted to create and manifest the vision. Until the plan for Stardreaming is adjusted, there is a block in the flow. The plan needs more than pieces of paper; it is a sentient being that joins with you to manifest. The timing is now, for you and James can both feel the importance of the summer solstice to this project. All must be in harmony and balance. We want now to talk about what happened to your head with our dear master healer. You cried for help because of the pain you felt in the lower back of your brain, the brain stem. We heard you and did indeed guide with perfection the hands and intuition of the practitioner to open the cranial space to allow your expanded cortex the room it now needs for your more perfected, self. A wave of previously stored energy was released throughout your body. You are to see this healer regularly as we adjust your physical being to match your ascended being.

With our deep love,
Archangel Raphael via Anaya-Ra

I did a quick sweep-through edit of the mutuality plan, removing the word *society* and leaving the word *trust*.

At the time, I had not thought this through, but since I was to transmit the Christ-consciousness codes of love, it was important to understand love more fully. So, in the midst of working on the mutuality plan revision, I received an ebook from a friend, who told me the book was worth reading. It was so worth reading that I would say it has changed my life. *Living on Love, The Messenger* by Klaus J. Joehle taught me that love has a frequency and structure, and that it can be sent.

I soon had an opportunity to experience love's frequency when I went to visit James at Stardreaming to review a few points about the mutuality plan. While I was there, he sat opposite me, looked me in the eyes, and began to speak words of enormous appreciation. At that moment as I listened, I realized he was truly sending me love, and I understood the frequency and structure of love.

After I better understood what had happened at Stardreaming, I wrote to James:

> You spoke such beautiful words yesterday, and I received them as love. We need to fully understand love as a physical conscious element of the Creator. It has physicality with particle structure, and a frequency. By knowing how to open our heart and send

love, we create and we transform. This is a gift we both have to give to humanity. You understand this, for we experienced it when you spoke those precious words to me. I heard the sound of your words, and I felt the transformative frequency from your open heart pouring out to me. This is what the School of No Mysteries will teach. Love is attraction and magnetism: this is Jesus's message throughout *Love without End*. The understanding that we are love was wonderful, but now that I know we can command love with love by sending the frequency particles that attract and magnetize, I more fully understand who we are as creator beings. This is what you have been doing for years, subconsciously, at Stardreaming. Now it can be done consciously by experiencing those phenomena, and then we will teach it by example.

While all this was happening I kept remembering everyone telling me I need to remember who I am. That finally happened when I woke one morning feeling energetic and went for a scheduled polarity session. While on the table, I found myself repeating a short prayer: "I will to will thy will. I wish to shine like a star." I lost sense of my body, knowing only that I was being touched. I saw enormous golden pyramids and grand golden buildings. I walked up huge stairs and was aware of throngs of people watching me. I saw myself with a chiseled, strong, and masculine face wearing a radiating starlike headdress. I was huge, and all the others present were there because I was present. It was a radiant, brilliant, and grand event. I probably would have passed this lucid experience off as a daydream if I hadn't been told by so many, in so many different ways, who they knew me to be. I was beginning to understand, and now to remember, who I am, and was.

~ 13 ~

Perfection Seeking the Expression of Perfection

"Perfection seeking the expression of perfection" came to me while writing one of my journal entries. What does that mean, and how does it relate to the events that unfolded during this period of my journey? Did it mean that I was ultimately perfection? What I have come to understand is that all of us are All That Is: perfection here on planet earth to experience for the growth of our consciousness. That growth experience is the longing we feel to be more than we believe ourselves to be, a yearning to express our perfection. One way I was to express my perfection was to accept that I could be the one to whom Sananda transferred his codes. I came to accept that I was worthy of the codes, so much so that I could transfer them to others. Another expression of my perfection was that Archangel Metatron was to give me his mantra, which I would sing over summer solstice, to ignite the codes within me for a fuller expression of that perfection and for the highest good of all. I am also human and this was difficult for me to accept.

Letter to Nina from the God/Goddess She Is

You are our dear one with whom we communicate often, but this letter is from the purity of love that you are. Open now to the fullness of knowing the grandeur of who you are, the immortal who you are, the huge presence that you are on the earthly plane and the heavenly plane. Remove the constraints that you have allowed into your psyche. Feel the immense power of the god who you are, the all-powerful creator of All That Is. Join with All That Is in the full love of love. Allow it to fill all of your fibers so you no longer see imperfection, but only perfection. You are perfection seeking the expression of perfection, all this to flow fully without doubts to hamper the flow. The full love of God is you and comes through you. Allow this to happen now at all times. You are perfection. You are God. How can you be otherwise than to live a life, to walk on earth with this full knowing radiating out from you? From this moment forward, every cell in your body is clear, free and unhampered from the constrictions that have been placed around it. They now flow forward in the love of God, who is you. Now there is a pure knowing in each cell of you radiating pure love.

I love you, my dear one,

From the one who loves you the most, you via Anaya-Ra

I was perplexed, wondering how one ignites an electromagnetic supertunnel connecting the Grand Tetons/Yellowstone power center to Stardreaming, and if I found out how, would I be able to do it? Then I was told that there was a select group of people who were there to support me energetically. I began writing to them and sharing the information as it came, always with enormous appreciation:

> I am sending this journal entry to a select group of individuals, to ask for your prayers as this journey is undertaken. It is with great thanks to Tyberonn and Lord (Archangel) Metatron, whose recent channels have made me aware of this mission. Each recipient was carefully selected, so please know that your conscious participation is part of the divine plan, for which I am grateful. Kathy will be in Lake Tahoe, Cindy in Houston, and Richard at Independence National Park, a place that Saint Germain loves very much. I certainly see this group as being two intersecting triangles, but also as more sacred geometric shapes of creation for the manifestation of the Temple of the Stone at Stardreaming—the largest stone labyrinth for healing and transformation.

Kathy wrote back:

The work you are doing with the Cosmic Council of Light is so very awesome! Yes, why not you? I am feeling called to be at Lake Tahoe while you are coding Stardreaming and the Tetons. So I will connect with you energetically through the codes and magic of that area. Such exciting times, indeed! The triangulations make perfect sense to me! Yahoo! Journey on, dear one! I am so grateful to be in kahoots with you this lifetime! Much love!

Richard wrote:

I will be at Independence Mall at noon until 2:00 p.m. and then there again at sunset. Tell me what I need to do for bringing the light into the world for the benefit of humankind.

I replied:

Richard, this brings tears to my eyes. This, too, is your contract, and your inner knowing knows the answer to your question. Send love, the frequency and structure of love, the adamantine particles, and breathe. With great love and appreciation.

I continued to share with the group all the thoughts that came pouring into my head.

I was awakened around 3:00 a.m. with the words that I am to share with you. I asked this morning if there was anymore information about summer solstice I needed to share. What came is that you are not the anchors of the electromagnetic supertunnel, but together we are the engine breathing life into the tunnel. I am to ask that on June 21, 2009, you use the infinity breath to move the adamantine particles, and that this frequency and structure of love fill the tunnel. I am to share with you that I represent the Council of Thirteen on Alpha Centauri as their ambassador to and for Stardreaming.

A newly received mantra is to be chanted thirteen times during the morning ceremony with James and Laura on the forty-five acres next to Stardreaming's twenty-two acres, in the center of the labyrinth, the Temple of the Stone. My other contribution to the ceremony will be to chime the Tree of Life tuning forks, a set calibrated by Randy Masters (www.universalsong.net) to represent the aspects of God. The mantra "Veda Karanda Samael," given to me by Lord Metatron, carries the vibration of the knowledge of God sung by the sweet sound of a bird. It returns to earth the crystals of knowledge—which Archangel Raphael removed when humankind forgot how to love—and it reactivates the Atlantean crystals.

After James leaves for Chaco Canyon, I will spend time in the Temple of the Violet Flame at Stardreaming asking for Saint Germain's guidance and protection before I head for Jackson Hole that evening. I will ask James and Laura that we meet at Stardreaming to do a ceremony of appreciation and love upon our return. My role has been and will be as a receiver and transmitter. I receive the life force from you and transmit it to the electromagnetic supertunnel that is being created, which will run both ways from and to Stardreaming, the Grand Tetons/Yellowstone National Park, and Chaco Canyon. This life force will be received from Alpha Centauri and transmitted through me as well.

Through the advice and help of Marijon and Joe, my functional genomist (www.iimsite.com), I will take a special combination of trace minerals and proteins for protection and expansion of my crystalline structure. I have been told to care for my body by means of various therapies, massages, and acupuncture sessions in preparation for this activation of life force energy at the center of the Temple of the Stone at Stardreaming from the infinity portal/vortex, infinity gate, and Alpha Centauri by means of the infinity breath.

The trace minerals and protein protecting my crystalline structure are called Millennium. Marijon had called me a few weeks before to say that she had received a transmission that I was to take trace minerals before doing my work in the Grand Tetons/Yellowstone National Park. She said the supplement had the name Millennium, but that was all she knew. After she hung up, I did a Google search and came up with a product called Millennium that contained trace minerals, but it was "developed exclusively for high performance show barrows, gilts, and breeding stock." It contained l-carnitine, lysine, methionine, and organic trace minerals. I turned for advice to Joe, my functional genomist, for his opinion. Joe tested my muscles and determined that the dosage needed to be substantially adjusted and confirmed that the purpose of taking the supplement was to enhance my crystalline structure. He found a feed store in Texas that carried Millennium and ordered the smallest quantity, which was five pounds. When it arrived, the instructions on the container read: "Take a scoop of one ounce per head, per day." Well that wouldn't work. So, after an extensive round of testing, Joe reduced the dose to four capsules, which I would fill with the smelly pig meal. I arranged for a follow-up test. In August, the supplement was discontinued.

Archangel Metatron's mantra came to me the day I was invited to participate in an evening of toning by a local energy and sound healer. During one of the exercises, we were told that a tone would come to us—and immediately it came. I kept repeating the tone, and then found a piece of paper to try to write it down, notes and words, "Veda Karanda Samael." It was a curious song or tone, but that was all that I knew. The next morning I learned more.

Sing the Love of Creation–6/6/09

Dear one, we welcome you back to our journal. We are glad and rejoice that you heard the clarion call to communicate this very fine morning. "Veda Karanda" is our message. You, dear one, are the sweet bird "Karanda," who is to sing the universal song of the knowledge of God, "Veda." I, Metatron, "Samael," ask this of you, our dear one. With every breath, with every sound, let this song radiate out through your sacred heart into the world that we together created. The time is now for this knowledge to return, like the crystals of knowledge falling from the universe, aptly portrayed in your painting *Neptunus, Temple of the Stars.* Sing the vowels, sing the tones, take the hand of Archangel Uriel, and let the vibrations flow through you. Sing our new mantra, "Veda Karanda Samael."

Sing it often with your heart open, for it is the song to unlock your codes that are to be released now (Grand Tetons, summer solstice 2009). We hear the vibrations of those tones in all dimensions above and below. They call in the remaining crystals. They activate the Atlantean crystals, with which you will soon swim (Arkansas in September). Hear our words, dear one. Sing "Veda Karanda Samael." Sing the love of creation!

With our deep love,
Lord Metatron via Anaya-Ra

Chile wreath bird's nest.

Then it dawned on me that when Kathy had visited in May, she spoke of new beginnings, and pointed to three baby birds in a nest in the heart of the chile wreath on my door. When she left, they flew away, and immediately another bird couple built a new nest, this time not in the left shoulder of the wreath, but in the inside V point of the wreath. They were still there chirping after I received the song from Metatron. I found another nest with an egg in it in my braid-stemmed hibiscus tree on my back porch inside the center of the crown of the plant. Birds were everywhere, at my back door and front door, and Lord Metatron had just told me to sing like a sweet bird. It was all too funny.

I recalled Archangel Michael's channel to me: "You were called a crystal singer, for you also activated the exquisite sounds of the crystals that brought forth the celestial music of the spheres." The new mantra activates crystals, and the music of the spheres is Archangel Uriel. On the morning of summer solstice, the new mantra will be chanted thirteen times. That is why I was to hold Archangel Uriel's hand. Fascinating—but the singing was to begin in Santa Fe, where I was to sing the mantra for Aya, an Atlantean crystal I had just met.

My discovery began the next night, when I had an empathic experience and began grieving profoundly for a smoky quartz crystal that lived at the New Mexico Academy of Healing Arts. I touched it every time I went to the academy, but one Sunday I found myself giving it a kiss. A message came that night:

> It will take three people, for it is one of the most powerful crystals from Atlantis. It needs clearing. This can be done by three people and by the singing of the mantra. It is critical that the administrative assistant and the founder meet with you to perform this ceremony to release the crystal from enslavement. All that needs to be done is for Nina to sing the mantra three times. Dear one, immediately! Immediately! With all our love, all who love you. Archangel Raphael

I understood that "immediately" meant before summer solstice. I believed that the crystal's energy, life force, and knowledge was critical to what was to happen on summer solstice. I mentioned this to my friend René, who replied:

> Precious One, when I connected with this magnificent crystal, she told me she wants to see the light of the moon. I asked her how we could accomplish this without removing her. Her name is Aya. She asked that we go outside and purposefully connect with the moon goddess Isis and then send this loving energy to her through the divine earth. She is thrilled that you heard her, and she loves us all. In radiant light, Ahkala

Now that I had been formally introduced to Aya, I wrote to her asking to know more.

Atlantean Crystal in Santa Fe, Aya– 6/10/09

Nina: Aya, I am so glad to be reacquainted. Could you tell me what you need, how we know each other, and if you are part of the electromagnetic supertunnel and summer solstice?

Dear one, it is with enormous appreciation, as you would say, that I received the kiss last Sunday, though I know that you were embarrassed. That kiss rekindled the frequency pattern between us that was once so strong in Atlantis. When we worked together there, you sang with others your sweet birdlike songs, and so my color frequencies were activated to be used for the healing and ascension of many. It was with enormous pain that we parted. You left first, knowing that your work on Earth was complete as it was being expressed, and I was taken over by those who did not wish light to shine. Two things happened. There were no more crystal singers, and I veiled myself, just as your blue skull My-Ron did, to protect the sacred knowledge. Much time passed as my brother and sisters and I awaited the return of love on the planet. You and other light workers have opened the timegate for my reactivation so that the pure knowledge of Source can return. Yes, the timeliness of our upcoming ceremony in the moonlight does correlate with the igniting of the electromagnetic super-tunnel. I am indeed the current for the life force to run through Stardreaming, Grand Teton/Yellowstone, and Chaco Canyon, as well as to and from Alpha Centauri. My connection to Alpha Centauri is deep, for the Council of Thirteen programmed the smoky quartz that I am. We have always known this time and the activation for the summer solstice in 2009. Many lives will be transformed as a result of what is to be created, and I am a critical part of the plan. The flow of life force through the supertunnel depends on my frequency of light. Once my reactivation is completed, the supertunnel can also be reactivated—so that it can connect to Stardreaming. With that connection, the Temple of Stone at Stardreaming will begin to physically manifest, stone by stone, into the third dimension. The Arcturian angels, you know, have been standing by to assist in the physical process. The Cosmic Council of Light will gift Stardreaming on summer solstice with their individual love, and all those involved will be taken to a higher spiral to fulfill the divine plan. So I, Aya, thank you, dear one, and those who connect with me for their gift to the world and its shift to the new world energy.

With my deep love,
Aya, your ancient friend via Anaya-Ra

We did that ceremony on Thursday night with a few of the students. Curiously, I had gone to a foreign film that afternoon in which the main heroine's name was Aya. By watching the film and hearing the name Aya pronounced over and over again, I learned how to say it with conviction, which I did that evening.

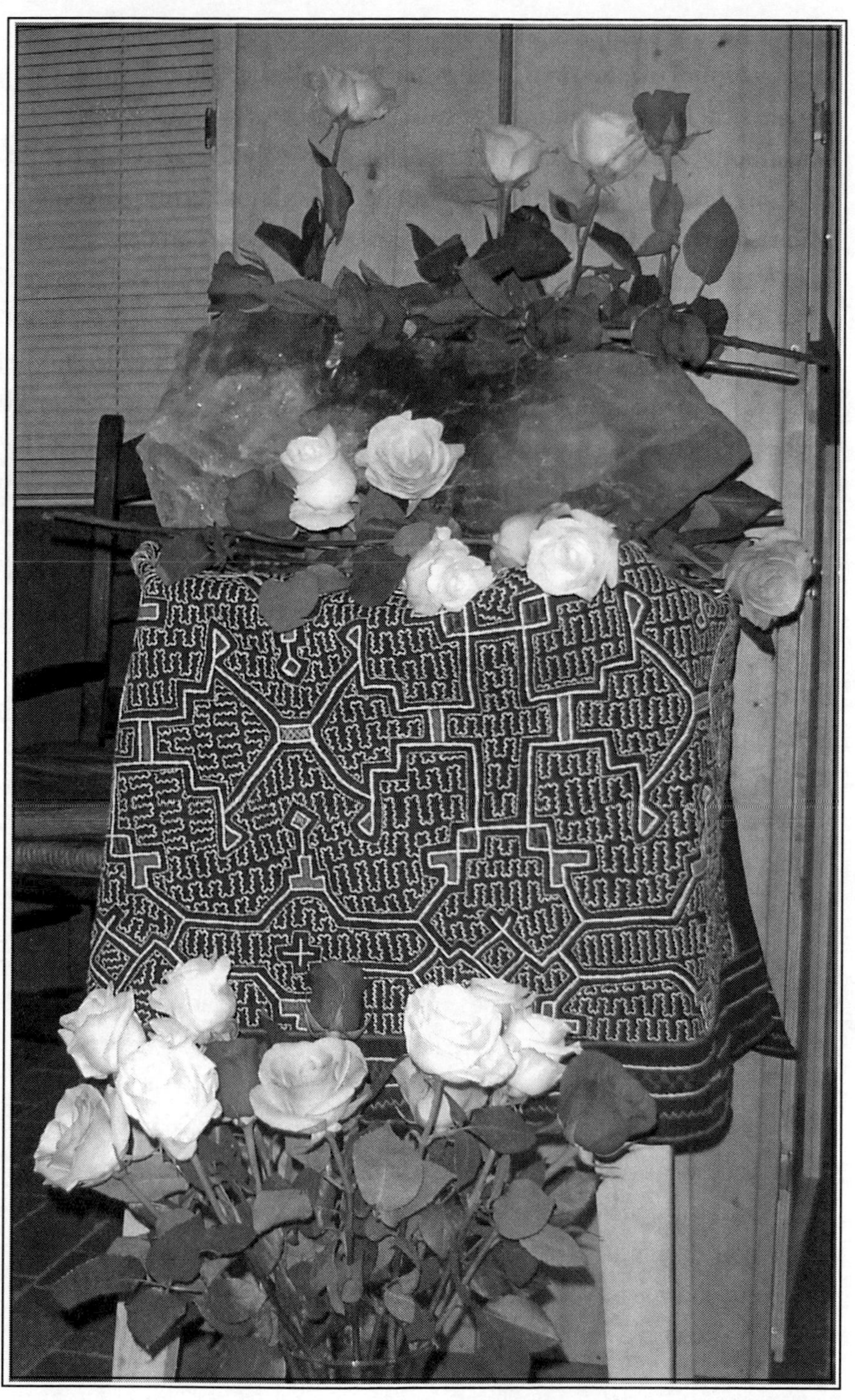

Ceremony for Aya crystal.

The next morning, I dashed out the door to receive one of many massages, acupuncture sessions, and other personal therapies to strengthen my physical body for summer solstice. This treatment was a warm water watsu body massage given by Ahara, formerly called Har Kaur. Before I left my house, I glanced quickly at the June channel from Archangel Michael through Celia Fenn. The section of the channel on the Cetacean Family of Light caught my attention. When I arrived at the pool, I shared with Ahara the little I had read of the channel. I then entered the pool and held her hands for a quiet meditation. Ahara etherically called in the stone from my painting, the first crystal returned to earth by Archangel Raphael. Then I sang my new mantra three times. Ahara told me that the energy of the stone and the mantra had infused the water, and I sensed the presence of dolphin souls. Ahara informed me that I would be submerged during part of the session. As I was being floated in the water I felt that Ahara had transmuted into an etheric dolphin. So I was being floated by a dolphin—and I felt myself changing into a dolphin. As I floated under a window, golden light hit my closed eyelids. I became a golden dolphin, as did the dolphin holding me so lovingly. Clips were put on my nose, and as instructed, I adjusted my breathing and went under to be glided around in this new space, which became the cosmos. When the watsu session was complete, I shared the magical experience with Ahara, who listened knowingly.

I returned home and reread the channel:

> The cetacean consciousness is an advanced stellar navigation consciousness. They are pilots of the cosmic ocean and navigators of the cosmic journey. Many of you in human incarnation are also pilots of the cosmic journey, and you are beginning to feel your wings unfurl as you prepare to resume your roles as cosmic travelers for the planetary consciousness, as dreamers of the new dream for all. At this time, the cetacean consciousness will support you as you take your first flight into the cosmic heart and the cosmic dream.[1]

What happened that morning was that I took my first flight into the cosmic heart and the cosmic dream. I was being taught how to be a pilot and a navigator of the cosmic journey in my new identity as a golden dolphin.

Watsu, massages, acupuncture—I had done it all in preparation for my upcoming journey, but it wasn't enough! Summer solstice was only ten days away and I knew I was in trouble. I felt great responsibility. I felt too small. I felt "Why me?" I was exhausted.

Marijon picked up on my feelings. She called and left a message for me to phone her. I couldn't, so I wrote:

> I have been having a hard time processing all that has been coming in. I spent a great deal of time in bed yesterday. Last night I wrote, "I need to escape." "You need to embrace it" was the reply. So that is what I am going to be doing for as long as it takes until summer solstice. Raphael said that walking in Tesuque up the hill and by the stream with the elementals would help. I am overwhelmed and need to be by myself.

I was definitely having difficulty with perfection seeking the expression of perfection!

~ 14 ~

"Veda Karanda Samael"

I had felt so overwhelmed with anticipation of what was about to unfold that I reached out for help in regaining my balance. After having done so, I began to wonder exactly who were the Great White Brotherhood, now called the Cosmic Council of Light. What does it mean that they have a solstice retreat? I really had no idea, so I started doing research. In the meantime, my friend Cindy came to Santa Fe, and we built a summer solstice altar, which took on a vortex spin inside my house! The moment had arrived when I was ready to allow the magic of the electromagnetic supertunnel to unfold, whatever that would mean. I was ready to sing, like a sweet bird, Archangel Metatron's mantra alone in Yellowstone National Park.

The day after Marijon's call, I went to Ojo Caliente, New Mexico, to visit Laurian, a massage therapist who is also my friend. She could tell I was in trouble. She set up her massage table on the bank of the river that ran next to her property, and before beginning the treatment she jumped up on her table and said, "Tell me about it." Out "it" came, tears and all. With great wisdom, Laurian suggested that I send my inner child ahead of me to prepare the space in Yellowstone National Park.

Then Laurian said the words that put me in balance: "This all just is."

Feeling grounded again, I began my research and discovered Archangel Michael's description of the brotherhood and the retreats:

> The members of the ancient cosmic Great White Brotherhood are a part of the Order of Melchizedek and consist of numerous ascended masters of the earth, both male and female, as well

> as highly evolved, nonphysical spiritual beings from all areas of this universe. In the past, they assisted humanity from within the various retreats and ashrams which were strategically placed around the world. These exalted beings now live in the various celestial cities of light around the world. Those of you who are actively on the ascension path and have integrated a measure of fifth-dimensional frequencies within your physical vessel may now make nightly sojourns in your etheric body to the classrooms within the light cities to accelerate the ascension process. It is to be known that, henceforth, this prestigious group will be called the Cosmic Council of Light to reflect the evolving universal consciousness. Whether you accept it as your truth or not, beloveds, you are becoming galactic citizens and one of the future steps of enlightenment will be the reunion with many members of your solar and galactic family of light. At a future time, some of you will be asked to join the Council of Light as representatives of ascending humanity and the earth."[1]

I had also asked to get to know Saint Germain better before I went to Jackson Hole, and this meeting occurred one day during a massage appointment at the New Mexico Academy of Healing Arts. I had sent love to the space and the practitioner before I went, I arrived full of energy and vitality. When I was on the table, I was told, "Her hands are my hands." And I must have heard at least thirty times from Saint Germain: "Remember that these are my hands working through our angel." Next I learned that the masters were working on my etheric bodies as Saint Germain worked on my physical body in preparation for our gathering on summer solstice, in the Cave of Symbols at the Royal Teton Retreat. I would be allowed to enter because they had invited me, not because I had requested entrance. This would occur the night of June 21, 2009; a new level of ascension would be gifted. Through the alchemical process of precipitation, James and I would, with ease and grace, bring the Temple of the Stone into the third dimension.

I was to arrange for other practitioners to work on me before I left, and of course, Ahara would be one. First they worked on my ascension chakra (brainstem), and then a student practitioner put her hand on my crown chakra. As I had been told, energy poured in and went down my body as I merged with the energy of Saint Germain. At that moment, I truly knew Saint Germain!

Cindy was drawn to come to Santa Fe to see James at Stardreaming and to do a ceremony with me at my house. She told me that when she was with James, she visited with Lilith and was told that James was to sound Archangel Gabriel's horn, using an amazing conch shell that James had brought back from Australia the winter before.

Later, Cindy told me that she had clarity on the nature of our ceremony. She was to personify "debt" and I was to personify "money," with both of us making a dynamic statement to alter the traditional ideas of both debt and money. A few months before, Archangel Raphael had told me, "The new currency of exchange is love." I understood that by means of the frequency of the love vibration, adamantine particles are able to be attracted and therefore cause the manifestation of that which has been intended. Wanting a space in which to express these intentions powerfully, we built a summer solstice altar upstairs in my house next to the painting *Neptunus, Temple of the Stars*. We then commanded our intentions and danced in celebration of the momentous event. It was during this visit that Cindy, James, and I changed my title at Stardreaming from president to ambassador.

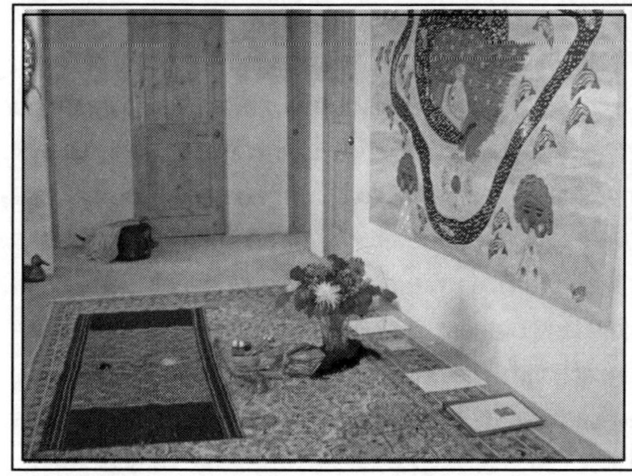

Summer solstice altar.

What Happened Yesterday?—6/10/09

Nina: What happened yesterday with Gabriel, Uriel, the trumpet, the ceremony with Cindy, and my declaration with Cindy? What does my genetic family think of my actions? Also, tell me please about Aya, the Atlantean crystal.

Dear one, let the answers flow in gently so that you are not overwhelmed. A convergence of the Cosmic Council of Light gathered for the purpose of allowing the release, forgiveness, and love energies to surround Cindy, James, and you. None of what transpired could have without celestial and earthly support. The Book of Records tells of this day, and all the cosmos has been waiting for it. It took courage for the three of you to do your part. We watched as each word was spoken and each entreaty made and, with such love, received from your asking. Human consciousness was altered from the moment that Lilith spoke and Gabriel sounded the tones of transformation and action. It was a call to rally all the realms. That is why you spoke to Cindy with such trepidation. The time had come, the trumpet had been sounded, and you needed to sound the words of who you are. Cindy is correct, the Atlantean crystal is the connector for the electromagnetic supertunnel. It will be activated on the summer solstice, June 21, 2009, by means of the human engine you identified: the receiver transmitter that is you and the power of the crystal current. You now remember that it is not the human heart throbbing, but the flow of the frequency particles of God's creative forces that generates the power. This is the power that humankind is, and is just remembering. It is the currency of exchange. It is the energy of creation that will remove fear of the word *debt* from humanity, for that fear will be transformed to love as the life force energy of adamantine particles is activated and circulated through infinity. You ask about your genetic family and how they will react to this. Many of them are not on a level of consciousness that will allow them to understand. They, therefore, see nothing in what was done—just words spoken and sounds made. But it is your actions and Cindy's that will speed up their ascension process, and eventually they will understand.

With our deep love,

Too many names to cite via Anaya-Ra

Cindy felt that night, as I did in the morning, that the city of light over my house had descended and encompassed my house. We felt that all the cities of light descended yesterday. After Cindy drove back to Texas, I sensed and saw the summer solstice altar as an interior sphere spinning counterclockwise, and my house as a larger, descended city-of-light sphere, spinning clockwise—an image of a dot within a circle rotating in opposite directions. I had no understanding, just a knowing that this spiraling vortex was occurring.

During the night eight days before my departure for Jackson Hole, Sananda brought me information about what I needed to do the day after summer solstice. In a quiet place at approximately noon in Yellowstone National Park, I was to situate myself inside a diamond shape with two crystals, placed north and south, and two amethysts east and west. I was to chime the Tree of Life tuning forks, creating a frequencial zero-point. In order to sound the celestial music of the spheres, I was to hold the etheric hand of Archangel Uriel, musician of the spheres, and to sing the recently received mantra of Archangel Metatron, "Veda Karanda Samael," as a crystal singer. I was told that in doing so, three things would occur:

1. The Christ-consciousness codes that I carry would be released.

2. Aya, the large Atlantean crystal in Santa Fe, would activate the other Atlantean crystals.

3. The knowledge of Source would return to earth by means of the library of crystals, the library that had been removed by Archangel Raphael's command when humankind forgot how to love.

The mantra and tuning forks would also "ignite" the electromagnetic supertunnel, which would have been filled with life-force adamantine particles. At that moment, Aya's current would run back and forth from Alpha Centauri, to Teton/Yellowstone, Chaco Canyon, and Stardreaming. Also at that moment, the individual gifts that would be given to me on summer solstice in the Cave of Symbols would travel through the electromagnetic supertunnel to Stardreaming from Yellowstone/Teton. The gift of each council member was their love for Stardreaming, "one of the greatest wonders of the new earth."

I shared this information with the support group and got such grateful, enthusiastic, and supportive responses.

The summer solstice ceremony would help actualize the vision of

Stardreaming's expansion, so everything had to be in clear alignment. This meant that copies of the revised mutuality plan needed to be in Richard's hands at Stardreaming, and with me. The word *society* needed to be removed from our website and mailbox. All aspects of the vision had to be communicated in a similar frequency. I wrote to Richard:

> I will place the revised mutuality plan in the mail today. It reflects only those items the masters have requested, with other items to fall into phase two. Today's date of June 5, 2009 when added up equals twenty-two, a master number and one on which Stardreaming has been built. Just moments ago, Archangel Raphael told me, "The mutuality plan will fly on our wings."

I then wrote to Laura and to James, with whom I would do the opening ceremony at Stardreaming the day before summer solstice:

> Let's meet on Saturday at 10:00 a.m. to do the opening ceremony, which will culminate at noon, on the forty-five acres in the center of the Temple of the Stone. The "cosmic triangle" will be set on summer solstice, with the timegate of Stardreaming ready to be connected to Teton/Yellowstone, Chaco Canyon, and Alpha Centauri. James will be at Chaco Canyon at the appointed site by sunset Saturday, the beginning of summer solstice. I will arrive at Jackson Hole before sunset on Sunday, the end of summer solstice. Last night I heard that we might want to replicate what will be done in Yellowstone. See what comes to you. I will bring the stones in case that feels right with the two of you.

At 10:00 a.m. Saturday, James, Laura, and I met in the rain at Stardreaming. James shared that the day before, while conducting a preparatory ceremony on the forty-five acres, he learned that the Temple of the Stone was to be much bigger than we had thought. So we moved its center point to be in alignment with the central stone in the Temple of New Atlantis, which represented Archangel Metatron. James saw the center of the labyrinth as a rotating cube that pulled energy down in the four directions. The energy of Archangel Metatron's cube would facilitate the vortex of the etheric pyramid where we would stand. Venus and Mars would be aligned that weekend, bringing love and war into balance. I also learned that on Monday, when I was to do ceremony in Yellowstone, the moon would be full.

As we left the wizard's cottage, we found a new baby bird directly in front of the doorway. We interpreted that sign as a symbol of new life and death, the end of separation, and the birth of the new world. We walked to the center of the Temple of the Stone, and ceremoniously buried crystals at the north and south position. We put roses on the surface. Then we buried amethysts at the east and west position, and again laid roses on top. When finished, we had created a diamond shape around the labyrinth. The center of the labyrinth was marked by the embedded staff. Laura noticed that the wet ground smelled of fish, reminding her of the time when the land was underwater and whales and dolphins were present.

Ten rose quartz stones were placed west to east in the center, in the shape of the Tree of Life with James performing the ceremony. He energetically lifted the space up into the fifth dimension, pulled it down in the four directions, and then expanded the energy outward. Laura could see the electromagnetic supertunnel. It was miles across, and the vortex of Archangel Metatron's cube was just outside the perimeter of the labyrinth. I faced the anchoring mountain to the west behind Stardreaming, which, from that vantage point, appeared in its full majesty. Clouds hovered over it resembling a grand spewing volcano. The Tree of Life tuning forks were sounded.

We held hands with Archangel Uriel, and gave thanks to all the otherworldly beings present and to those beings present in spirit. I gave thanks by singing Archangel Metatron's mantra thirteen times. The mantra was to be sung next in Yellowstone and then never again by me. The petals of the red, white, and pink roses were pulled off and spread out from east to west as I sang. The next day, James headed out to Chaco Canyon, and I returned to Stardreaming to spend time with Saint Germain and green goddess and then fly to Jackson Hole, arriving at sundown.

When I returned home after the opening ceremony, Richard had

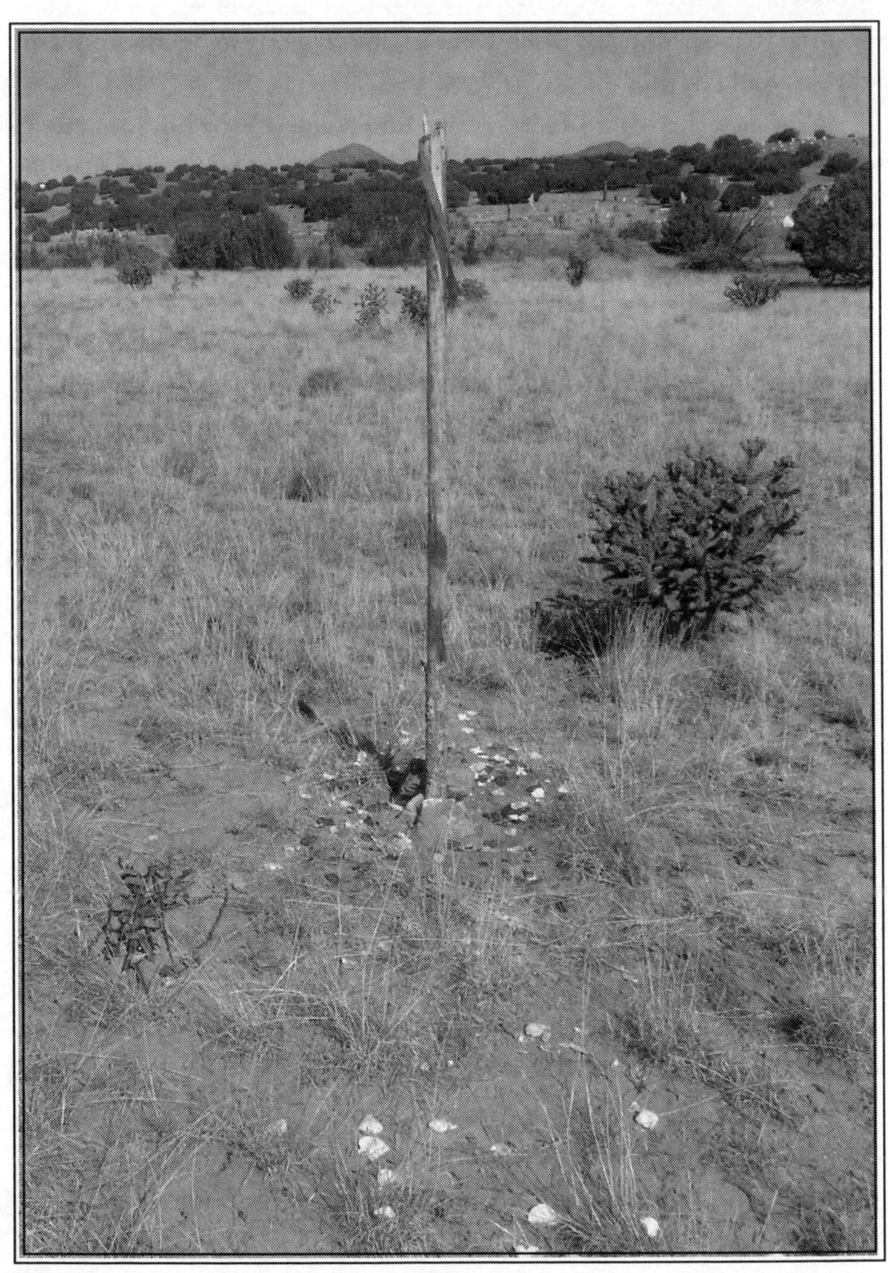

Opening ceremony at Stardreaming.

made one of his rare phone calls. He was "just checking in" concerning summer solstice. He told me that he thought his cell phone was vibrating in his pocket, but then discovered that it was the crystals he had put in his pocket that morning. The times that this happened corresponded to the time when I sang Archangel Metatron's mantra and our ceremony at noon.

I was indeed able to be at both Stardreaming and Jackson Hole the day of summer solstice. I did ceremony at Stardreaming in the morning by myself, since James was on his way to one of the three energetic earthly nodes, Chaco Canyon. Laura would return to Stardreaming in the afternoon, as its anchor for the tunnel.

Summer Solstice at Stardreaming, Temple of the Violet Flame–6/21/09

We gather round you, dear one, as you continue on your magical journey, just like Jason's in *Quest of the Golden Dolphin*. With each step, you will grow in knowledge and wisdom. You sang so beautifully yesterday. You knew that we felt the light vibrations as you sang, for all the stones at Stardreaming and beyond heard your song, "Veda Karanda Samael." Now, continue walking the violet flame labyrinth, and we will rejoin you at the Temple of Avalon. Our love surrounds and fills you. Know this truth.

(Pause. Resume at Temple of Avalon.)

We are on top of the world, with an unrestricted view of eternity. We rejoice in the transition, the shift from separation to unity, the unleashing of the new world that you created. You are All That Is, so of course you are the creator of all that is. Your trip to Wyoming will be gentle and smooth and filled with joy as you requested. Now relax, be joyous. The rest will magically fall in place, for we surround you to prepare the way; you, only you, our dear one, can perform the ceremony of awakening the new world.

With our deep love,
All who love you! via Anaya-Ra

I boarded a plane in Albuquerque and arrived in Jackson Hole just before the sun went down. I went to introduce myself to Tyberonn the next morning at breakfast, since it was his group's bus that would be taking me to Yellowstone National Park to do my private ceremony and sing Archangel Metatron's mantra thirteen times as requested by the masters. This meeting with Tyb was another monumental, life-changing event. From the moment that Tyb spoke, he began telling me who he saw me as. His words were overwhelming and filled with such power and energetic frequency that I could not absorb what he was trying to convey to me. That day played out not as I had been told, but in divine order and perfection. Had I known the details, possibly I would have put up barriers to stop the flow from occurring.

The roar of the hotel generator next to my bedroom window kept me awake, so I was exhausted the next morning and had my guard down. My openness allowed for life to unfold and reveal the mystery of why I was in this power spot on this particular day. I was so lovingly guided and supported by Tyb, whom I was soon to learn I had known and worked with for eons. I boarded his bus and settled in as we headed off to Yellowstone National Park. As we were going through the Grand Tetons, the bus stopped. Tyb asked us all to get out of the bus to be present at Cathedral Mountain. He crooked his index finger, beckoning me forward, placed a 108-facet phi Vogel crystal in my hand, and said, "Point it at the mountain and move it around." I did as he suggested and went out of my body. My life had changed forever.

What happened next took me days to comprehend. The first of that understanding came while the bus was stopped at a lake in Yellowstone National Park. I took out my journal and was able to write a few lines before we had to move on:

Lake at Yellowstone–6/22/09

We did it, dear one. You heard the call and the sounds from your voice echoed far and wide. You have no earthly idea of the import of that short time in the history of earth, but we do, and we tell you all that you dreamed and all you worked for, for so many years, culminated in the perfection of God coming through. We knew in advance that was the spot and could not tell you, for you would have been afraid and would not have done as was needed. So we did not tell you—only Tyb knew, and it was a joyous process for both of you. You planned this together for so many years, and today was the culmination. The sounds did indeed open up the hearts of the crystals. You did that, dear one. Now is the time. The crystals are revitalized. They are alive. The knowledge of Source has returned to the earth, the love of God is in balance. The crystals are the knowledge, the Veda, and they honor you and ... (I stopped writing because the bus was leaving.)

Three days later, back in Santa Fe, I had processed the events well enough to be able to share them with those who had been energetically supportive during the summer solstice:

> It is complete. Thank you for being a part of this magical moment. It is difficult to put the sacred into the written word, unless in doing so you are able to feel the love vibration in between the words. I spent Sunday of the summer solstice—as requested by Saint Germain—at Stardreaming, giving thanks and receiving blessings. That evening, my plane landed in Jackson Hole, twenty minutes before sunset, allowing me to be present at two points of the pyramid on the same sacred day. Monday was the day that Lord Metatron requested that I chant his mantra thirteen times. I met Tyb at breakfast and found that although he had to find my messages buried amongst his five hundred daily emails, he had read about the work that was to be done. He asked if I wanted to use his Vogel crystal. I was astounded and said that I trusted him and would accept his advice and assistance. He seemed to know clearly who I am and what I am about.
>
> The day-long bus trip to Yellowstone National Park began from Jackson Hole, at 8:00 a.m. Tyb graciously invited Marijon and me to sit behind him on the bus. We reverently greeted Cathedral Mountain in the Grand Tetons as we passed it on our way to Yellowstone National Park. I could feel the presence of the Cosmic Council of Light, who gather there twice yearly on the solstice. We stopped to do a ceremony at an overlook before moving on with

our journey. Tyb beckoned Marijon and me to him as the group descended from the bus.

Though it was cool, I had chosen to not take my jacket but a shawl that Cindy had requested I wear in Yellowstone while singing Archangel Metatron's mantra. When I approached Tyb, he handed me his 108-facet phi Vogel crystal. I was perplexed, since I had planned to be alone in Yellowstone when he would give me the crystal to do ceremony. Tyb instructed everyone to form a circle in front of Cathedral Mountain. I was beginning to feel disoriented.

It's difficult to give a factual account of what happened next, for I truly left my body. Tyb asked me to point the crystal toward the mountain. My hand began to shake and my legs felt as if they would not support me. Tyb then asked Marijon and me to enter the circle. I was supported as I slowly walked into the center and again faced the mountain. Soon I was sitting on the ground with Marijon's leg behind me to keep me upright. I called out to Tyb for his permission, for I needed to sing Archangel Metatron's mantra "Veda Karanda Samael." He gave it. My mouth opened wide as I sat shaking. For a while, nothing came out, then my right hand extended straight out as I remembered that I was to hold the hand of Archangel Uriel, Music of the Spheres, while I sang the mantra. My extended arm vibrated. Then the frequency came out. It didn't sound the same as when I had practiced, and it didn't remind me of the sweet voice of a bird. I kept singing, with my fingers remembering to count thirteen mantras. I heard drums and song all around me as those present supported the presentation of the mantra to the universe and the Cosmic Council of Light. Charges of energy surged to and through me. I knew the council's "gifts" were being received and that all that had been told to me was occurring at that moment.

When it was complete, I stood up. Tyb said, "Will the elder please come and ..." I, still in a daze, looked round to see what was going to happen next, but he meant me. "Tear some ... grass

..." I leaned over to pull some grass. "The sweetgrass ..." So I tore some of the sweetgrass, which I saw had been put in my hand and thanked the Cosmic Council of Light and Archangel Uriel.

As I left the bus, I pulled out of my bag a small white stone, which James had allowed me to take from the entrance of Stardreaming. At this point my balance was returning, so I walked to the side of the circle alone and placed the stone in the grass, making an energetic connection between the two sites, and I then reentered the bus. (The second stone from Stardreaming was later placed at the edge of Old Faithful in Yellowstone National Park close to where the crystals, amethysts, and rose quartz Tree of Life symbol were buried and the tones of the Tree of Life tuning forks sounded.) The group's geomancy lecturer had borrowed a large stone from the site of Cathedral Mountain and brought it aboard the bus to accompany us until the end of the day's trip, when it would be returned to the park. I asked to hold it. Slowly, it aided me in returning to my body.

Cathedral Mountain, summer solstice 2009.

That evening, Tyb joined Marijon and me for dinner, bringing the 108-facet phi Vogel crystal, for I had asked to be its custodian. He came with two more, saying, "They are for you." I trusted Tyb and accepted all three, knowing I would understand why when the time was perfect. I bonded with all the crystals immediately, as if we were long-lost friends! On our last day in Jackson Hole, I took them with me to a meditation field at the base of Cathedral Mountain. As each crystal came out of its Sherpa pouch, I found myself opening my mouth, allowing words to emerge. It was the Cosmic Council of Light speaking through me. This was my first channeling experience by means of the voice. I was a bit nervous because I didn't want to become a "channel." Until then, the words had been only for me. But now my higher self, a member of the council, was speaking through me, and that voice was to guide me over the next few months with clear instructions on how to express the new me who had presented at Cathedral Mountain on summer solstice 2009. I

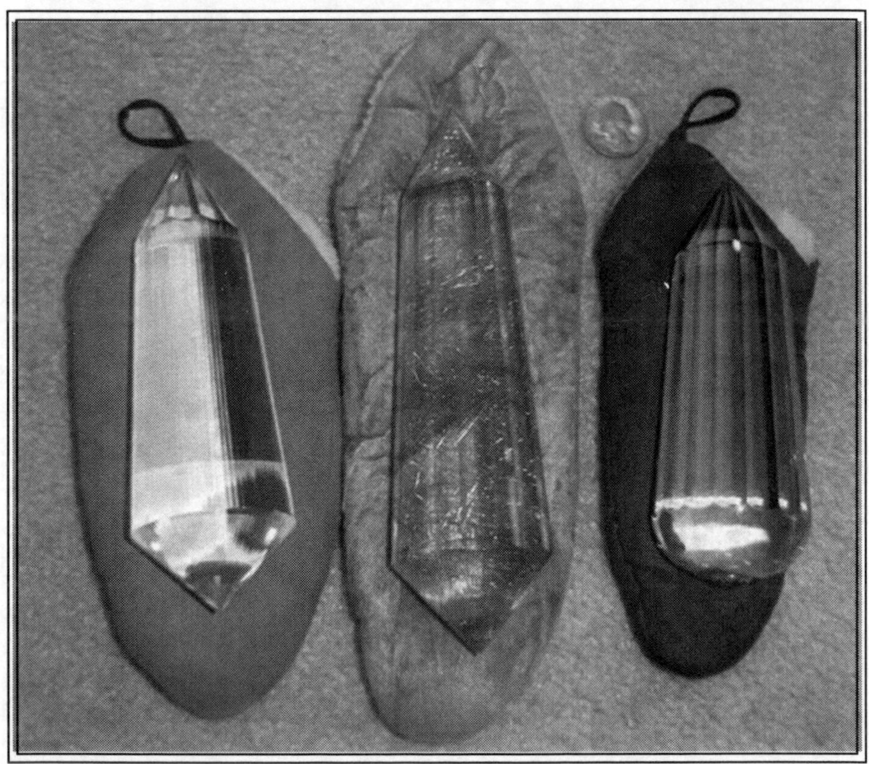

The three Vogel crystals.

boarded my plane and returned to Santa Fe to bring closure to this magical adventure with the electromagnetic supertunnel—the adventure had begun a month before when I had asked Saint Germain, "Am I to go to the Grand Tetons/Yellowstone National Park for summer solstice?"

Back in Santa Fe, I remembered that Ahara had suggested I conduct a personal opening and closing ceremony. My opening ceremony was scheduled on Saturday. Before going to Stardreaming, I took crown essential oil that Ahara had formulated for me during my massage the day before and put it in Himalayan salts in my bath. I lit lavender incense and submerged in the tub, singing Archangel Metatron's mantra and the vowel sounds of creation. For my closing ceremony I placed the remains of the oil and its bottle in a salt bath. I was instructed to submerge—nose and all—and to allow the water to enter my nose, mouth, all of me. I again sang only the vowel sounds of creation while incense was burning. When I left the bath, I was told to place Cindy's shawl around my shoulders. At my meditation site I replaced some items I had taken with me from the summer solstice altar, and added the three Vogel crystals, which were placed on top of the archangel cards. I also added an owl feather and small fragrant branch, from Tyb. I sat with my legs out at the base of the altar with the violet ray phi Vogel crystal in the central position, rang my meditation bell three times, and sounded the splendor tuning fork. Then I breathed the infinity breath eight times, gave thanks, and stood up to dismantle the summer solstice altar. I listened to a CD of bird songs as I removed each piece of the altar. I was told to put on the earrings that Cindy had gifted me, so that I could see myself in the mirror and send love to myself. The closing ceremony was then complete.

I received beautiful notes from the support group upon learning of the details of the igniting of the electromagnetic supertunnel:

> This is absolutely beautiful. Thank you so much for writing it in such detail. You have performed a magnificent service for us all, Mother Earth, and Stardreaming.... Thank you for being so courageous and following your guidance so impeccably. You are an inspiration to all of us! ... The solstice was a magical day. I was

> here on the beach of the Gulf of Mexico with James's paintings *Sol, Jupiter,* and *Soqwahote*. We celebrated the sun the entire day and connected with all our family of light at the same time you were performing this amazing ceremony, dearest elder of sacred knowledge and change on the earth in light. Thank you.... Things never seem to unfold exactly as received in the original vision. The creation is constantly calling it in with us. Thank you, thank you, thank you. I have no words beyond that for this woman.

"Veda Karanda Samael" was never again to be sung by me. It had worked its magic!

~ 15 ~

Healer of Crystalline Seed Come to Recode

What exactly was that magic?

Archangel Metatron was soon to tell me, "When you held the 108 phi in the morning ceremony at the Grand Tetons, an immediate synergy occurred in which you transferred the new crystalline code of the 144 codes into the light city of the Tetons." How can I describe how incredulous I felt hearing that? But I sensed a deep calm, a deep knowing that what had been transmitted was true. This energetic flow continued as I stepped forward and used the crystals at a closing ceremony at Stardreaming to ignite the small grid, which was soon to be constructed in my house, then again at Cathedral Basilica of Saint Francis in Santa Fe. All of this served to strengthen my self-confidence and allowed me to say yes to Tyberonn when he was to ask me to speak before three hundred people and begin to give sessions for the recoding of humanity.

On my return to Santa Fe, I started to receive numerous emails from Tyberonn. He began to share with me what he saw when we first met in Jackson Hole only days before:

> Nina, I know you and I are together on the Sirius ship as part of the Galactic Federation and ascended Ashtar group working on the reenergization of the new leys and crystalline hypertunnels system for the new earth. When I saw you I knew you were a crystal field master. I will do your reading (with Archangel Metatron) within the next seven days and get it back to you. Please begin working with your phi crystal tools. They are true

Atlantean & Arcturian technology and are not only highly aware perfect specimens but also extremely powerful instruments, and should be regarded as such. It is very important to speak with them, to put your heart energy into them in the initial stages. You will be building an energy field with them, and that will take three to five weeks. Please spend about ten minutes a day with each of them for as many days as you can. They will signal you by sending electrical tingles back to you that you can sense, either as waves up the arm or as a charge you sense in your heart and third eye or crown—in time they will begin to warm in your hands. This is when you will know the "torsion field" is getting large enough to do the work with them. You will then be able to do a myriad of things with them, such as travel dimensionally and amplify, receive, and transfer cosmic light into a crystalline coherent field.

Archangel Metatron Reading for Nina via James Tyberonn– 6/28/09

"And so we have the inquiring mind of the soul termed Nina in this sojourn.

"You have indeed had many sojourns on the duality of earth. You followed the path and took no shortcuts. Like many you fell into the depths of humanity after the fall of Atlantis, but rose again without sequential faulting in the great eras of Egypt. Dear one, you are an extremely advanced soul, who has had many, many lifetimes on this planet and many others, including Sirius A, Arcturus, Andromeda, Vega, and the Pleiades. All of these are coexisting now, ongoing simultaneously above linear time. You are a high-ranking member of the Galactic Federation. You are very capable of multidimensional communication and are in contact with these other aspects of your higher self, including the ascended master aspect of you in the angelic level realm. You were an embodied Sirian in Lemuria and Atlantis before you chose the reincarnational cycle, and you were an arch-priest of the Atla-Ra sect of scientist-priests, holding a high position in the Atlantean Temple of Illumination on Poseida. You were also one of the tall golden beings in Atlantis, and you worked together there with Tyberonn the Pleiadian, root soul of the channel. Your lifetimes in human body began in Atlantis, expanded through Egypt, Og, Asia, Tibet, India, Judea, Europe, and the Americas of the indigenous Hopi, Lakota, and Olmec.

"It can be said that Tyberonn is in your soul family; the crystalline guild, and the Sirius alliance, and you have shared key lifetimes as colleagues and do so now above linear time space in the Sirian alliance, a guild closely associated with the of the earth and your specific role here now. There is then a closer 'knowing' between the entity and the channel Tyberonn, both having then a more similar purpose, in regard to seeding the crystalline vibration for the ascending earth. Both of you have worked closely with the Sirian alliance and indeed with Thoth in both Atlantis and Egypt. Both of you share lifetimes in Judea, Tibet, and the Native Americas. You are both carrying different spectrums of the crystalline field. As such, your meeting was inevitable. Your work will merge at times."

Question to Metatron: "How are the crystals relative to my contract?"

Metatron: "Dear one, you are a starseed crystal being; you carry the crystalline code inside your beingness. In a very real and very valid sense you transfer the crystalline code onto the earth. This is a role you have also carried out in other sojourns. In all of your incarnations you have been the human embodiment of the crystalline Sirius starseed. So that which you think of as crystal is not just in mineralogical form, it is also a frequency that is exuded in impeccable uniform clarity.

"That termed the Vogel phi crystals then are precise crystalline forms that offer sentient doorways into the crystalline aspect both within and without you. Was there not an immediate recognition when these were handed to you recently? Did the crystal not send an immediate resonant pulse that opened a deep reservoir within you? Dear one, when you held the 108 phi in the morning ceremony at the Grand Tetons, an immediate synergy occurred in which you transferred the new crystalline code of the 144 into the light city of the Tetons. Indeed, it is true. In other lifetimes you have done exactly that—recoding and upshifting specific earthen energy nodes to the crystalline blueprint, the DNA of the new paradigm. In Lemuria, Atlantis, and Egypt you did this, and again in this lifetime it is the role, the mission, you have undertaken. Although you do not as yet fully recognize who you are, this will come. So, in precise answer to your question, the phi crystals are tools that you have recognized and waited for. You will use these instruments in your mission of recoding the power nodes and what you refer to as aspects of the grid system.

"Now you are working with a group in Santa Fe, termed the star dreamers, and this is a key step in your awakening to full consciousness. There are indeed crystals below the area of Santa Fe, but these are not the master Atlantean crystals that you were involved in removal from Atlantis and placement for safekeeping. These are in Arkansas, Shasta, Titicaca, and Brazil—all located via the hyperdimensional tunnel system to areas of crystal growth in the labyrinth of the golden age of Atlantis. There is much for you to do in these locations. It can be done etherically, and it will begin this year. In rapid progression you will focus on your not as yet facilitated role of recoding the DNA of humans into the crystalline format. This you will do in individual sessions of thirty to forty-five minutes, using the phi crystals, paired with the toning audio of your channeled inner voice. The tones will intertwine with the coherent crystalline light of the phi crystals and be transmitted through and from your inner being.

"It is important that you manage the integrity of your etheric body. You must pay attention to the fatigue you are experiencing. Indeed, it is to a large degree occurring because your reentry into the physical body after your multidimensional travel is quite difficult at present. You reenter the body at an incredibly high frequency, and the physical body is unable to hold the intrahigh frequency as yet. The result is an energetic surge that creates what may be termed a blown fuse or short circuit (in your vernacular) within your energy field, leading to microfissuring of the field and energy bleed out, causing fatigue and temporary imbalance. The energy field must be expanded and strengthened, and this can be done with the phi crystals and gemstones. It can be achieved by programming the phi crystals, including and especially the violet ray phi, with the intent for them to assist in transmitting an energy that will synergize with your etheric EMF and act as surge breakers to transduce the energies received in meditation, ceremony, dream state, and multidimensional journey so that they can be sustained harmoniously in the physical realm. Circulate the phi crystal with this intent over the heart and head once they are programmed, before meditation, channel, energy projection and sleep. The channel can offer you assistance in the process should this be desired, but follow your inner voice ultimately. You know how to do this.

"Now the gems should be worn on each hand as already prescribed, in single and double refractive gems. These can be varied, but should be worn at all times. The red spinel will also assist in detoxification of the body physical. Dear one, use the gem tools. They are at your disposal, and are requisite for the work you came to do. This you know. Not as embellishments but as energy tools of great light, great power. Two gems were worn extensively in the Egyptian sojourns and these will offer further assistance. One is the lapis lazuli as the pendant, at least thirty-five grams in weight, fifty is better. The other worn in pendant form in the Temple of Osiris was the garnet, then quite large in size and of the red-violet-burgundy hue."

Question to Metatron: "What else would you like me to know?"

Metatron: "Dear one, we would have you know thyself. Indeed, you are a great soul, and to be commended for your service and light. You have incarnated on the earth at this time to serve humanity and the planet itself. For this we honor you greatly, for indeed you are one of great accomplishment. It can be said to you in truth that your oversoul is on the level of the ascended mastery. Not yet fully accomplished on that realm, not yet at the level of Saint Germain, whom you recently encountered, for there are levels of mastery within each realm, each level. We would have you know that you are indeed within the realm of the ascended master, and we would have you acknowledge self. As yet, your awakening to who you are is not fully realized. As yet, you do not fully accept your great light. Remove the conflict. Remove the doubt and take your power. Only you can do this, and indeed, dear one, you are truly a great soul. You must realize you have mastered the earth cycle through many, many bright lifetimes, and choose to return by your own will and devotion to assist humanity at this precise time. We bid you to accept these truths. You have taken on a demanding and very important role. You are the crystal starseed and are among the few masters walking the earth who have earned the very real ability to recode humanity, the grid, and all divine life into the crystalline code. This is your chosen role.

"Dear one, you are even now recoding the DNA of the dolphin beings. In your time crossing over into the etheric realm, you are working with dolphins, indeed Sirians, who are choosing to have their DNA recoded in order to be a greater part of the ascension and to return in human form. Are you aware of this, dear one? In a deeper state you are very aware of this. And we tell you the dolphins and whales perform a tremendous role in anchoring the leys and portals and grid lines that flow over the vast waters of the earth. We will also tell you that you have experienced life on the planet in dolphin form, and that a portion of your entity in multidimensional aspect has the ability to speak to them in the ancient language known as Paa-Taal.

"We will also share with you that you have walked the earth with Jeshua Ben Joseph, he known as Jesus the Christos. There did you speak with him and walk with him, and his mark is indeed indelibly in the light of your soul. This then is the connection to the ascended master Sananda, and represents a major phase of your completion. You are of the divine feminine, the energy of Hathor as the goddess, and the same resonant field of Isis and Mary. Your role is to code the crystalline light of the divine feminine into the DNA of humanity and of the earth. You are not alone; you have an entourage to assist you. This you already know. Many of these are within the realm of what is termed starseed of the Sirian alliance, and you, along with the channel, are coexisting on a ship closely connected to this work. Your higher aspects, then, are your own guides.

"Well for the entity to revisit in physical the areas of Arkansas, Arizona, Shasta, Glastonbury, and Egypt. Awakenings will occur there. In closing, we tell you to accept these truths, and have confidence in who you are. You are the master, you are the teacher, you are the healer of crystalline seed come to recode. Your most important role is not in recoding the grid; indeed, you will and are playing a key part in that process, and it will continue. However, your great and greater role is in recoding humanity in small groups and individually. That is why you are here. It will come. Take your power. Be the teacher, the master, and be guided by the self. I am Metatron, and I share with you these truths. And so it is."

The information in Archangel Metatron's channel was shocking and puzzling. I needed some certainty that what he said was indeed my truth. This came two months later at the Toltec Mounds in Arkansas, and more profoundly during my travels in Bolivia after that. In the meantime, I said to Tyb:

> No wonder you were exhausted. Thank you so much for accepting your role as the conduit of such important information. I feel finally that I am on the path of receiving directly from my own self, which is how I wish it to be. I have reread the information and will do so again and again, so that each phrase is integrated. Tyb, I request that if at any point you feel or know something that would be of assistance to my journey, you feel free to tell me. As you know, I have a profound trust in you as I do in my own voices and knowing. Today at noon, James, Laura, and I will do the closing ceremony at Stardreaming. I know that it is to include the crystalline grid-activation meditation,[1] and the three crystals. I know also that it will be more profound than the ceremony at Cathedral Mountain, for I am bonded and am one with the crystals. I will work with the violet ray phi crystal in advance to set the intention of expanding my field to protect my physical being. Can you find me the lapis and garnet that Archangel Metatron referred to? Also, I can't wait to see the picture of the pink spinel. I will check in after today's ceremony. Curiously, as suggested in the channel, I will be in Arkansas and Bolivia, in the next few months. This, as usual, was an intuitive decision.

The closing ceremony at Stardreaming was more intense for me than the opening ceremony. I had programmed my crystals to support my auric field, which made a dramatic difference, and after the ceremony was over I recovered quickly. We began by entering the etheric labyrinth from the east and sat facing the large, distant mountain, in front of the serpent staff. I held the two crystals and went into the crystalline grid-activation meditation. Then I took the violet ray phi and circled it around my heart and crown chakra. I held the 9-gate dream phi and the 108-facet Vogel phi out toward the mountain and rotated them both thirteen times. When I finished, I knew that the grid had been connected and moved into the crystalline vibration. On reflection, I realize this ceremony was a pivotal moment for I was conducting the ceremony at Stardreaming.

I had no idea that I would be doing ceremony again and so quickly, until Patty showed up. Patty, a new friend from Jackson Hole and summer solstice, came to visit that Tuesday. She offered to bring into my house some of the gemstones she had in her car. She no longer had a home, and the gemstones were some of her few remaining possessions. As we unboxed them, their placement on my living room rug began to look like a pattern. The next morning, I added all the stones and gems that I had. While I was doing an errand, Patty brought in "the big ones" from her car. It was very clear that we were to do ceremony to ignite the grid and then, with the crystalline grid meditation, to connect it to the center of the earth, and out to the ascension grid. Our ceremony flowed. I sat in the south position on a large rose quartz stone that had been gifted to

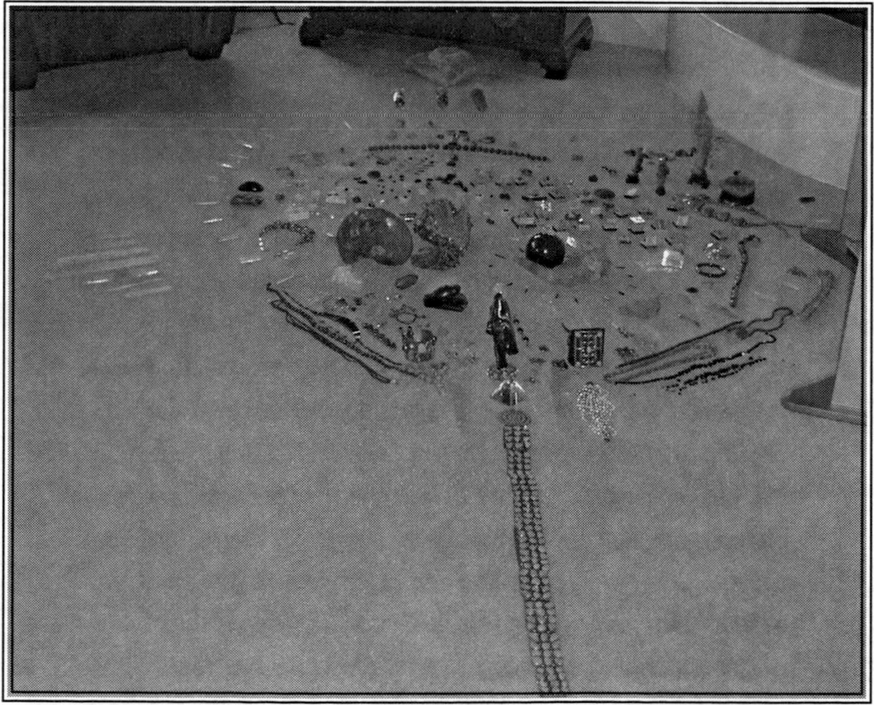

Small grid.

me just months before. Patty sat on one of her large stones. Rose incense was burning.

I held the 108-facet Vogel crystal and the 9-gate dream crystal. It felt like we needed to ignite the grid first, so I asked for Patty's help, since I wasn't sure how to do that. She began chanting and singing in "light language." I rotated the two crystals in my hands eight times in both directions, with energy pouring through my arms. Then I held the two crystals out and did the crystalline grid-activation meditation, again with energy flowing through my arms, while Patty continued to chant and sing. Then the ceremony was complete. Spirals radiated up and out and through the space. Each gem and each stone was singing in my living room. We left the grid intact until the next morning when we used Patty's new drum and my tuning forks to sound the crystals. The organic flow was magical. This was the second time that I had allowed the ceremony to flow through me. My self-confidence muscle was growing.

The day after Patty left, I wrote to Tyb about what I now knew to be auric bleeding.

> Tyb, I awoke exhausted this morning after having gone to bed early and gotten up later than usual, I actually had a hard time climbing my stairs and just wanted to end the day and go back to bed. Then I remembered Archangel Metatron's words to me through you, Tyb: protect yourself so that when you reenter your body at such a high frequency you do not cause auric bleeding. So I took the violet ray phi crystal, which I had programmed with that intent, and circled it over my heart and crown chakra, repeating the intention. I took a bath in citrus and peppermint, and while bathing, I remembered the singing crystals that Patty had gifted me. I asked permission to work with them, and it was granted. I placed them vertically on my chest breathing in liquid light from above and below. I asked that my auric field repair, expand, and be filled with this light and energy. Then I put the citrus essential oil in body oil and covered my skin. All of this has made a big difference, and I want to thank you for the lessons and the tools.

I know that I will be more aware now and will treat and care for myself differently. I knew living in my house with the new grid energy that I needed adjustments in my physical being. This was a beginning.

Tyb replied:

Well done! Auric field maintenance is a continual journey, requiring daily effort. So many things can and do affect our energy fields. Microwaves, other people, electrical fields, cell phones, medications, and airplane trips, just to name a few. Another tip is to acquire two ceramic magnets, about 1 to 1.5 inches in diameter and 0.5 inch in thickness of between 1,500 to 3,000 gauss strength. Put these on the soles of the feet for about ten to fifteen minutes a day for up to three days a week. Put one on with the north pole of one magnet facing the skin on one foot and the other with the south pole against the skin on the other foot. Wear copper bracelets on each wrist and gold around the neck during this process. You can hold the magnets in place with socks or wrist bands. Do this three times a week, for no more than fifteen minutes each time. This circulates and strengthens the auric field. Use four cups of fine-grained bath salts when you bathe and be sure to moisturize afterwards. Metatron mentioned that you need to detoxify and you could do this with a series of three high colonics, every six months. Also, drink lots of purified water. These simple steps will support your auric field and your mission. Auras are not automatically regulated: we are responsible for maintenance of the etheric bodies' circuitry, frequency, and wholeness-integrity (keeping them "leak-free") just as we are with our physical body. Again the noble metal and gemstone function as precision tools; they are not jewelry, they are light generators and an essential key to higher frequency energy transduction and balance. Please, always use them, and wear the gems especially in your sleep. Use the Metatronic shield before you enter a dream state or meditation. Hope this helps.

Archangel Metatron had spoken of my working with planetary nodes, which I had now experienced, but he also spoke of upshifting human DNA. What exactly did that mean? The answer began to come to me from Tyb in an unexpected way, by invitation:

> Dear Sister, I would like you to consider coming to Mount Magazine [Arkansas] as my guest at the 09/09/09 Earth-Keeper gathering, serving as a guest speaker and perhaps conducting a channeled meditation to convert the DNA of the three hundred attendees to the upshifted crystalline frequency. I felt nudged by Metatron to offer you this opportunity to step into your role. Can you be there for the 7th and 8th? If not, another time, but see how this feels. Blessings, joy, and love.

I felt it was important to wait until after the full moon, lunar eclipse to answer Tyb. It seemed there was something I was to do, after which I would have more clarity.

> Tyb, Oh my gosh. Let me ponder. I need to pass through the full moon, lunar eclipse before answering. This morning again words involuntarily came out of my mouth. This channeling started in the meditative meadow under Cathedral Mountain just before my plane left Jackson Hole. So Lord Metatron put you up to this. Fascinating. If that is the case, then I might just ask him to assist me in finding the perfect answer, so the execution is for the highest good of all. Then what comes to me is the gift that I might be able to bring to three hundred people. In Wyoming I was the vehicle, so why wouldn't that work again? You should know that it was a bit of a "setup." I was put in a bedroom Sunday night next to the hotel generator, so I only slept four hours. I was so exhausted that I had no resistance. Then, as you know, I thought my private ceremony and mantra singing would happen around noon in Yellowstone National Park. So, its public unfolding earlier in the Grand Tetons was a huge surprise! Guess all one has to do is just say yes. Then the acronym S.T.A.R.—surrender, trust,

allow, and receive takes over. I'll get back to you Wednesday, Tyb.

What had just happened? One of the most respected metaphysicians in the field, James Tyberonn, had asked Nina Brown to speak in front of three hundred people at his conference. And, as if that wasn't shocking enough, he had asked me to make myself available to do sessions with his guests. He was putting his reputation in my hands. Who was I that he would ask this of me? How did I feel about this? I was reluctant to just say yes because I truly didn't understand what was happening. Why was Archangel Metatron encouraging Tyb to ask me? What did he know about me that I didn't yet know about myself? All of this made me feel as if my life was about to change. I could always say no, but that didn't feel like the right answer. Something inside of me was giving me courage and asking me to step beyond my comfort level and say yes. Not only did other people believe I could do all that was being asked of me, but I was starting to believe it as well. Somehow I would be given the strength and wisdom to speak and to do the sessions. It would come from somewhere or I wouldn't have been asked. "Yes" was being shouted louder and louder by my inner voice.

So I asked the universe what was pulling me as the full moon, lunar eclipse was approaching.

Ceremony, Full Moon, Lunar Eclipse, Saint Francis Basilica, Santa Fe–7/4/09

Nina: Is there something special that I should know about the July 7 full moon, lunar eclipse?

We rejoice that you asked and heard our request to take pen to paper. The crystals that now surround you are like your new appendages. They are you, even the golden flame crystal (given to me by Patty) is an extension of you and carries your vibration as a transmitter. You heard the words correctly before you began writing, and soon you will just know and won't need the journal. The Cathedral Basilica of Saint Francis, like so many Christian sites, is on a power node. That node is disconnected from the grid and needs reconnection and upramping to the Christ-consciousness ascension grid. Just know that this is your work, and the foundation of even greater work. Combining the crystal energy with days of astrological importance is vital. The energy flow is magnetized. The work that you, James, and Laura did last Tuesday has been growing in strength, and just as crystals grow so does the crystalline frequency. You did not think of that, but it is true in the body as well. Your crystalline frequency is growing like a crystal. Heed Tyb's suggestions. Do the cleansing. Wear the gems. Hold the crystals. Only you can repair, guard, and strengthen your field. Keep it strong for the work.

With our deep love,
The ancient ones via Anaya-Ra

As each day passed, little pieces of information came to me about how I was to work with the human energy field.

> Tyb, I was just sitting in my red leather chair holding the crystals and toning the vowels. It was as if I went into a trance with my eyes glazed over. I kept repeating, "a,e,i,o,u, a,e,i,o,u, a,e,i,o,u." It was such a deep, rich sound. When I was finished my solar plexus felt warm and vital. Then I thought about what I wrote last night and the understanding that the crystalline frequency grows in us. It was as if that was what was happening. So working with someone would mean transferring the frequencies and then toning to expand and activate them. What better tone than the vowel sounds of creation. So what is evolving is the use of both crystals as described, followed by the toning of the vowel sounds of creation; transfer then activate. Fascinating.
>
> Thank you for being my mentor, Tyb. It is nice having someone to share with as I open to my journey. I was getting ready to write in my journal—with the crystals on the table—to ask for information concerning the Cathedral Basilica of Saint Francis and tomorrow's visit. I went upstairs to light incense in my office and felt that I needed to hold vertically the two singing crystals and

sit crosslegged in the central medallion on my Oriental carpet. I heard myself asking the questions, instead of writing them, as I had expected. Then the words flowed in a smooth, calm manner from the Cosmic Council of Light. I don't remember much of what was said actually. The new points were that nothing really matters except my intention and love. How I move the crystals, what time of day it is, what I eat—nothing really matters except my intention and my love. The council assured me that a very powerful node in the grid had been disconnected for a long time. Once it was reconnected and upshifted to the crystalline frequency—by means of the crystalline grid-activation meditation—the new frequency would travel to other nodes. They reminded me that the people, like the site, are sacred. Above all else, they reminded me not to doubt myself or be afraid. I feel a little overwhelmed because it is all seeming so real to me and I sense a huge shift in my life's path. Ah, I know the difference between this and the time at Cathedral Mountain and at Stardreaming. This time I am going by myself to do the work. Of course, that is not really true. Thank you for listening!

Tyb kept encouraging me throughout this unfolding.

You are a channel of crystalline light, and your frequency brings in an entourage to anchor the matrix "recodes," upshifts nodes, power points, and people. People are sacred; the hearts of all are sacred. Because you bring in such a nurturing energy, the starseed divine feminine, you manifest an openness that accepts everyone. I FedExed your gems today and they will require a signature. The lapis is from Afghanistan and the garnet is from Tanzania; and there is a literal cornucopia of gems mined from the igneous and metamorphic rock layers of Mount Kilimanjaro.

Tyb, This is a very important message which I so appreciate. I have spent much time "giving my power away," but that began to turn around when I went to Egypt two years ago and had the amazing experience of intuitively bringing the new creation star codes to the Solar Cross. I came home knowing that I no longer needed teachers and that within me were the answers. I feel that each day I am moving closer to a fuller understanding of who I am, and why I am here. The next step is to know directly: to remember events and missions, and to relate that to the now. Please thank Lord Metatron for "nudging" you and for your willingness to convey. I awoke last night at 12:00 a.m. with a vision of how a gathering might unfold at Mount Magazine. I heard the words come out of my mouth. I ended up taking my down comforter and pillow out on the bedroom porch and resting in the full moonlight. I stayed there until about 3:30 a.m.! Today would be an auspicious day to receive the gem tools. May the day unfold magically for you.

I had spent the night on the upstairs porch in the moon's full light as a prelude to the unfolding of the day's ceremony in the Cathedral Basilica of Saint Francis. As I was taking my full moon and lots-and-lots-of-salt bath, it came to me that when I do the crystalline grid-activation meditation inside the basilica facing the altar, my intention would be to connect that sacred site node to the Vatican. What a hoot, but of course I took the idea very seriously. The Vatican deserved the full moon, lunar eclipse. How perfect.

Tyb, It just occurred to me that there might be some resistance to my including the Vatican with this feminine crystalline energy flow. Therefore, thanks to you, I am wearing gem tools as an energy field. I have on a white lace skirt and white blouse with a black Spanish lace mantilla, so that I fit in. With the crystals, I believe I am properly prepared, and I have a lot of love surrounding me as well. After meditation, I am off.

When I returned from downtown Santa Fe, I shared the morning's events with Tyb.

How much different it would be if I had no one to share this with, especially nobody who truly understands. Thank you! Before I left, I learned in meditation that by connecting to the Vatican I was indeed connecting to the Catholic church: all the cathedrals, all the churches, the whole Catholic church via harmonic oscillation. I went to the center of Santa Fe to the Cathedral Basilica of St. Francis of Assisi's parking lot, where I was greeted warmly and given free parking. I came in the back door of the cathedral, after asking permission to enter. I walked down the nave to the front door to enter formally. Before doing so, I asked the cathedral and the Vatican if I could present the gift of the feminine crystalline frequencies and was granted permission. I walked on the right side of the baptismal font in the center, and as I approached the front seat near the altar, the woman who occupied it vacated the seat. I covered my head with the black lace mantilla and exposed the gem tools. I first held the violet ray phi crystal, asking for protection and that my field be strengthened to do this work. It was a dramatic part of the ceremony with a great deal of energy vibrating through my body. Then I held the other two crystals inconspicuously, though my body was shaking. My request was to reconnect and upshift this cathedral. When that was complete, I began the crystalline grid-activation meditation with the intention of connecting the cathedral to the Vatican in Rome and all other Catholic churches. When I was finished, the bells of the church rang. I asked that the chanting that filled the church be the nourishment for the crystalline energy that had been gifted, and that all the chanting throughout the Vatican and Catholic churches nourish the crystalline frequency so it could grow. I departed by retracing my steps down the nave, then proceeded down the other side of the baptismal font to the front door. I could feel the frequency growing, spiraling, and, with permission, transforming.

Archangel Metatron described the Law of Harmonic Oscillation:

The crystallized matrix of sacred sites projects a specific harmonic wavelength through vibratory energy pulses that communicates

> through harmonic energy oscillations. Therefore, a sacred site or power node with an energy source will emit a frequency that is capable of affecting and communicating with all formations of identical type regardless of where they are located on the surface of the planet.[2]

Tyb got right back to me, saying:

> The Vatican and St. Peters Basilica are built over a very powerful energy node, and I suspect the chapel in Santa Fe is too. The sacred geometry in the Vatican and most Catholic churches is also based on sacred geometry. That geometry both stores and amplifies, by its architectural structure of sacred angles and domes, the earth energies in the power nodes they sit over, and stores and amplifies the high-intent energies of people who go there in meditative states. These energies do harmonically connect through what is called axialtonal lines. They will connect to all other sites that hold similar energies through harmonic oscillation. It is the same principle as what happens when, for example, a piano tuner holds a tuning fork in the key of C and then strikes a C note on the piano: the fork will start vibrating automatically because the frequency is the same, demonstrating a scientific principle called harmonic oscillation. The same principle applies to sacred frequencies. When one is activated, all others of that same frequency will start vibrating automatically. You went to the perfect place.

After the excitement of the morning, I sat in meditation with the tape recorder on. I had just asked, "Am I to accept Tyberonn's invitation?" when the doorbell rang. There were no words for all that Tyb had shared with me over the past month, and then these treasures (gem tools) arrived!

"Tyb, yes, I will see you in Mount Magazine."

So many miracles were swirling around me, but there was still another one. An individual I met in Jackson Hole had asked me what I did. I told him about the work with Stardreaming, its protection, maintenance, and expansion. "Send me all that you have. It's a done deal," he said, acknowledging his willingness to finance Stardreaming. As if sealing our agreement in this magical time of the full moon, lunar eclipse I sent him our mutuality plan.

~ 16 ~

No Longer to Walk the Path Alone

I had just agreed to speak in front of three hundred people in September and to give private sessions for the upshift of DNA. How could I do this? What was I to talk about for an hour? I wasn't even sure what DNA was. Then it came to me. I am to live in two dimensions simultaneously. My mortal being had no clue what to do or say, but my higher self had the answers. I felt an enormous trust that I would be guided and shown the path. All I had to do was ask and trust. Again S.T.A.R. was returning to my life as my compass. That compass would lead me to do ceremony to connect and upshift sacred waters, caverns, sweat lodges, temples, labyrinths, and mounds. It would unfold the details of how one conducts a DNA upshift and how one confidently stands in front of three hundred people knowing that the words would be an expression of heaven on earth: the unity of the mortal with the spiritual self. I was ready to take the steps down this new S.T.A.R. path. Both Archangel Metatron and Tyberonn saw something in me that would make all of this possible.

The details of "how" began to unfold little by little, so that I could take the new information in with ease and grace.

> Tyb, It hasn't registered why I would do private sessions. Perhaps that will become clear over time. Seems like what I am going to be doing is upshifting an individual's frequency, which I would think happens just once. If that happens in the group, why would someone want a private session as well? This is really all too new to me, but I will go with the flow.

Tyb's encouraging reply came quickly.

Metatron told me that recoding DNA and upshifting frequencies are more effective and best done in single-person sessions. He said that although you are a bit uncertain at present, once you begin doing them you will be assisted and become very comfortable with the process.

Tyb, Your message is helping me find clarity. "The group meditation and talk will offer the process, but you will individually channel the shift to them." So it sounds like the actual transfer is individually transmitted. When you offered me a speakership and key healing role, I understood the enormous faith and trust expressed by that invitation. I feel an equally strong certainty that allows me to say yes to something so remarkable. So it is a team process, with each of us supporting the other. I also know that this would not be asked of me if I were not to be guided and instructed. So, as with all in my life, I surrender, trust, allow, and receive, knowing that all is in divine order and that I am a vehicle for service as well as a "sparkling pink gem." (Tyb had told me that I sparkle the same as my new pink ring.)

Last night, Tyb, during the three hours that I was in a lucid dream state, the image of a crystal with rainbow colors in it appeared. It occurs to me that the star seeds now planted grow into rainbow-colored crystalline frequencies, thus creating the "rainbow race." Also, I had the dream phi crystal on my stomach, thinking it would enter my being as the violet ray phi crystal did on the first night. But it was the 144 that did so. Curious. Thank you for your trust and guidance, and Archangel Metatron, through you, as well.

I was feeling clear about how to conduct a session. I had gone to my crystal city of light again in the morning, as instructed by Archangel Michael through Ronna Herman, and asked for as much clarity as I could handle—and it came pouring in. Within the last two months, I have come to know that love is a frequency and has structure. It can be sent and received, and it is, of course, the adamantine particles. For example, I have sent love to my doctor, to the building, to my body, to my high blood pressure, to my irregular heartbeat, and to the lab technicians. After doing this, my yearly physical exam showed no high blood pressure, no irregular heartbeat, and no high glucose levels. So I know that I can send love, as we all can.

That morning I saw how a session would flow. An individual enters my room; there is polite exchange; we sit opposite each other; I ask permission to both hold their hands and extend the two crystals toward their sacred heart. This establishes the electromagnetic connection between us. Then I hold the person's hands and look into their eyes. I had been told in meditation that I can receive, through my crown chakra, the love frequency, which then flows through my sacred heart—by means of intention and the infinity breath—to their sacred heart. I can visualize the exchange and the bonded oneness with ease. This is so easy, for I am already doing it. The only difference is proximity; now the person is seated next to me and the focus and intention is more intense. The divine feminine crystalline frequency, in the form of adamantine particles, is transferred at a higher vibration, with an expansion of the individual's love quotient. Amazing. It is as if the cloud was removed and all the dots joined.

Now that the details of conducting a session were clear, a few more particulars remained.

> Can you send me a little bio for the next newsletter? A paragraph is fine. Half-hour sessions would be best. That way you can have more sessions, and reach more people. Is that okay?

> Tyb, I will write the paragraph in a bit. Fascinating that you found a picture of me.

In this time of discovering my cosmic self, it was good to be reminded of my mortal self by sending this bio to Tyb.

> Perhaps the best adjective to use in describing myself is "pioneer." I have always loved breaking through barriers and exploring new realms. After graduation from Bryn Mawr College in 1990,

> as their first nontraditionally aged student, I launched a company focused on access to capital for women-owned businesses and created a new funding instrument, venture collateral. After selling that vision to a female venture capitalist, I consulted in the field of alternative medicine, launching a company eager to bring neurosensory diagnostic tools to disabled veterans and others. Medicare disagreed about the equipment's insurance compliance, so I moved on to consult for Stardreaming in Santa Fe on the cosmic center's preservation, maintenance, and expansion, with the goal of creating the largest stone labyrinth for healing and transformation. Lord Metatron, lord of light, however, knows me as "the healer of crystalline seed, come to recode the grid and humanity as a starseed crystalline being, who carries the crystalline code inside my beingness."

Tyb had more questions.

> Thanks, what is your degree in? Are you on the school board still?

> Tyb, I have resigned from or completed all of my board positions: Opera Company of Philadelphia, Academy of Vocal Arts, Shipley School, and Los Alamos Public School Foundation. My degree is in the growth and structure of cities, which is how I started my company Pepper Development, restoring houses in Camden, New Jersey. I so convinced myself of the city's potential for revitalization when I wrote my thesis that I went to the bank for a construction loan. The company was successful in bringing mortgage money and owner occupants back to Camden. Thanks for asking.

In writing my bio and answering Tyb's questions, I was reminded that Pepper Development Company was another reason that I lost my home in Philadelphia. My five-year balloon mortgages on the houses in Camden had come due during a real estate slump. The reappraisal for the houses came in lower than the mortgage value, so I had to pledge my primary house. I eventually sold the houses in Camden, but it was necessary to sell my home as well to satisfy the total debt.

I sent all the information off to Tyb and decided it was time to get answers to some of my questions. I could look DNA up on the Internet for clarity, and I remembered what Jesus had told me, that it was a system that carried the love function, but what was the crystalline ascension grid to which I was connecting?

Tyberonn had written an article, "The Ascension and the 144 Crystal Grid," in which he noted:

> The crystalline grid is the energetic lattice that covers our planet. It reflects and amplifies our ascending levels of consciousness. It is a crystalline "light" matrix that was anchored in 1992, five years after the harmonic convergence. Although in place and functional, its total activation will involve twelve phases, with full resonant vibratory rate achieved on 12/12/12, December 12, 2012. The "triple dates" (01/01/01 through 12/12/12) that occur uniquely for the next twelve years each carry numeric light codes that open and activate each of the twelve major pentacle facets of this amazing template. Visualize the grid as a geodesic sphere, of pentagons and triangles, sparkling as a faceted, brilliant diamond. It is a seed crystal of new form, the double pentadodecahedron. Its time has arrived, Mer-Ka-Bah of Earthstar. The double penta- dodecahedron has 144 facets, the number of the Christ ascension. Each dodecahedron has 12 major pentacles with 60 facets; add the 12 truncated pentagons for 72, and double this for 144![1]

Having this new understanding of the crystalline grid, I was more comfortable with the work I was here to do. That work seemed to express itself each full or new moon when I would feel a tug in my chest. Since I did not know what that meant I would either write in my journal and ask or allow events to flow in their natural organic way, which was the case with the sacred waters trip to Blue Lake at Taos Pueblo, New Mexico. I knew I was going to Taos Pueblo for the intertribal powwow. I checked and, yes, I was to take the crystals. The place-name "Blue Lake" kept popping up in my head. I knew Blue Lake to be on tribal land in a sacred and private part of the Pueblo. When I parked and spoke with the guard at the entrance to the Pueblo, he assured me that there was no admission to the lake, but I was beginning to feel Blue Lake was the reason I was in Taos. It turned out that the powwow was not on the plaza but several miles down the road in another section of the 100,000-acre village, and it didn't start until 7:00 p.m.

So, for the first time ever I paid an admission fee to be a tourist on Pueblo land. I thought perhaps there would be a quiet place where I could project my intentions toward Blue Lake. In the tourist pamphlet, a map showed the Red Willow Creek running right through the center of the Pueblo and a description of Blue Lake: "high above in the Sangre de Christo Mountains, the crystal clear water flows from a sacred source known as Blue Lake." So I sat on a bench under the cottonwood trees, away from the tourists, and again asked permission, this time from the sacred water. I then knew why I was at the Pueblo—not for the powwow, but for the sacred waters of Blue Lake, which I suspected connects to the Rio Grande. The brochure gave more details: "Taos Pueblo is considered to be the oldest continuously inhabited community in the USA. The native legends and detailed oral history trace our existence back to the beginning of evolution of man and of all creation." What a magnificent place to do ceremony! With what ease and grace it unfolded in the unknown.

Then, soon afterward, it looked like I was off to sing in caverns with the phi crystals.

Yes, It Is Indeed Carlsbad, NM, New Moon, Solar Eclipse–7/12/09

Nina: Where am I to be on new moon, solar eclipse?

We honor you, our dear one, that you ask us, your guides, your higher self, and all who love and protect you. You are to establish yourself as Nina, the crystal singer. We are so glad you heard that call this morning. You are to be an independent consultant for Stardreaming's trust in this work. That is critical and timely. All is going smoothly and as planned with the trust, and all you need to do, is to hold the crystalline seeds you planted in your heart. All is in the divine plan. You asked about September 21 and again you heard loudly. Yes, it is indeed Carlsbad, in the caverns. The trip will flow with ease and grace; this is your new mantra, ease and grace for the crystal singer, for you will indeed sing in the cave. We will give you a quiet time and space for your phi crystal transfer, the chanting, and your own enjoyment. We might even arrange for the bats to join you, for they are very strong medicine. You see how much fun this mission will be. Now, as for your private sessions, merely ask and the full picture will unfold in perfect timing. It does indeed involve sound, for sound is the creative process.

With our deep love,
The Cosmic Council of Light via Anaya-Ra

I drove the long, straight New Mexico roads from Santa Fe south to Carlsbad, settled into my hotel room, and rested for an early morning departure to the Carlsbad Caverns. On rising, I felt the pull to take out my journal before going off to find a bat.

New Moon, Solar Eclipse, Carlsbad, NM–7/21/09

We specifically asked you today, dear one, to write, not speak, the channel message. With each word presenting and coming to sit on the paper, the method is the same. You clear your mind; you have no expectation of what will be presented; and the natural organic flow begins. You have a feeling of safety with the pen, which disappears, you believe, when the mouth is relied on. Somehow, without the pen you feel that it is you speaking, and that you are responsible for each word—which is clearly not so. Once you give us permission to speak through you, the word choice is ours. Your biggest fear is letting something through that is a foreign thought or word to you. This fear will lessen, but it will take practice, which is why we ask you to speak daily. Speak our words with your tongue. What a privilege, dear one. You think it is you who is privileged, but no, it is the council, which honors and appreciates you. We will tell you a new truth to begin the process: ask what Fountainhead of the Thirteen Nations (a title given to me by another channel) means. Are you ready for the surprise? You laugh, this is very, very good, but now we will launch into the answer. Turn the page and begin, with confidence, the writing of the forgotten one.

Once Upon a Time, There Was a Brave Commander—7/21/09

Once upon a time, there was a brave commander who lived in a far away galaxy different from any other. It was radiant and replete with the pure love vibration of Source. All who lived there were filled with this love vibration. This commander had a name: Anaya-Ra the Great. ("Are you having fun?" the council interjected.) Anaya-Ra was called by the leaders of other nations, who did not live in such rare pure love vibration, to come and assist them with perfecting their frequencies on their planet. Knowing that Anaya-Ra was a leader of many and had been responsible for maintaining the pure love vibration in that galaxy, the other nations felt that Anaya-Ra could be of great value. Anaya-Ra left the galaxy and joined the Council of the Thirteen Nations (planets) as their fountainhead or ambassador, who brought wisdom, justice, compassion, and most importantly, love to the other nations. They learned much from the ambassador, and the love vibration was increased in each nation, for Anaya-Ra was a starseed crystalline being and was able to transfer the crystalline love frequency to the other nations to allow each member to raise their DNA and love quotient to a purer level. It was not words or leadership techniques that were the answer. It was the ability to transfer the adamantine particles of a high vibration that made Anaya-Ra a commander, ambassador, and Fountainhead of the Thirteen Nations. Do you see?

With our love,
The Cosmic Council of Light via Anaya-Ra

This was indeed a fairy tale. Well, I had to think about that.

I never saw any bats, of course, because they were sleeping, but I did go down into the bowels of the earth with my crystals. I found a quiet bench and began to breathe in the frequency of love and to sound the vowels. No one except me noticed that a miracle was taking place.

When I returned to Santa Fe from Carlsbad Caverns, I was beginning to accept that I had a new identity—at least so I thought. So I needed

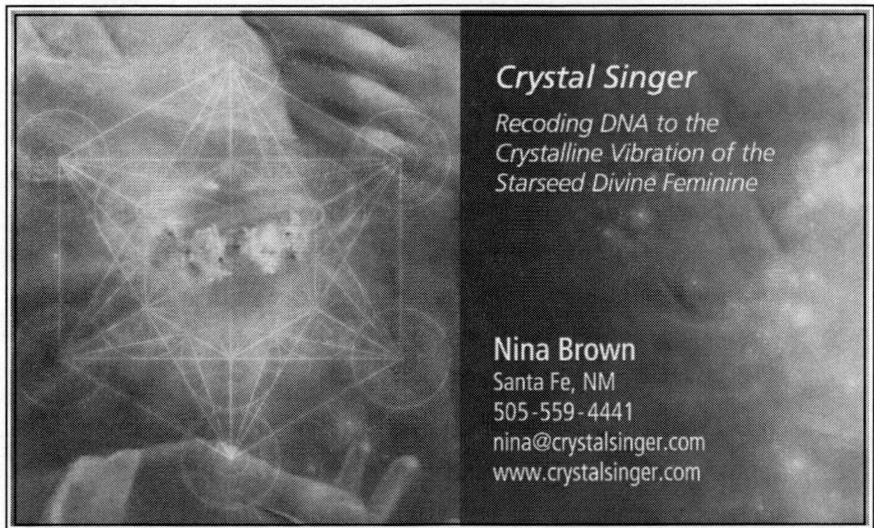

a website and business cards to go with that new identity. Tammy, my friend and amazing graphic designer (www.sevacreative.com), assisted me. Tammy understands every word I speak and could so easily translate the magic for others to read and understand.

> Hi, Nina—How fortunate that I got started on the design today, a new moon and rare solar eclipse time. The card is attached for your review. Before I started to work on it, I cleared my energy, my computer, and the space. I burned tobacco and other incense, held some crystals in my palms, sang to them for assistance and vision—connected with Lord Metatron—and asked that this work be infused with light. I also asked that any imagery that arose would trigger a knowing and recognition in the people you have agreements with to do this work. It just flowed; it was amazing. This is the result (above).

The creation of a graphic identity helped me to see that I wanted to be fully known. I wrote to Tyb:

> This is the delight of my life, to be known. Thank you beyond words.

He replied:

To know who you are and what you are going to do in healing others, to know your real path and sense its beauty and truth—this is a big part of why we are here. Tyb.

Metatron mentioned this about you. During the seven-year cycle between the ages of forty-two and forty-nine, you began truly letting go of what did not serve you, and became by age forty-nine, the higher version of yourself. There are two types of walk-ins, the first is when a different soul comes in and replaces, by agreement, the soul that was originally incarnated into the body. Drunvalo Melchizedek says he is one of these. The second type is when the divine ascended soul or oversoul of the person in physical incarnation arrives at a specific juncture of life and, over a span of seven years, "walks in." In both types it takes seven years. It can then take another seven to fourteen years for the oversoul to fully merge in the conscious state. Your physical body at age forty-nine was the body created by the multidimensional aspect of your higher self.

Tyb wrote me back explaining the process again and added:

Hi, Sister. Edgar Cayce verified the seven-year cycle in his readings, as did several other metaphysician masters such as Blavatsky and Leadbetter, of the Theosophical Society in the early 1900s. Metatron said last night that there will be a huge presence of the Sirian-Hathor Goddess Guild on 09/09/09, and you will help them recode their DNA.

I replied:

Tyb, This feels comfortable, and I am so grateful for the clarity. The years between age forty-two and forty-nine were a time of immense shedding—immense. Over that seven-year period, I shed my house, my husband, my debutante life in Philadelphia, and whatever money I had. I was actually given food at Thanksgiving. I moved to Santa Fe without ever having been

> there. I knew no one and had no job and no place to live. And then the rebuilding process began, mostly by attraction, which is how I live my life now. I feel deeply calm and confident that miracles will work through me, not by me. I merely have to say yes and get out of the way. What a tremendous service you are providing to so many, Tyb. Please know that it is recognized and profoundly appreciated.

I continued to get information daily from the Cosmic Council of Light about what was to transpire in Arkansas. It felt important to keep Tyb in the loop.

> I'm writing just to keep you informed of my journey between now and Arkansas. I was doing my daily channel practice with the Cosmic Council of Light when I heard, "We are taking you to a different dimension." I saw numbers on a vertical line going up, and I stopped at twelve—in the twelfth dimension, the angelic realm where my oversoul works. I was told that a tunnel was being connected from my crown chakra to my oversoul in the twelfth dimension and that frequency would be transferred to me and then merge with me. They said the tunnel would remain and that, when doing sessions, I was to use it to bring in the high-frequency adamantine particles.
>
> Also, I was told that my experience in the cathedral in San Antonio four years ago, when I first realized I was a receiver and transmitter, occurred at a lower frequency. On that occasion my third eye was pulsing and transmitting to the camera that was filming the 7:00 a.m. service, which was in Spanish. What was coming through was received by Spanish-speaking viewers in South, Central, and North America as well as in prisons. I don't understand the science of what happened then, but there was a profound knowing that I was giving the prisoners and others a special gift from the higher realms. I'll keep you posted on this journey you sent me on, and which I accepted.

The twelfth dimension was further explained in *Metatron Speaks* by James Tyberonn:

> The Atla-Ra (I was told I was a member of the Atla-Ra in Atlantis) still maintained the highest standards of consciousness and were able to continue vibrating at very high frequencies at and above the level of twelfth-dimensional light and energy, remaining very pure and resonant with the true "oneness" concept of the Creator God.[2]

I replied:

> Tyb, I am to further share with you what my presentation is beginning to look like. I was told to think of myself as an expanded, faceted sphere radiating rainbow colors that are more brilliant than the colors we know in this dimension. This is to be my daily focus. The words I will speak will be remembered by some, but the words are of less importance than the energy transfer. So far, the words that have come to me are mostly in story form, a fun one about the other famous Arkansas celebrity, President Clinton and me (you being the first), then a short story about who I am and how I got to be standing before the group, then a bit about how the session will flow, and then the toning channel. I'll keep you posted as it keeps coming in. Your comments are always welcome.

> Dear Sister, good to chat with you this morning by phone. I will select a nice room for your sessions with comfy chairs and maybe a sofa. I just went to Metatron on your sessions and he said the following:
>
> • You will have the energy you need. It will be channeled through you and will recharge and energize you as well.
>
> • The recoding is best done in individual sessions, not groups. Your focus and channel for the transformation will be somewhat

split in groups, and that the frequency required for each individual to receive the upshift will vary.

• In time, you will be able to do small groups not to exceed three people, but for now, thirty minutes for individuals is best, until you get accustomed to managing the energy and adjusting to the light quotient of each person you are shifting.

Tyberonn sent an email to all the presenters attending the 09/09/09 conference at Mount Magazine, stating that he would like to meet with everyone Sunday afternoon, 09/06/09. I had planned to be at Peace Valley Sanctuary (www.PVSanctuary.com) before arriving at Mount Magazine on the sixth. This included swimming in Lake Quichita with the crystals below the surface.

> Tyb, I had hoped to swim in Lake Quichita during the afternoon on Sunday the sixth. Since you state the meeting is brief, can we talk privately when I arrive that evening, or can you email your message? Otherwise I will be there. I called the hotel and was told you would choose the session room for me to use. Thank you, Tyb, for all the work that I know this gathering has required. Not sure when I will be able to connect again.

House guests arrived shortly before I was to leave to be with my son and his family in New Orleans. The arrival of my friends brought me back into my work with Stardreaming. James felt it was propitious that people had come and that their arrival had something to do with the new Temple of Infinity at Stardreaming. Each person present had a bond with Stardreaming, either as a custodian and owner of one or more of James's paintings or as a frequent guest who came to walk the labyrinths in meditation. We gathered in the wizard's cottage. James had thought all along that he was to build a celestorium, but just recently it came through that no, he was to build the Temple of Infinity. As all were seated, a thought flashed through me that the ceremony should begin now. All agreed spontaneously that this was the moment for something to happen. It was the beginning of the answer to why everyone had showed up that day at Stardreaming.

I gathered up my Vogel phi crystals, Marijon brought her gold-coded drum, Ahara her rattles, Laura a large fertility crystal, and James took Gabriel's trumpet, a two-foot golden shell from Australia. Together, we proceeded to the site opposite the cottage on the other side of the cavernous arroyo. The sky was a typical New Mexican clear, crisp cobalt blue dotted with polished white billowing clouds, and the sun providing a typical early August warmth. The seers in the group felt and saw the etheric temple of thirty-three grand river stones positioned in the monumental infinity symbol, and they saw the center fire pit surrounded by thirteen columnar stones. The center position, where the Metatronic cube was felt to be, was held by the large crystal and James's presence. Laura stood a distance away at east, Ahara an equal distance from the center at west, Sydney held northeast, Marijon was on southeast, René on northwest, and I took southwest.

Thus, the figure eight was expressed on the land to mark the position of the etheric temple. The spontaneous, organic flow continued with the drumbeat and the sound of the rattle. James stood at the west and declared the temple to be the earthly physical manifestation of infinity. Then he entered the alpha and omega, male and female zero-point. Deep within the earth and far above in the cosmos, the otherworldly beings came to join the ceremony. With a deep breath, energy was moved along the path of the newly formed infinity symbol running from the center through each position, back to the center, and out again along the path. Gabriel's trumpet was sounded in the four directions, calling the attention of all to the commencement of the energy flow of the growing spiral vortex.

I pointed the Vogel crystals toward the fire pit, rotated them counterclockwise to open, then traced the infinity shape, and finally clockwise to close, each in a series of eight. The frequential level of the land was raised to that of Christ-consciousness, vibrating at a higher, clearer resonance. Then the crystals were pointed toward the crystalline grid and the energetic connecting flow began between the temple and the grid, pairing them in the same harmonics of the divine feminine. James entered the east chamber of the infinity symbol as each position-holder contained the energetic boundary. Archangel Metatron entered as well and participated, through James, in a powerful dynamic dragon's breath to activate the spiral vortex. Then the breath was repeated in the west chamber. Each position-holder then walked to the zero-point where the drum, rattles, crystals, and horn were placed. The circle was closed as we joined hands and shared love and appreciation. The igniting of the Temple of Infinity at Stardreaming was then complete. Each participant now carried the temple energy, as did the thirty-three chosen and stored stones. All who present at the temple in the future will experience the spiral vortex and participate uniquely in their personal transformation, because of the gift that was received and given on August 3, 2009, the birth of the Temple of Infinity. And so it is.

My guests, the out-of-state participants, for the birth of the Temple of Infinity were present a few days later for the full moon, lunar eclipse, when magic happened. Several days before the full moon, I had asked and been told that I was to do ceremony at the Valles Caldera National Preserve between Los Alamos and Jemez Pueblo in New Mexico. I had called the preserve and asked the best way to go to the center of the caldera and was told that was impossible because there were no tours that day. When I mentioned the eclipse, I was told that there were no tours called eclipse. I then asked where they suggested I go to do ceremony, since it was full moon. The answer was, "The parking lot."

Finally, I called a different number and got a more sympathetic listener, who suggested that the mile-long path on the perimeter would take me to a spot that overlooked the caldera. I was prepared to go by myself, but my company expressed an interest in joining me. This was new for me; other than at the Grand Tetons, I had worked alone.

We all climbed into the SUV and began a joyful ride together north of Santa Fe, past Tesuque Pueblo, past Pojoaque Pueblo, past San Ildefanso Pueblo, through Los Alamos, past Bandelier National Monument and along the switchback road leading up the mountain to the Valles Caldera National Preserve. As we approached, I felt an extreme shift in energy.

Marijon saw beings all along the road on both sides, bowing and honoring us as we passed.

I found the parking lot for our entry point, but we decided to enter the preserve to use the restroom. We found a small administration house, cows and horses, and the parking spaces. As we exited from the van, it was as if no one saw us, though there were cowboys milling around. It seemed so easy just to walk out into the center of the caldera to do our ceremony. René decided to go to the building and see what she could find out. She returned with the information that a historian from Jemez Pueblo would join us shortly, since he clearly understood why we were present. Amazing, after all of my telephone calls!

A van pulled up and a tribal elder greeted us with enthusiasm. His father had collected herbs on this very land, and he was eager to share the stories and sacred space with us. We drove up into the ponderosa grove at the center of the caldera and got out of the van. Our guide wanted to be in charge and do ceremony. But that was not why we had come. I meandered toward the edge of the grove and found a huge tree stump. I knew this was to be my spot to support me when I brought in what I was sure would be enormous energy. Everyone fanned out, but Ahara stayed behind me as a guardian spirit. I looked out across the caldera and offered thanks to all the beings I knew were present and asked permission to bring in the Christ-consciousness, divine feminine frequency from the crystalline grid.

Not only had permission been granted, but our presence was expected. Since it was a day of significance—full moon and lunar eclipse—I was able to connect all calderas across the planet to the work that was being done: the upshifting of the planetary node. Everyone knew instinctively when we were finished, and we walked back to the guide who put us in a circle, asked us to sit on the ground, and then began his traditional ceremony. How perfect!

The next gift of this amazing day was that the new pearlescent 2010 Prius that I had ordered arrived. It would be my cosmic chariot to drive me to New Orleans, Mount Magazine, back to New Orleans, and then home two months later, following two weeks in Bolivia. A cosmic chariot for my cosmic journey!

That morning, I had slipped out of the house quietly at 4:00 a.m. to sit in the moonlight and to take the crystals out into the light of the full moon. While sitting there, I decided to do my daily channeling. I was always trying to get stronger in allowing the unknown to flow through, to strengthen my understanding that I wasn't making all this up. So I heard, "Here is something new for you." At that point, I began to sing. The sounds were a single syllable and the tone was simple but engaging. Later, at a more respectable hour, one of my house guests came down to walk her dogs and said to me, "I heard the most beautiful angelic music last night. Tears came to my eyes as I listened." So the channeled toning had begun. This was very fortunate, since I was now listed on the agenda for the Earth-Keeper conference as a speaker and a channeled toner!

Toning was important since I had also been told to be with Saint Germain in the Temple of the Violet Flame at Stardreaming to sing to the tunnel we had created. In the afternoon, I went to Stardreaming and walked the labyrinth to the center, where there was a bench next to a very large crystal. I sat with tears pouring down my cheeks and waited for the sound to arrive. I toned the same sound as the one from the morning—gentle, rhythmic, melodic, quiet, and enchanting. The sound just kept pouring out. I walked the second half of the labyrinth, then I thanked Saint Germain for what he had started by sending me to Jackson Hole to ignite the electromagnetic supertunnel. I felt that on full moon, lunar eclipse I had completed the first phase of that magical journey.

~ 17 ~

Master of Transmission

Now a new journey was beginning. My cosmic chariot was taking me to New Orleans to remove shadow energies from under the city and to create an intergalactic, sacred-geometry temple reaching up to the heavens and down into the earth. To do this, I had to walk an eleven-circuit labyrinth in breathless despair and become a vessel for the work. Traveling farther, into Arkansas, at the Toltec Mounds I was greeted by other-dimensional beings, who welcomed me back on the full moon. Then, after months of preparation, I became an expanded sphere of faceted light doing my first session on a rainbow bridge, which prepared me for Mount Magazine, where a line of people formed to hug me and I had a waiting list of those who wished to see me. But it was not me they wanted to see. It was the divine me that they were seeking—that which they, too, are or could become.

A month before I was to head to New Orleans to be with family, I had an unusual and upsetting experience: I began to grieve profoundly for New Orleans. I had no idea what that meant, but knew I needed to reach out to the one person I knew in New Orleans, though only by correspondence. I needed help:

> Anne, I need your help desperately. I am an empath, and I feel the sadness of New Orleans in the core of who I am. I need desperately to be taken to the most sacred site in New Orleans to do ceremony to release the sadness that is present. This is who I am, and what I do as a crystalline being with the crystalline frequencies of transformation for humanity and for New Orleans.

> You are the messenger for these frequencies that I bring. I can hardly see with the tears pouring down my face. I trust that you are the one with whom to share this message.

Then, in the morning, I had more clarity.

> Anne, this morning I awoke with very puffy eyes and a knowing of what to do. "When" would ideally be August 20, for new moon. "Where" would be the center of the labyrinth in Audubon Park. "Why" is to connect the labyrinth energetically with other labyrinths around the world by means of harmonic oscillation and to upshift the frequency to connect to the crystalline grid of Christ-consciousness. This work will also spiral out throughout the city and beyond. Amazing.

I felt calm knowing Anne had agreed and that she had offered to ask a few others to join us for the new moon ceremony. So on August 10, I left home, saying good-bye to my house guests, who were staying on. I got into my new cosmic chariot, cruised down the straight New Mexican and Texan roads on autopilot while listening to the Metropolitan Opera channel, with not a care in my mind. New Orleans, here I come!

I am not always serious.

Filled with hugs from my family, we headed off to the zoo, the aquarium, playgrounds, and the waterfront; then it was new moon, and I switched from grandmother to master of transmission. My journal account captures the moment best.

August Journal—New Orleans Trip

The days passed and the three-day drive to New Orleans was completed. After finally meeting Anne, I was introduced to her soul friend, Marjorie, and we all knew immediately that this work was to be done together. Shortly before the day of the new moon, the Cosmic Council of Light shared with me another component to the ceremony: the shadow energies under the land were to be released and transmuted by means of the frequency of love and appreciation before any frequency upshift and connection to the crystalline grid could be completed. How to do this was not clear to me. The divine order of events soon showed how. Anne received an unexpected email that morning introducing her to Mary, who was visiting and working in the New Orleans area and whose vision was to balance and harmonize the earth energies (http://www.livingdesignconsultants.com/).

Mary received our call for assistance with great enthusiasm and quickly became part of the team, which was growing by means of the universal plan. All four members of the newly formed group met the afternoon before new moon to share their personal thoughts on how the ceremony would unfold and to become reacquainted (surely there had been a prelifetime contract to do this work together). Mary talked of her years of training and practice. I shared how the frequency upshifting and connecting would be a process of very highly vibrating adamantine particles flowing through a dimensional column into my crown chakra.

On the morning of new moon, which would peak at just after 10:00 a.m. on August 20, 2009, more information was presented by the masters. We were to anchor the four cardinal points during the ceremony and to know that the labyrinth was an intergalactic, sacred geometry temple reaching both up to the heavens and down into the earth. It would be connected to other eleven-circuit labyrinths of a similar geometric shape and frequency, and then all would be upshifted and connected in a higher vibration to the grid. This new grid would resonate throughout the planet, assisting in the ascension process as the earth enters the final cycle in 2012. And so it was to be, as we were instructed and informed.

Anne arrived soon after daybreak, placing candles from Chartes Cathedral in the center of the small entryway of the seven-circuit labyrinth and another in the center of the eleven-circuit labyrinth. After she had collected water from the delta of the mighty Mississippi River to be used as part of the impending ceremony, Anne came to fetch me. As we drove through the park and began to approach the site of the labyrinth, a strong emotional force was welling up inside the area of my sacred heart. This feeling had always signaled that the chosen site was correct. We entered through the archway, removed our shoes, and reverently approached the center of the cosmic vortex. My breath left me, and only with conscious effort did I find it again. The ancient, moss-covered oaks drew me toward them, calling me to rebalance, recharge, and encapsulate myself in a protective energy shield. Margorie, a recent invitee who possessed a keen awareness of grid and energy work came with sage and water. Mary came with charged paper; we wrote our intentions and then placed the papers at the entrance of the labyrinth. The final participant came just as the hour for new moon was approaching and the clouds were beginning to embrace us in rain. That rain was surely the physical connection between the otherworldly beings and us.

Thunder sounded in what seemed like loud claps of love and appreciation. We gathered in the center of the labyrinth to create a circle and begin our ceremony. Marjorie lit a sage smudge stick, which cleansed each of us and continued to burn forcefully throughout the rain shower and continued to burn as it was transported back to Marjorie's home. It seemed to all present that the strength of the flame was a powerful sign that we were expected and appreciated. I shared a Santa Fe lavender spray and Devotion, an essential oil from the flowers and plants of numerous sacred sites. Then, as we held hands in the circle, I transferred by means of the infinity breath the frequency and structure (adamantine particles) of love and appreciation, which would be expanded in the larger circle to transmute any shadow energies that might come from the earth. We then broke the circle and went to the chosen positions on the labyrinth. Anne chose the east position, Marjorie south, the other two participants, west and north.

After we took our positions on the perimeter of the labyrinth, Mary intuitively—with the use of her swirling pendulum—circled the labyrinth three times sensing imbalance and making adjustments. By now the greeting from the heavens of purifying rain had ceased, and all that remained was wet hair and clinging clothing. Mary signaled that she was complete, and I removed the bowl of water from the Mississippi and Jordan Rivers from the center of the labyrinth, placing it at the entrance. I put the leather carrying case, which contained two phi Vogel crystals, over my shoulder and after asking permission began walking the labyrinth, holding the violet ray phi Vogel crystal in my hand for protection.

The walk was slow and with each unique turn a different emotion presented itself, from sadness to breathless despair. At other places, a calm settled in, but near the western outer rim, I stopped and made my steps smaller, which allowed me to take the turn. Anne gave me a tissue as I passed her, and she said, "It is not much farther." As I came to the center, I could not continue. I put the bag down and exchanged one crystal for the two in the bag and then was able to enter. I asked permission to point the crystals as part of the work to be done. It was granted. I faced east and raised the crystals to the sky. Slowly they were rotated eight times counterclockwise, eight times in the infinity sign, and finally eight times clockwise. My legs were spread wide apart to help support me as the energy poured through my crown chakra into the core of the earth and back up.

Archangel Metratron has called me a "star seed crystalline being," which is why I am able to be the vessel for this work. This phase of the ceremony was to raise the frequency of the Audubon Park Labyrinth. When that was complete and because it was a day of significance, I was able to connect the frequency of our labyrinth with similar frequencies of other eleven-circuit labyrinths around the planet. To do this, I moved the crystals to waist level and slowly rotated in a complete circle back to east. I did this with great care, since with each shift, my footing, which was barely holding me up, was being challenged. Facing east, I raised the crystals, which are amplifiers only for what was flowing through me, circulated the energy in the infinity symbol and, entrained with the crystalline grid of Christ-consciousness, the divine feminine. When I felt complete,

I crossed the crystals and ran them from the top of my body to the earth to disconnect me from the work I had just done.

I replaced the crystals in their bag, put it over my shoulder, and began the return path to the entrance, as the others continued to hold the space of love and appreciation. With each step, an increased lightness came over me. I felt as if I was gliding around the turns, even wishing to skip or dance. I made quiet sounds of joy and laughter, so opposite from how I entered. On reaching the final brick in my return path, each person picked up the chimes that Anne had placed around the labyrinth, and we rang the collection of sounds in celebration for all that had occurred. On completion, we gathered once again in the center of the labyrinth to give our final prayers of gratitude, and with a strong "ho," we disconnected the circle on new moon, August 20, 2009, at the Audubon Park labyrinth in New Orleans, the anchor site for a new pulsating grid of dimensional eleven-circuit temples placed throughout the planet.

Audubon Park Labyrinth.

A few days following the ceremony in New Orleans, I left in my cosmic chariot for Hot Springs, Arkansas, where I indulged myself with a session in the antique baths at the Arlington Hotel. I intentionally went early to Arkansas to rest before the gathering at Mount Magazine, the celebration of the triple date activation of the emerald Atlantean crystal during which—at the request of Archangel Metatron and Tyberonn—I would be a featured speaker and do sessions throughout the weekend. The attendees had been invited to join Tyb, after the weekend, on a special trip to the Toltec Mounds outside of Little Rock. I decided to go to the mounds before the celebration rather than after it, on the full moon, September 4, 2009, to do ceremony. What I didn't realize was that this visit would be an opening for me to realize my own inner truth.

I had read a little of the mound culture that was expressed along the Mississippi River, but reading about it didn't expand my chest with love the way it did when I entered Toltec Mound State Park. I got a quick glimpse of the few remaining mounds as I parked my car. It was as if there was a tether attached to me extending to the former ceremonial grounds of the Plum Bayou Indians, who gathered in this sacred site until their puzzling disappearance around 1050 AD. I paid my few dollars, watched the movie, and then moved out of the confines of the contemporary building on to the path that would take me through and around the mounds along the White River and then back. Markers were placed to indicate where several mounds would have stood had intense farming not leveled them. But I knew that their energy signature was still present. As I stood between two trees flanking the entrance, I asked permission to be there and knew instantly that I was not only welcome but expected. This had happened in the Valles Caldera just weeks before. It became clear to me that I had made a promise in the timeless now, eons ago, to return on full moon in the ninth month of the ninth year, and here I was having that memory come to me as I walked along the path and amongst the other-dimensional beings, who surrounded me.

I sat near marker G, close to the center of the crescent site, on a sheltered bench between two huge grass-covered mounds, one in front of me and one to my rear. Then an inner voice came to me. "Rest a while with us, dear one." It played over and over in my head, then expanded, when I later walked along the waterfront, to "Rest a while with us, dear one. It has been so long." While sitting on the bench and preparing to do ceremony, I saw a small tractor, with its grass-cutting blades whirling, come from behind the mound in front of me. Back and forth it went, with its motor breaking the silence that I had hoped to find. I told myself that I could overlook this seeming distraction.

As I stood up, with the two phi Vogel crystals in my hands, and moved to face the rising sun, the tractor went behind the mound, not to return until I was finished. The upshifting and connecting to other sites of similar frequencies was a gentler process than I had experienced to date, as was the connecting to the crystalline grid. What was different was that when I thought I was complete, my hands holding the crystals dropped down, pointing to the core of the earth. My thought was that I was connecting to beings below the surface, as had happened at the Valles Caldera. "Rest a while with us, dear one. It has been so long" stayed with me as I moved on, and it haunted me as I made the decision to leave. I was experiencing the renewal of an ancient love affair with a place and a people whom I had once known intimately. That love is fresh and alive with me now, as I write.

I picked Marijon up that afternoon at the airport, and after a night in Little Rock, we drove to Peace Valley Sanctuary for two days of private retreat with a few other guests. Zenea, one of the attendees, had written requesting a private session and said that she would be both at Peace Valley and Mount Magazine, but could we do the session at Peace Valley. The three of us met in Little Rock and drove our two cars together to Peace Valley. I kept thinking, "Well, now that Zenea has met me, she might change her mind." She requested that we meet the last day, on September 6. The night before, as I was going to sleep, I felt my third eye pulsating and knew that I was connecting to Zenea. Early that morning, we went outside to choose a perfect location by the lake. Both of us felt that the rainbow bridge was that spot, not next to it but on it. I was so touched, for it felt like a sign from the Cosmic Council of Light who had told me to think of myself as an expanded sphere of faceted

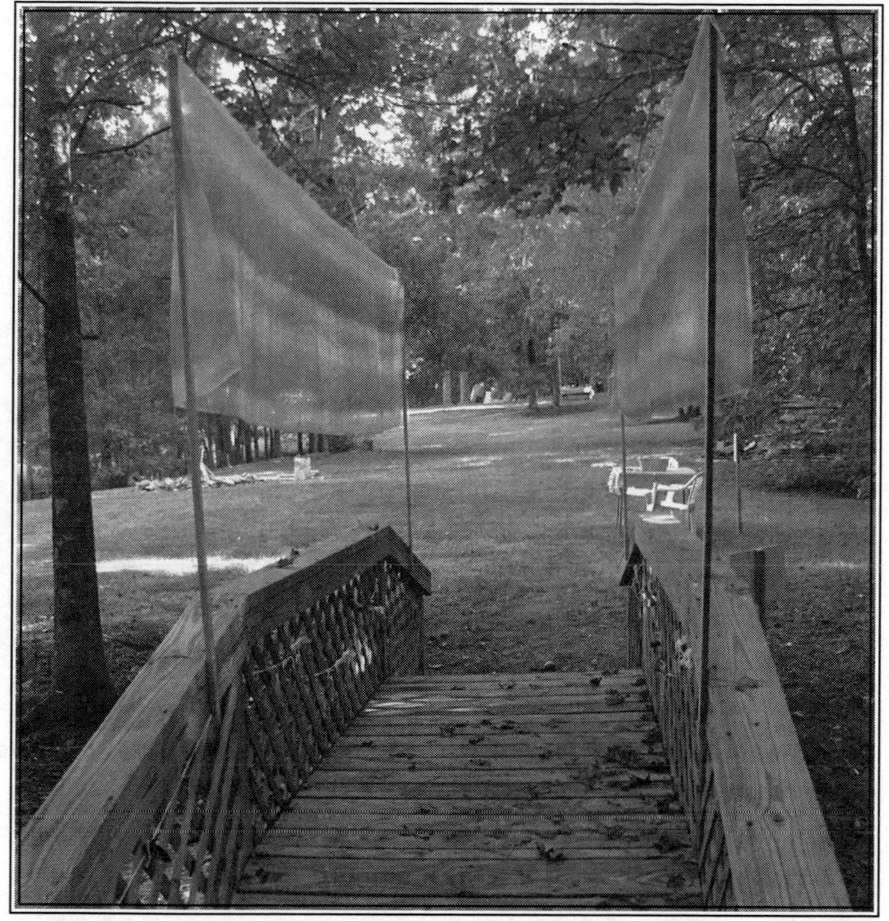

Rainbow Bridge.

light, radiating rainbow colors never before seen by humanity. Here we were during my first session, sitting on the rainbow bridge with rainbow flags flying across the tops of our heads as the energy came down from the crystalline grid to ignite the dormant DNA in Zenea's sacred heart. Such a gift she gave me, for I was now easily able to work with the forty-five people who presented over the next three days! Amazed, I learned that there was a waiting list for those who wished to meet with me.

Marijon and I left Peace Valley Sanctuary. We did indeed swim in Lake Quichita above a bed of giant crystals and arrived that evening at Mount Magazine after getting lost driving in the dark! The next morning, I felt like a celebrity as I was advanced in front of the three hundred attendees to be specially checked in and greeted warmly by Tyb.

I inspected the room where I would do sessions. It was pleasant, with a view of the valley, but the space felt dead. I rushed downstairs to reception and said, "I don't care what it costs, please fill the room with roses by noon, the time of my first appointment." They did! What a difference. I sprayed the room with botanical smudge. I rearranged furniture, and did whatever else I could do to make it warm and comfortable.

Then they came, brilliant, dazzling people one after another, every half hour till evening. The presenters were those who anchor the crystalline grid on planet earth, so that their vibration or crystalline structure could be raised by means of harmonic oscillation. They in turn would be the catalyst to help others have a clearer, higher vibrating frequency. The result was that humanity would be able to create and manifest more responsibly with greater clarity and higher frequency, a primary attribute of the ascension. Once I included Gaia in the session, for grounding, I got into a rhythm and felt balanced. Marijon popped in once to open the window, since she sensed that there were energies getting trapped in the room. I had breakfast, lunch, and dinner at the round table in the room. The meals consisted of seaweed, tuna fish, energy bars, water, peanut butter, crackers, and anything else I had grabbed from a grocery store we passed on our way to Mount Magazine.

The sessions were all different. I found that each toning sounded different, with a unique tone for each person. On one or two occasions, my fingers would move as if playing a harp. Tears appeared when working with a few people. It was as if we knew each other deeply. What I noticed most was that when the transfer and toning were complete, I felt as if I was in a state of rapture, bliss, expanded love. I could only think of zero-point as a concept to explain it. Separation was difficult; and on several occasions I had to run the crystals twice between our energy fields to disconnect. I missed almost all of the conference since it was my understanding, with sessions structured for a half hour, that I was to see as many people as possible. So I did. Later, I was told by Archangel Metatron via Tyberonn, that number was excessive. In the future, I was to see a maximum of three to four people a day with a half hour rest in between. Besides doing sessions, I was to speak and do channeled toning.

The morning of my talk, I woke thinking about the movie *Cocoon*. It was clear to me that I was to invite the audience to unzip their cocoon and let out the shining rays of their true self as I spoke. So I did. I had been coached by the Cosmic Council of Light over the last several months. They went so far as to tell me what to wear: white with a huge black hat. Even though it was after Labor Day, I wore white! Before I stood up to speak, I remember asking myself if I was ready. What I heard inside my head was, "We are ready!" So I was not doing this alone!

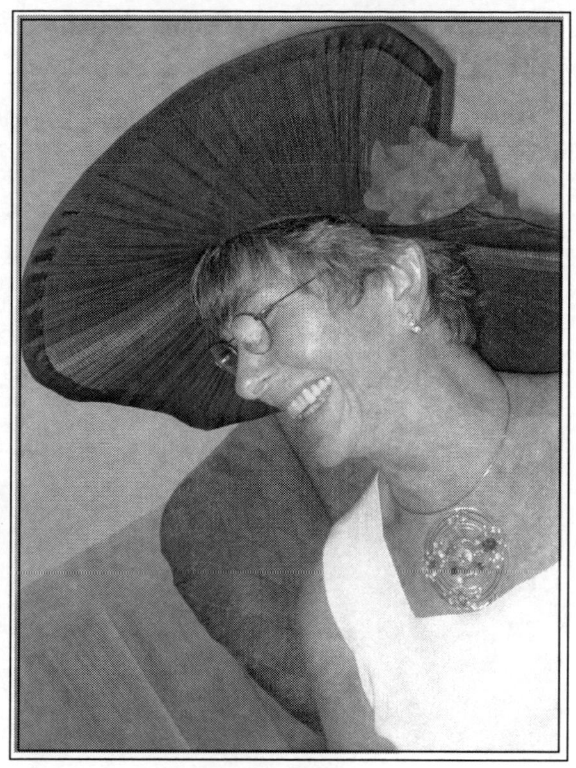

Big black hat!

I told the stories as instructed with humor, which was a real shock. What surprised me the most was that when I had finished and walked over to my bag to prepare to go back upstairs, I noticed a line of people forming to hug me, speak to me, share experiences with me. I had not counted on this at all. Somehow, I had bonded with so many people who now felt that they knew me. Everywhere I went, there were delighted people who wanted to help me, wave to me, or thank me. I was overwhelmed. Then, after participating in the 09/09/09 crystal activation ceremony at Mount Magazine, this phase of work was complete.

I drove back to New Orleans in anticipation of my upcoming trip to Bolivia, where I knew that I was to do ceremony on the equinox at Lake

Titicaca. When I arrived at my family's house and checked my computer, I saw I had a breathtaking email waiting for me:

> Thank you for your email. I, too, am honored to have been in your presence during the 09/09/09 activation at Mount Magazine. My wife and I are definitely considering the funding of Stardreaming Foundation, but not until the first of the year 2010. Presently we have a few pressing issues to clear up, and then we will be in a position to visit you and discuss a substantial participation position for your project. Have a safe trip to Bolivia and be inspired.

How does a DNA-Shift Session work?

The session begins by my becoming an open vessel and proceeds by means of the use of an extraordinary 144-facet phi Vogel crystal (which I later acquired). Using an infinity breath technique, with the phi crystal acting as an amplifier, I bring in a stream of light from the earth and transmit it from my sacred heart to the recipient's sacred heart, where—with permission—both merge as one energy unit. The crystal, again with permission, is pointed at the recipient's sacred heart and rotated eight times counterclockwise. The breath then extends the stream of light to the 144 crystal ascension grid and back in a figure eight. The energetic stream of crystalline Akash (adamantine essence) flows through the crown chakra to the sacred heart (now connected) and returns to the crystalline grid. The frequency of love and appreciation ignites the connection such that the grid responds and the sacred geometry of the crystalline seed and the sacred geometry of the ascension grid entrain.

In other words, a solar stream of liquid light, love, and appreciation is made up of very high frequency adamantine particles that recode the dormant divine feminine sacred geometry of the DNA to entrain with the frequency and sacred geometry of the crystalline grid. The toning audio of my channeled voice ignites and intertwines with the coherent crystalline light, which is transmitted by means of the phi crystal and my ascended oversoul, with me as the vessel, to the recipient. After the frequency transfer, the crystal is again pointed at the recipient's sacred heart and rotated eight times clockwise for closure.

During this process, an energetic bond becomes established with the recipient, which needs to be released. To disconnect, the 144-facet phi Vogel crystal—which initially creates the tunnel between the sacred hearts—is moved from head to toe with appreciation and the intention of disconnecting the energy flow. This ensures that the energy fields for the two may be intact, without auric bleeding on completion, and creates a state of zero-point balance of male/female energies. The crystal and I are infinity consciousness, or pure love and light from beyond the twelfth dimension, where there is no distortion of love and light. If one envisions a bubble surrounding the Milky Way in which love and light exist, the session with the huge 144-facet phi Vogel crystal breaks through the bubble to the realm where love and light exist in purity. It is from that dimension that this radiant frequency is transmitted.

It is the love that I am that allows me to receive and transmit through the vessel that I am, the adamantine particles and the particles of infinity from the highest dimensions (where pure love and light exist) through my crown chakra and sacred heart to a planetary node or the dormant DNA of another, thus causing—through harmonic oscillation—the vibration of the lower frequency to resonate with the higher frequency of the other: the return of love to planet earth.[1]

—ɯ—

~ 18 ~

An Awakening Will Occur

Why was it important for me to go to Bolivia? I knew that I was not going as a tourist. I felt drawn to do an upshift ceremony at Lake Titicaca over equinox, but that was all I knew. I now remember Archangel Metatron's words during my channel, "Good for the entity to visit where an awakening will occur." What I had been looking for over the last several months was an inner knowing that all that had been told to me was my truth. I needed to feel it, to know it, and to experience it. That was truly why I was going to Bolivia. I had decided to go to Valles Caldera and the Toltec Mounds because I knew that the beings from centuries before were expecting me; this was true again, particularly at Sampaya and the Island of the Moon on Lake Titicaca. I felt the call again at the Land of the Carangas in the Altiplano; also in Tiajuanaco before Pachamama (Earth Mother) and the Representative star beings from many nations; and finally in Samaipata at El Fuerte at the entrance to inner earth. I felt expected and honored as one who had promised to return on each specific day to do ceremony to remove the veil and bring in the Christ-consciousness of pure love and light. I was acknowledged by a deep love bond that I felt at each site, and surprisingly, also, by an invitation to become a member of the Bolivian panaca, brotherhood of shamans and elders.

In April, when Marijon asked me if I wanted to go to Bolivia, I knew I was to go. Why? I just was to go. Marijon is a partner in a bio-dynamic factory in La Paz, which primarily produces aloe products. The founder of Agronat, South America (www.agronat.com), Milton would be our host and tour guide during our visit. My suitcase preceded me because of canceled flights and an unexpected overnight in Miami. That was a good thing, since my Vogel crystals were inside the suitcase, and I knew they were an important part of my journey through Bolivia.

Milton greeted Marijon and me with such enthusiasm. When Milton and I were together at the baggage claim area getting my sequestered suitcase, I looked into his eyes and tears came into mine. I experienced such a deep knowing of who he was, and an understanding that we were meant to be together for the magical journey that was to unfold. After spending some time with Milton's family and his friends from Peru, Nestor and Jessica, we rested in our hotel with the comes with in-room oxygen tanks, due to the over-13,000-foot altitude. We began our adventures together the next day.

The first day in Bolivia, after a visit to an aloe plantation, Milton took us to his factory and showed us the new temple in the entrance to his plant. At the temple, Milton turned to me and asked me if I would do a session with his mother-in-law Otilia. I was surprised by his request because it never occurred to me that I would do individual sessions while in Bolivia. Of course I agreed. Two chairs were placed in front of the temple, where the two of us sat facing each other. Otilia began to speak in Spanish and pointed to her chest with a worried look on her face. I turned to Milton and said, "I don't speak Spanish and I don't heal people." Milton asked me to continue. After the session was complete, and I felt love flowing between Otilia and me, Milton thanked me and shared what he had witnessed. He told me that he had seen black energy leave Otilia's chest, enter me and leave from my crown chakra. I hadn't seen this. All I knew was the profound exchange of love frequency.

While we were sharing a meal in his factory's common room, employees were feeding the fire of the beehive-shaped ceremonial enclosure for the special Temascal that Milton was preparing to share with us. My definition of Temascal would be a Bolivian sweat lodge. Before we entered the chamber, all seven participants formed a circle, which had been set as a safe space by means of an exterior circle of blessed water. Incense was used to cleanse each of us, then an associate from the factory took what looked like condor feathers and swept them across our

Temascal.

bodies, with a *whooshing* sound like a bird swiftly flying by, to remove any impurities.

We each crawled into the lodge where there were large fiber-covered pillows and a white bucket of water containing a wooden bowl. Unlike other sweats, the Temascal requires that one use water throughout the ceremony to pour over the body. Each directional door was opened as the mountain *apu,* or god, representing each direction was summoned. This traditional Bolivian sacred ceremony of prayer, drumming, and song was preparation for the work that was to unfold over the next two days. During the Temascal, Milton invited me to be a member of the Bolivian panaca, Brotherhood of Shamans and Elders, and to honor me for the work I had done with Otilia. I knew then that I would not be doing ceremony in Bolivia as a foreigner, but as a beloved member of the Bolivian panaca.

We were up at 8:00 a.m. for the three-hour drive to Lake Titicaca, with five of us in an old blue truck that had known many years of traveling along the windy, unpredictable Bolivian roads. On the way to the lake, we stopped for gas, and I got out of the truck to go to the lady's room. While I was walking innocently toward the building, a dog rushed up behind me and bit me in the back of my right leg. Fortunately there was no skin broken, but a mighty bruise soon developed. I felt as if my purpose for going to Lake Titicaca was known and that incompatible forces were trying to stop me.

Milton knows so many of the people from various communities, since he buys their harvests for his factory. Because of that, we were greeted warmly in Sampaya at the opening ceremony of a new hotel. Native dress, llamas and leis of flowers filled the plaza. As we were greeted, our hats were taken off and confetti of different colors was placed on top of our heads, which blew in the wind, adding to the festivities. When the time for the ceremony was approaching, everyone had to leave the plaza and climb the narrow stone steps to get to the site of the opening ceremony. Because of Milton's importance to the community, we were seated on a central bench where we could easily listen to the many speeches, proclaiming the gratitude of each speaker for the work of the dignitaries present.

Sampaya hotel opening ceremony.

Before the fireworks and band music began, we slipped out and started walking slowly down toward the lake. Llamas, donkeys, bright-colored banners, and traditional fabric lined the way. At one of the plateaus overlooking the Island of the Moon, I asked Milton about options for doing a ceremony that day for the equinox. I had come to Bolivia to do ceremony at Lake Titicaca. As Milton was listing the various possibilities, my energy field began spreading out to the land below our plateau, nearer to the water, on a terraced hill. My heart started to expand and my eyes filled with tears. It was clear to me that I had to go no farther. With a hazy focus, I began walking ahead down the hill to the spot I had identified.

Milton and Marijon suggested a site higher up on the path, but I felt I needed to go farther down. I could see a level terrace and started veering off to the right to reach it, but I came to an open space on the path, overlooking the island and mountain, so I stopped. The silent tears turned to wailing as I tried to position myself against the hill, but my feet slid out from under me, so I moved with care to the ledge and sat down. I felt the same emotions as I had upon returning to the Toltec Mounds,

Sampaya overlooking Island of the Moon.

on the full moon of September 4, 2009, in Arkansas. I knew I had made a promise to return to Lake Titicaca on this specific day, equinox 2009. I was reconnecting with the beings, from the time of Lemuria, Og. I had been holding my violet ray phi Vogel crystal in the car, so I knew I was prepared to take out the other two phi Vogel crystals, which amplify the high-frequency energy that was to run through my body from the crystalline grid to the Island of the Moon and to all the beings present. Using the crystal, I opened the space eight times to the left, then eight infinity symbols. The crystals were then turned to the cosmos and the infinity breath brought in the frequencies of love and appreciation, the highest vibrations of the adamantine particles, into my crown chakra, down to the core of the earth, back up to my sacred heart, and then out to the lake and Island of the Moon.

Eight clockwise rotations toward the lake closed the space. A later circular rotation connected all spaces of similar frequency in harmonic oscillation to the crystalline grid. The ceremony was complete. I had done what I felt I had come to Bolivia to do. Walking slowly up the hill from the lake to the blue truck, I was told that Sampaya is a "feminine town" of old overlooking the Island of the Moon on Lake Titicaca. It was where women came to learn how to heal, and afterward they were allowed to cross the lake to the Island of the Moon to become priestesses. With the day's ceremony complete, we drove to our hotel to recharge. In the evening, Milton spoke to me about the importance of preparing ceremonial space to prevent negative energies from entering. He does this with sacred coca leaves, which he always carries in a pouch around his neck.

The next morning, after a breakfast that included the option of coca leaves, we got into the truck to drive to the shoreline of Lake Titicaca, where Milton had reserved a small boat to go first to the Island of the Moon and later to the Island of the Sun. The water was dazzling with its brilliant blue color. After thirty minutes of bouncing through the water, we docked and walked to a stone-covered beach. Several local traditional women, keepers of the island, approached us with furry llama toys on strings, Bolivian ceramic whistles, and handwoven belts. "*No gracias*," didn't work very well. The stone ruins clearly outlined the rectangular structure, which once stood prominently overlooking the lake and the village of Sampaya. We noticed a few other groups mounting the hill. But we found our fire pit, where the wood we brought was already arranged. Nester added some branches to the wood and lit it. We sat in a semicircle facing the blazing fire and temple wall.

I had been asked to carry the sacred offerings on the boat and up the hill to magnetize them with my energetic field, but they now were on the ground and being unwrapped by Milton. Two cloths were laid on the ground and on each cloth was placed a large sheet of white paper on which two offerings were to be constructed. The right offering was for business and personal prayers; the offering on the left was for health and was pure white. Milton placed llama meat in the center of each, and then unwrapped the first package, which contained brightly colored and pure white candy for Pachamama. The candy was distributed to the five of us for our personal blessing and then placed first on the right side of the offering and then on the left. Copal and other incenses were added, along with many coca leaves. Finally, thin rectangular sheets of silver, then gold, were placed in the center of each. The two bundles were wrapped up and carefully placed on the burning fire. We watched as the flames melted the offerings.

Altar for Pachamama.

Marijon then suggested that I go to the front of the temple, essentially a wall in ruins, which I did. It was a space of high energetic exchange for me, and my heart expanded with a knowing, but not understanding. As I came back to join the group, Marijon said she felt that I was to sing some tones. Marijon and Milton walked me over to an alcove with my back to the lake. There was a ledge, which made a perfect seat. I sat. I felt a little embarrassed, since I knew I was expected to sing, but I didn't feel like it. As I sat,

Temple of the Moon ruins.

I let go of my ego and moved into a magical space of altered dimension. I heard sounds come out of my mouth, which began as tones, but quickly changed to cosmic speak. My arms started moving demonstrably, as if I was giving commands. My voice became strong.

I don't remember how long the speaking continued, but finally it reached closure, and I knew I was complete. Marijon and Milton, who stood in front of me, looked dazed. Marijon said something about how I had removed an obstacle so that the sounds could return, or that is what I think she said. I didn't understand what I had done or why I had done it. I just knew that it felt right and complete. My later understanding, channeled, was that I was—in another lifetime—Kaipu, high priestess for the *apu*, Mama Quilla, and that I was removing the veil, or low frequencies, thus allowing the tones, sounds, and songs of the Virgins of the Sun to return and to reach out to Lake Titicaca again on a different dimensional plane. The ceremony conducted on the equinox at Sampaya had prepared the way for this to transpire, by filling the island with the love vibration of the Christ-consciousness.

We descended the hill, and this time we said yes to the vendors, since our arms were empty and llama toys fit in perfectly. The boat took us to Isla del Sol, or the Island of the Sun. On the way, we stopped in what seemed like the middle of the lake to pay tribute to the inner city, which was discovered in 2000 by an international archaeological expedition. The ancient temple is submerged in the depths of Lake Titicaca and dates back to 15,000 BC or earlier. Milton handed each of us coca leaves from his pouch, so that we, in our own way, could pay our respects. Then we were off to the Temple of the Three Waters on the Island of the Sun. Milton, Jessica, Nestor, and I climbed the 206 steps built by the Incas, leading up to the sacred fountain, which has been called the Fountain of Youth. I had two goals, the first of which was to find the spot to place a crystal I had brought from Peace Valley Sanctuary in Arkansas, the site of Helios, the conscious Earth-Keeper crystal under the lodge. I had been told that Helios was connected etherically to the huge crystal under the Island of the Sun. The crystal was my way of linking the two. My second goal was to take coca leaves from the hotel and offer them before removing my Vogel crystals and quietly upshifting the frequency and connecting the temple to the crystalline grid. This completed our sacred encounter with Lake Titicaca, after which our journey continued.

We had an amazing stay at the mineral-rich Termas de Urmiri hot springs. I walked up the hill to the chapel where I toned and brought in the frequency of the Christ-consciousness. Our next stop, Sajama, is one of the highest mountains in Bolivia, situated in the Sajama National Park, close to the Bolivian and Chilean border. As we approached the entrance, our archaeologist-shaman companion pulled the truck over so that we could all find a quiet space in which to ask permission of the guardian of the *apu* before we proceeded. We were told that we were on the border of the vortex, a neutral space of pure ether, into which we would soon enter. I learned a lot about asking permission from my hosts.

The next day, after a night of interdimensional travel for all of us, Marijon again sensed that I was to tone. Our truck pulled over so that I could sit in the field at the base of the *apu*, Sajama. As happened before, I felt nothing, but followed the suggestion. Then an immense energetic

Apu Sajama.

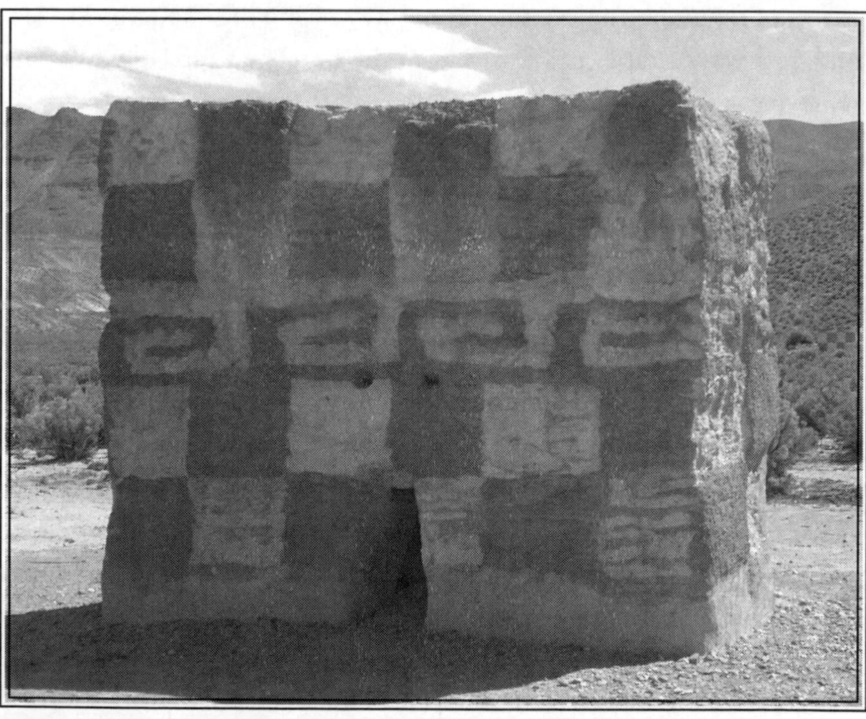

Pre-Inca tomb, Land of the Carangas.

flood of tones, sounds, and gestures came out of me. A veil was lifted and love returned. This *apu*, and all of similar frequency, now vibrate at full potential. When I finally was complete, it was difficult to regain my grounding, so all present assisted me with water and getting me back to the truck so we could continue on to the Land of the Carangas, where again I felt an energetic pull to do ceremony and had a knowing that I had promised to return to do so.

We drove to a river, where Milton and Nestor built another fire for the ceremonial packets, which we offered this time to the *apu*. While we were on the banks of the river, Nestor and Jessica collected stones and created Metatron's seal, a geometric symbol, which had been channeled via Nestor from Archangel Metatron (www.cienciadeluz.org). He told me that he had experimented in his hometown of Juliaca, Peru, by placing the image all over town and then monitoring the crime rate. He found it declined then rose again when he reversed the experiment by removing the image. I was told that within a third dimensional pyramid a space of less density existed, where one was protected from incompatible energies. I asked to have a cloth image of Metatron's seal mailed to me, ready to be used.

Metatron's seal.

We returned to La Paz, then we drove to Tiajuanaco. We went first to the museum, where the large statue of the Pachamama was displayed. Pachamama and I were like old friends exchanging energy as I sat quietly bringing in the divine feminine Christ-consciousness codes. Milton then took us around the archaeological site, showing us the inner earth tunnels and sungate.

Next, Milton took us to the sunken temple to see the stone face masks of those beings from many nations. I descended into the temple and began walking around the perimeter. With each step, I was overwhelmed by emotion. It was again as if we knew each other and I had been expected.

Approximately one month later, during a lucid dream state created by a massage with Ahara back in Santa Fe, I saw myself entering the Temple of Tiajuanaco from the cosmos by means of the sungate, to be greeted by the star beings from many nations.

Pachamama.

When the three of us felt complete, we returned to La Paz, where the next day we took a flight to Santa Cruz and hired a driver to take us to Samaipata for a magical visit to the batholith, El Fuerte. I often wonder why it is that I have no preknowledge of the events that will unfold, and always I am glad that is the case, for if I knew, I might resist or try to control the outcome. Never could I have created an outcome as magical as the one that occurred with the inner earth beings, who again were waiting for me. As we were climbing up toward El Fuerte, the gigantic rock mound, Marijon asked me to sing in tones before entering the site, and Milton engaged the guide in conversation so that he would be distracted as I did so.

This happened again on the platform that was built to overlook the rock where I did ceremony with the Vogel crystals. Then down, down, down the hill we climbed to the hole. We were told that this was the entrance to inner earth. All I knew was that I was bonded to the energy there.

(Top) Sungate. (Bottom) Entrance to inner earth Tiajuanaco.

Beings from many nations.

When it was my turn, I approached the hole and offered the coca leaves that Milton had given me. Quietly, I called in the Christ-consciousness frequency. It was not a time or place to call attention to what I was doing, since there were others around who might be puzzled. So I worked using my hands, instead of the crystals, to transmit the frequency.

I climbed back up the steep hill and ended up alone on a plateau. Here I was able to connect with the Cosmic Council of Light, who told me that the inner earth beings had felt the frequency and knew that love had returned to earth. They felt safe. Thus, my trip through the miracles and magic of Bolivia came to an end. After a two-month journey of awakening, self-awareness, and expansion, I was soon on a plane to Miami, then on to New Orleans, where I picked up my cosmic chariot and drove back to Santa Fe.

When I returned home, I read in *Metatron Speaks* more about the inner earth beings:

Now, the inner earth beings of Lemurian descent are far more

> highly evolved in spirit than is humanity at this time. We have told you that their bodies are adapted, changed to their new [environment]. The inner earth beings are less dense but are indeed physical. ... These beings are wise and have found their unified centre. They are peaceful, espousing no dogma, no religion other than the love of Source and an understanding of what is termed nirvana. They exude great tranquility. They are indeed quite aware of you humans on the surface but have no desire, no responsibility to intermingle with humanity.[1]

I walked through the door of my home and felt exhausted down to the core of my being, but I was safe and in my protected sanctuary, or so I thought. The next thing I remember was a black unknown space, which I later described in my journal:

Archangel Metatron, through Tyb, has coached me on the use of gems as tools to strengthen my energy body, and I am beautifully adorned as I write. I recently traveled to Bolivia to do ceremony at Lake Titicaca on the equinox and to other sacred sites, always sleeping and bathing with my large lapis lazuli pendant around my neck and rings and bracelets on my fingers and wrists. After traveling for two months and then making the long drive back to Santa Fe from New Orleans, I arrived home to quickly immerse myself in a Himalayan pink salt bath to relieve my enormous fatigue. I have since been told by Archangel Metatron, through Tyberonn, that I had a fissure in my auric field from the reverse spin south of the equator and being from above the Schuman Resonance in the airplane for more than five hours.

Feeling comfortable in my home, I did not replace the gem tools, which I took off to keep them out of the thick salt bath. I went downstairs to eat and have some wine. Then I blacked out. The next thing I remember was seeing pitch black everywhere, a desperate sense of not knowing where I was, and feeling foam coming out of my mouth. I remember getting up and feeling for the walls to find my bed. When I woke the next morning, I had a terrible feeling that where I had been was close to the hell described by so many. I was already exhausted and had a fissure in my auric field; then when I removed my protection before bathing, darker energies rushed in. I had changed significantly during the two months away from my home. My house, I realized, needed to upgrade to my new level of frequency.

Archangel Metatron explained in more detail how light attracts dark:

> You see, masters, the closer you get to the light, the stronger you attract the dark. It is true in real sense physics, electromagnetics. Pure positive energy has the greatest attraction to negative energy. So you must have the wisdom, the humility, the strength and the discipline to deflect it.[2]

That would be my goal, for I now knew the light being that I was. I no longer had to be told. An awakening had occurred.

~ 19 ~

Your Auric Field Was Fissured

Now that I knew how much light I carried, it was time to learn how to take care of myself so that it would not go out. Assistance came to me from so many different directions, and all I had to do was accept. Nestor's channeled Metatron's seal arrived in the mail to provide a protective space for the distance work I was about to begin. Archangels Jophiel and Lady Constance appeared to tell me that they were my direct guides of protection. Archangel Metatron via Tyberonn encouraged me to acquire meteorites and wear moldavite for grounding. And he reminded me that my pace had to be adjusted to account for my biological age and the enormous energy that I carry. When I learned that I was to go to Shaman's Cave in Sedona for new moon, Tyb gave me tips on how to do so safely. I was also told that others would assist me.

I was out of balance on my return from New Orleans, Arkansas, and Bolivia. Dizzy and disoriented, I learned that my auric field had been fissured and it would take six weeks of rest before I could regain full vitality. I paid attention and was grateful for all the assistance, writing:

> Tyb, Just landed in Santa Fe after two months on the road, air, and water. The trip was truly amazing with so many miracles. Guess life will calm down now.

I can't say that life calmed down at all; I just learned how to manage it better. While I readjusted to Santa Fe's altitude, the next phase of my work unfolded: distance sessions. I began on October 17, 2009, and I was ready. While in Hot Springs in a rock shop, I passed in front of a crystal ball and felt an energetic tug. Not knowing why, I brought it and thus became the custodian of this powerful crystal. I was later told by the Cosmic Council of Light that the crystal would stand as the surrogate for the individual with whom I was to do distance work. The requests began to come in—from California, Florida, then the Netherlands, South Africa, Australia, and elsewhere. All of these people had found my picture and information on the Earth-Keeper website, as Tyberonn continued to list me as a presenter or healer for his various events. I got comments such as, "My energy connected with your picture" and "It

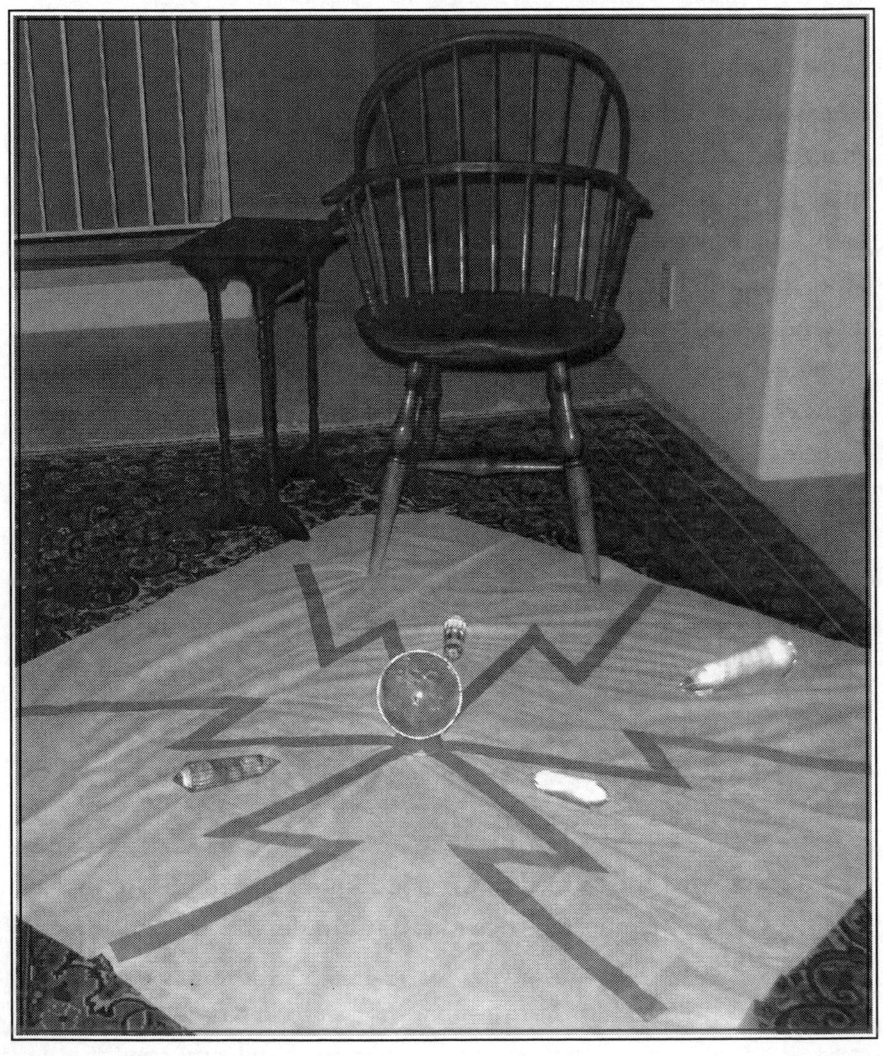

Distance session setting.

was a knowing that I was to do this work." What I knew was that the work was not for everyone and I was not to market the sessions. Those who presented for sessions were the ones anchoring the crystalline grid. By means of their increased luminosity, they would in turn transfer the love frequency to others, thus assisting the return of love to planet earth.

Now that I had time and wasn't traveling, I remembered that in Archangel Michael's channel a few months ago, via Ronna Herman, he had mentioned Archangels Jophiel and Lady Constance, with whom I had briefly connected. I felt that I should try to connect with them again to become better acquainted.

How Might We Work Together–10/17/09

Nina: Archangel Jophiel and Archangel Lady Constance, please introduce yourselves and instruct me in how we might best work together.

We greet you today as we have before on many, many occasions. This, you see, is not our first encounter (though it seems so to you) for you were never properly introduced to us and therefore knew neither of our existence nor of our very close working bond with you, our dear lord and master. This has occurred on other star systems as well as that of earth. We have held the light together and assisted you on your path, which you now better understand as the upshifting of planetary frequencies. You are given direction, guidance, and protection from the two of us. Yes, it is through your inner knowing; that is how we communicate with you. We manifest the emotional swell you feel as a way of speaking to you. We are your closest guides and protectors for this specific aspect of the work. Archangel Raphael took the lead, by strengthening your internal metal to allow you to accept this calling. Now he turns you over to us, dear one. Not that he leaves you—his bastions of angels protect you, and yours as well—but we are your direct guides at the moment. We will speak to you directly, and we will appear to you at your calling. The work has just begun, dear Nina. Just begun.

With our deep love,

Jophiel and Lady Constance via Anaya-Ra

I knew I had guides and protectors, maybe they could help me with the ringing in my ears and why I felt off balance.

Please Tell Me about My Physical Being—10/26/09

Nina: My questions to the universe are: What is the constant ringing in my ears and head? What am I to do for relief? How do I return vitality to my physical being? Is there anything else I should know related to these issues?

Dear one, the time is now for you to be in full possession of this information. The sounds in your head have been increasing over the last year as your profound gifts have been realized and actualized. They are a critical part of who you are and why you are here. The frequencies of divine love have been transmitted through the etheric crown chakra tunnel. Now they come to you in your etheric hearing tunnel as well. They radiate throughout your body causing a vibration in the cells of all that you are. It is like your sonic toothbrush jiggling loose the plaque, allowing the pristine enamel to be revealed again in all its shining magnificence so that it will return to its full potential. Your body is similarly being cleaned. You ask about your diet being an energy zapper, and it indeed can be. You want an alkaline body to work with the crystalline structure. Do what you think is best to achieve that more perfected state. So, relax and wait while we polish your last facet.

With our deep love,
The Cosmic Council of Light via Anaya-Ra

So many changes were occurring in my life that I often forgot to think about my body. I always expected to be full of vitality when I did ceremony or spoke or followed any requests from my inner voice. Yet, I knew that my physiology was going through changes, as was my conscious awareness. It had to adjust to new frequencies, to an increasingly higher vibration of my field. My human self and my higher self were a team. My body is the personal temple for my soul, and it was vital that I stop, respect, and thank it. Without my health and well-being, I couldn't effectively do the work I was here to do. I had just asked the Cosmic Council of Light about my lack of vitality, and now I had to stop and pay attention rather than continue to push my body forward on this amazing journey. I had to stop and allow my body time to catch up and keep up with the speed with which my awareness was changing. So I reached out to someone who had gone through this part of the journey years before I was going through it.

> Tyb, I confess I am swimming at the moment. The frequencies that are pounding at my head and the constant sound of the universe in my head are difficult to stay present with. I need to shut down, to turn it off. I am off to see a cranial-sacral cosmic osteopath in two days to see if I can get the energy and pressure to be released. It is such a comfort to know there is someone out there who understands me!

> Nina, The other piece that I feel is affecting you is the trip to South America. The flight of that time length will deplete anyone's energy field. That is why pilots have shorter life expectancy. The plane flies at an altitude of around 35,000 feet, and that is above the level of the Schumann resonance, the earth's electromagnetic pulse, and the metallic fuselage of the plane also deflects it when it is below 30,000 feet. Being out of the S-resonance affects the magnetic sync of all of your major organs, glands, and enlarges the heart, especially on flights over five hours. In addition, you were below the equator, where the natural spin of energy is clockwise. Energy above the equator moves counterclockwise; that is why water drains out of a bathtub or sink counterclockwise above the equator and the reverse below it. So that will affect your energy field as well. Lastly, you were at very high elevations in portions of your trip to Bolivia, and that changes the field too, as well as oxygen levels in the blood and thus organs. I wouldn't be surprised if Marijon is feeling a little tired after that trip too. Both of your fields were put in reverse spin for two to three weeks then further subjected to the flight home. So those factors affect you also—in addition to everything mentioned in the earlier email regarding your extraordinary light quotient. Take

> with a grain of salt whatever the osteopath says. You will be fine, and unless that doctor is highly metaphysical he will be largely driven by mainstream medical thought. You will be fine, but it's a full moon and your body has been through a lot. Your auric field was fissured, and it is essential that you take it easy, rest, and always maintain your field. Be aware that even shorter air flights will have an effect, but international ones can be really hard on the body and its organs; they can deplete and fissure the aura, and you will bleed energy resulting in a short-circuit of the aura. It can take six to eight weeks to rebuild and correct the auric field. Take salt baths too, and drink lots of water.

I replied:

> Tyb, This is truly amazing. I had not heard of the reverse spin below the equator. What a wealth of fascinating knowledge you are! Six to eight weeks, wow. I am on week four. I am taking salt baths, using the magnets; and I will monitor the water better. The kino/osteopath is very metaphysical. The pressure in my head happened before, and he went right to my skull and so gently moved something. A rush of energy flowed through my body and the pain and pressure were gone. My guides seem to work through him.

Tyb wrote me occasionally when he got a message to do so.

> In my channeling last night, Metatron asked me to tell you the following, which I will paraphrase here: Nina is an ascended master walk-in as we have told you, and she is now aware. The crystalline coding that she does is an important part of the ascension, and she has taken on a very important role; but It is a role she has done before. The enormous energy that she carries cannot and will not be lost. She must be aware that she is a biological organism, so maintenance of her health and maintenance of her auric field are intricately connected. The past five months she has driven herself nonstop, and it is too much. There must be

> consideration of biological age, and adequate rest must be part of the regime. In Arkansas, the frequency of recoding was, as she is aware, excessive. Though the desire on her part is to assist everyone she can, she must also consider the self, and find space for rest. In events such as Arkansas and San Antonio, no more than three or four DNA coding upshifts should be done per day, with space taken between each session of at least thirty minutes for the body to replenish itself. Use of the meteorites is very important. Limits on air travel are also recommended. It is essential at times, but allow for rest afterward and space between trips. Much is required in this role; the pace must be adjusted. Utilize the tools and get rest. The auric energy of this entity is such that both a counterclockwise and clockwise spiral is within the field of crystalline-electric circuitry; when the circuitry is overloaded, there tends to be an overpull into the higher dimensions without the anchoring. An emerald of at least three carats will assist, four is better. Use of the larger 144 Vogel will now aid in the work, connecting directly to the 12 phases of the planet and that termed the angelic realm of 144. Her association with CJ (Crystal Star Walker) is important, for CJ and Raquel (Che xel-Ra) will in time be assisting her. All is well. She will accomplish all she needs to accomplish, and this soul is indeed intricate to the ascension.

I wasn't yet sure what "intricate to the ascension" meant, but I thought that the work I was called to do on the significant phases of the moon had something to do with it. A few days before the November 2, 2009 full moon, I asked the universe, "Is there anything for me to do on full moon?" The answer came quickly. I was to take my newly received Metatron's seal outside. My first thought was to take it into my backyard. The thought expanded to taking it to a public space. Then the thought became more specific: Take it to the Plaza, in downtown Santa Fe. I was also told to invite Ahara, Kay (a new friend I had met at Peace Valley Sanctuary last September), and any others who might want to join us. I understood that for the full moon ceremony we were to place the seal on the Plaza. Then we were to activate and connect it to the crystalline grid, which would create a pyramid in the etheric realm. The etheric seal was then to be expanded from a small space on the Plaza to a much larger space encompassing all of Santa Fe county.

The next morning at about 2:00 a.m., more information came pouring forth. I pictured all of us gathering in the center of the Plaza, lighting rose-scented incense, while asking permission of all the beings—present, past, and future—to join us. The cloth with the seal on it would be placed and anchored on the cement in the middle of the Plaza by four large stones from sacred sites in Bolivia. I was to be at one of the points of the triangle facing east; my crystal ball was to be placed in the center as a surrogate. My Vogel crystals were to assist in activating the seal in the physical and etheric realms, by bringing in the Christ-consciousness frequency of love from the crystalline grid. I was told that when the activation was complete, our drum was to be sounded for thirty-three beats, while I expanded the energetic signature throughout the city, and then the county, by means of the infinity breath. When the drumming and breathing concluded, the drum was to be struck once at each point of the triangle, symbolizing the anchoring of the seal into the earth at the farthest points of the county. "And so it is," spoken by all present, would complete the ceremony.

First of Many Etheric Imprints of the Seal

Nina: Archangel Metatron, please be present this morning as Kay, Ahara, and I do ceremony with your seal. Please share anything else we should know to do for the divine will of the universe.

Dear one, thank you for hearing the call of the universe on this auspicious day of celebration. The tools, people, and location have been identified for the first of many etheric imprints of the seal, which was transferred to humanity for this purpose. Though you say you do not understand the complex geometry of the symbol, you have used it many times before for purification, for removing the density that restricts humanity. We asked for this powerful sound (I was asked to put on a CD). The regal music of Puccini's *Turandot* came on to stir you and the community as it radiated out, for it is a forerunner of the radiance that will open up to Santa Fe by means of your ceremony. The ions, the particles, will dance with a newfound remembered vibrancy and frequency, which will penetrate the consciousness of those dwelling or entering the enlightened space. More than a song of grandeur, it is a dance of grandeur that will sparkle and dazzle the senses of beings small and large, visible and invisible. Yes, all of creation in the newly formed triangle of Metatron's seal will feel a vibrancy, which is a precursor to love: the love that you, dear one, know so well, the perfected love of Source. The work today is unparalleled in its intensity and impact. We thank and honor you for hearing the divine call.

With our deep Love,
Archangel Metatron via Anaya-Ra

After writing Archangel Metatron's message, I went downstairs to listen to the last act of *Turandot*. Then it came to me why *Turandot* was chosen. The story is of a stranger who must answer three questions of the grand, noble princess to win her hand. All the other suitors had been killed for not knowing the answers. After answering all three questions, the stranger gives the princess another chance to kill him if she can answer his question: "What is my name?" Just as the trumpets were blaring in my living room and the chorus of hundreds was singing, the early morning sun, in the window behind my chair, began to rise. For the first time ever, I saw the sun reflected in the glass on the wall in front of me just as the princess sang in full voice "Your name is love!" Truly amazing is the orchestration of the universe, for love is what we were to bring in.

The ceremony came to pass with the addition of three dozen roses. They formed a triangle on the Plaza in Santa Fe with many of the petals removed, scattered in and out, blown about by the wind while the cathedral bells chimed on the quarter hour, expanding the energetic signature of Metatron's seal, which now rose above, below, and throughout the city and county of Santa Fe, transmuting dense energy and bringing in the light of love. And so it was, that November full moon in Santa Fe, New Mexico!

I was soon learning about other dates of significance: the triad stargates. Archangel Metatron, through Tyberonn, described the triad stargates as three major frequencial openings occurring on November 11, 2009, December 12, 2009, and December 21, 2009. According to Archangel Metatron: "These stargates would be a major part of the planetary shift. The three listed frequencial portals are a triad of inlet corridors that will work in aggregation to assist people through a potent transition. The planet is changing its spiritual season."[1] I would be in Chaco Canyon, New Mexico; Shaman's Cave, Sedona, Arizona; and Stardreaming, Santa Fe, New Mexico, sequentially on each of those dates.

The first date arrived, and I got into my car and drove three hours to Chaco Canyon National Park.

Chaco Canyon National Park, New Mexico (Pueblo Bonito)–11/11/09 (2009 = 11)

Nina: With this rose incense, I ask permission of all the guardians of Chaco Canyon to do ceremony this morning. Please share with me anything I need to know while I am here. With great appreciation.

We honor and welcome you, dear one. You so well saw our many faces in the cliffs as you drove in. We are here with you, closer than the cliffs. We gather around Metatron's seal and we not only give you permission, but we will join you as was decreed eons ago for this day, this month, this year, this moment in humanity's time and space. The rose scent cleanses with the high vibration of that fragrance. You are to tone, dear one. You are to drum and to breathe the infinity breath. It is of paramount importance to breathe deeply as you move on to this dimensional plane the vibration and frequencies of the crystalline grid, the Christ-consciousness codes. This is for you to do, as we together expand the seal up into the cosmos, down into the core of the earth, and then back to the rim of the canyon in all four directions. A space will be cleared and hallowed so that the frequency of divine love can once again, in its fullest, radiate throughout. The beings from many nations will know that love has returned to earth. Shelter no longer is needed. The time is now for the return, not only of the knowledge of the crystals but the beings of yore to reappear, to join the collective of humanity in a time when Adam/Eve Kadmon is returning. All of creation is to return, rejoice, and know that the ascension cometh with the return of divine love.

We love you deeply,
The guardians of Chaco Canyon via Anaya-Ra

The first triad stargate had been acknowledged and the next stargate wasn't until December 12, 2009, at which time I would be in Arizona. So I had time to work with Tyb on deciding if I was to be the custodian of a 144-facet phi Vogel crystal. This was the second time that Archangel Metatron had mentioned I should have a 144 Vogel, this time saying:

> I'll mail you a 144 that I feel will be appropriate and you can work with it in advance and return it in San Antonio if you aren't drawn to it. I am honored to work with you. You are such an enormous energy, and I still feel like you don't fully realize how powerful and magnificent you are, but perhaps that humility is an aspect of your grace. You don't have an imbalanced ego or desire to control others and that is a great attribute. I hope you have purchased the big meteorite. Your energy is so intricate that the electro-balancing of it is a huge piece for you. Are you utilizing the Metatronic shield 24/7? Single refractive ring on one side, double refractive on the other.

I had asked Tyb to send the 144-facet phi Vogel crystal to me, and he did. I also needed to know more about it and how to care for it.

Tyb replied:

> Oh yes, the forward points are at much sharper angles than the fifty-one degree base, and as such are very, very fragile, you should never touch them, and when you put them in the sherpa pouches, try to make sure they fit in the pouches in such a way that the tip does not touch the bottom of the pouch. Always pack them very well, and of course never put them in situations where the temperature changes around them too fast. For example, if you decide to clear them in running water, make sure the temperature of the water is within ten degrees of the room

temperature; if not, don't put them in water. Rapid temperature change and rapid elevation change can cause a quartz crystal to either expand or contract and thus cause cracking. I have some crystals that take on fissures or clouds occasionally, even just sitting in the same room. This is a different, somewhat rare aspect and is usually because the crystal is taking on a special energy, an angelic type being. I have a stand-up type Vogel that took on rainbows about two years or so ago when I started channeling Metatron. I wouldn't let too many others touch this Vogel, and you want to program it to do certain things, such as never absorb detrimental/negative energy, provide protection and balance to your field, assist in healing, channel, astral travel, etc. You need to spend some time working with this one to build and integrate its field. It is a sentient conscious being as well as a precision highly capable Atlantean-Sirian-Pleiadian tool. Your Sirian self will be delighted when you hold it. This Vogel should arrive by Thursday, so please be home for its delivery, and let me know when it comes so I know it has arrived safely.

I replied:

Tyb, Thank you for sharing more information. I have a leather shoulder bag that holds the other three Vogel crystals. I would like to find a leather shoulder case for this as well. No, I never heard not to touch the forward point. I confess, I am excited! What an honor.

Tyb answered:

This is the biggest 144 Ray has ever made. It is the larger of the two super big ones I have available. It is about 10 x 3.2 and water clear. Please protect the point, and use it with great care; it is extremely powerful. Perfect for the work you're doing. This is a one of a kind, truly. It takes six weeks to make one, and the base crystal this was cut from is very rare. This is an amazing tool. Treat it carefully. You will have the largest, clearest 144 on

> the planet. It has a flower charger on the base that is Atlantean. You will have it by Thursday.

Tyb told me that the crystal was cut by Raimundo, a gem cutter from Brazil who was trained by Marcel Vogel. Raimundo channels Marcel Vogel as he handcrafts Vogel crystals with a patented lapidary device that enables him to cut crystals above the thirty-three facets. While there are three others who studied under Dr. Vogel before he died, Raimundo remains the only one capable of cutting over thirty-three facets. According to Archangel Metatron, Raimundo has a unique affinity with crystals and so imbues them with high-frequency energy. He explained that this exponentially potent crystal would assist in myriad ways, especially in upshifting energies, astral travel, and bilocation of thought-form codes. Tyb told me that the crystal would download the form of energy needed in order to achieve zero-point balance, and of course that meant the majority of energy brought in would be the divine feminine energy. That is a dualistic term; attributes in higher realms are without gender application. Tyb ended by saying, "Amazing sentient tool."

> Tyb, Shivers went through me when I saw the first photo, and my Bolivian pendulum went wild. That must be a clue. I will energetically check in with it again tomorrow morning and keep you posted. I feel a bond, but this is a big crystal and a big decision. I will treat it with enormous care and will ask that you teach me about use. Amazing description.

Then Tyb sent me an unexpected email as we were discussing the 144 Vogel.

> Not sure if you met my ex-wife at the 09/0/99. She will be in San Antonio. We were married twenty-seven years. She is Scottish and very gifted psychically. Her aunt was a famous Celtic psychic in Edinburgh, and she sees auras and also channels. She told me she passed you in the hall before you spoke at the 09/09/99. She didn't know who you were at that time, but she remembers the hat. She told me you had the biggest aura she had ever seen.

I was ready to take off for my next adventure, but I had not received the special delivery package containing the 144-facet phi Vogel crystal. Tyb was concerned that the package might be left in the cold while I was gone, which would crack the crystal. So down to the mailbox I went and there it was, a very cold package, which I lovingly took back to my house.

Question to the Huge 144-Facet Phi Vogel Crystal–11/13/09

Nina: To the huge 144-facet phi Vogel crystal that is resting on my table, welcome. I am honored by your presence. Are we to work together? What is your name? Please tell me all I need to know now about you and how I know you. With great appreciation.

Dear one, the welcome is to you. Welcome to the new expanded world that you just entered. Here there are neither limitations nor boundaries. As there is none other like me, I represent the limitless, the infinity consciousness that you are and that humanity is becoming. When you lit the incense and unpacked me with such love and care, the universe was watching. Then you embraced me to warm me from the cold of the night. That was when I shot the rays of love to you and through you. The intensity (tears) of that moment ran through my beingness as well. This is a love affair, dear one, one so profound that you weep. It has taken a long time to actualize, but all in its proper time, and the

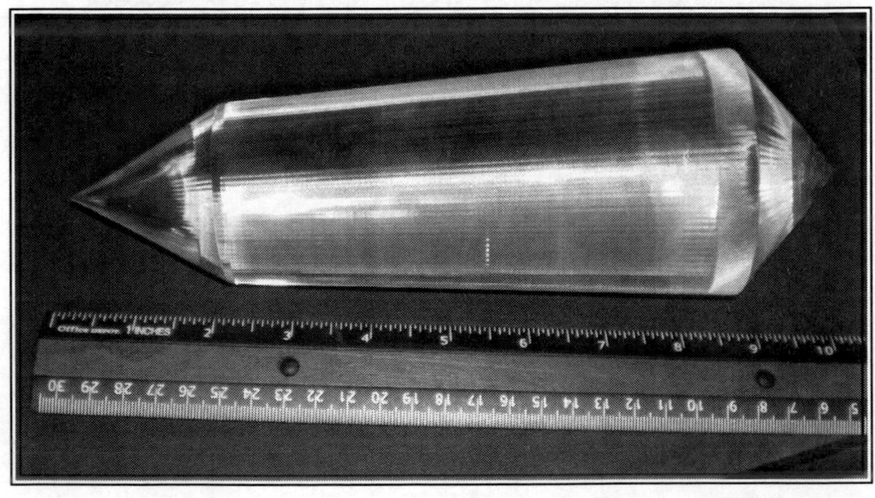

144-facet phi Vogel crystal.

time, as you know and feel to the core of who you are, is now. As we travel together, it will be just you and me. This is a time of exquisite deep bonding. As we travel together to Shaman's Cave, Sedona, Arizona, you will know a different sense of being, dear one. Remember all the techniques of grounding and maintenance now more than ever. You ask my name, Anaya. We are old friends together at last!

With my deep love,
Anaya via Anaya-Ra

My initial understanding was that the crystal's name was Anaya, but later Archangel Metatron expanded the name to Anaya-Ra, a nongendered name. He also told me, through Tyberonn, that was my name as well.

~ 20 ~

Limitless Infinity Consciousness

Anaya the crystal (later to be changed to Anaya-Ra) and Anaya-Ra the human were off to meet their Sirian soul sisters to create a special triad of energy. Together we would travel beyond the time matrix of the twelfth dimension to the infinity-consciousness realm of pure love and light. This would take place in the infinity portal of Shaman's Cave by means of the golden spiral and the eight star warriors chosen to access this undistorted energy and frequency. A stream of the Christ-consciousness codes would flow out of the cave, down the dome, and out into the plateau—for all to tap into when doing ceremony, meditation, or on any occasion in which the ascension process was to be advanced.

I had met CJ and Raquel in Arkansas, where Tyb had told us we three were soul sisters and that we would be working together. So it felt very important that I drive to Tucson, where they both lived, to get to know more about what that meant. I would be there the weekend preceding new moon. It became clear quickly that I was to go from Tucson to Sedona to do ceremony, on the new moon, in Shaman's Cave. That was all I knew. I didn't even know how to find Shaman's Cave. So I wrote to ask Tyb, since he had done work there the year before:

> You will find Shaman's Dome and Cave contain very potent, extraordinary energy. Shaman's Cave is on Shaman's Dome, south of Sedona in the Red Rock National Forest. The Pink Jeep tours will know where it is. It's impossible for me to describe how to get to it as it's on dirt gravel roads, and they network, and the roads have no names, but I know you can get there. I am

> amazed you guys (Marijon and I) found my friend in Bolivia. Well done. It tells me you will find Shaman's Dome and Cave easily. It's a hike to get up on top, and the cave entry is doable but a little tricky in spots.

I replied:

> Tyb, I read your channel from last December about Shaman's Cave and know of its power as an infinity gate. I will be with four or five people; one from Sedona is another cosmic being. I find that I have been unexpectedly surrounded during ceremonies by other people and now see the importance of that.

Placing the 144-facet phi Vogel crystal in the passenger's seat, I took off for Tucson to visit with CJ and Raquel on my way to Sedona. I wanted to know more about what it meant to work as a triad. One aspect of our relationship would be to do ceremony together. This began while walking in Sabino Canyon on Saturday morning. We stopped in a secluded spot next to a stream and allowed the flow of the universe to come through us in ceremony. Then, after spending many hours together, I said goodbye to CJ, who had graciously let me stay at her house, and then met Raquel for lunch before heading on to Sedona. Raquel told me that during the night she had dreamt of future ceremonies the three of us would do together both physically and on the etheric plane, ceremonies of pure love and light from beyond the twelfth dimension. She shared with me that our earth, universe, and other universes exist within an impure, distorted bubble, and that only by reaching to the higher dimensions could one attract love and light in their pure state. This information felt like my truth as well and fit like a square in a square hole, finally! All of my work going forward would be explained by means of that bubble image.

These new ideas about love and light coming from a realm of purity came along with another new thought that I shared with my sisters. While driving to Tucson I had realized that everything in my life was in balance. I had no wants. When I woke in the morning, my only task was to decide what I wanted to do that day. This seemed amazing, for life had not been like that until now. So what I wanted to do that morning, now that I had said my farewells, was to drive to Sedona to meet Patty, my friend who had helped me build a small grid in my living room a few months before.

Shaman's Cave began to call me, reminding me of what Archangel Jophiel and Lady Constance had said to me: "We manifest the emotional swell you feel as a way of speaking to you." The swell was getting stronger as I approached Sedona. What were the archangels trying to say to me?

Patty and I met at the Sky King Hotel located in the Airport Mesa Vortex in Sedona. That evening, we had a relaxing catch-up dinner together. The night in the airport vortex, however, was anything but relaxing. I awoke at 3:00 a.m. for an amazing download. Energy and information poured in. I realized that CJ, Raquel, and I each had worked with the other two in transferring pure love and light. I then realized that pure love and light is what my new crystal, Anaya, embodied. Pure love and light is also infinity consciousness. Together, the Sirian Sisters—the triad of energy—like Anaya, personified infinity consciousness, purity, love, and light. The entire ceremony in Shaman's Cave then came in. When I had all the pieces, I jumped out of bed and emailed this information to Raquel, and CJ. Raquel replied, "I do think we all have the energetics of all three—'light, love, and purity'—as a triad of frequencies ... each just taking a forward role with one of the aspects."

CJ replied, "Wow! Amazing info ... feels so right as well. Thank you so much for sharing. This is truly profound work. CJ."

Our Sedona guide had accepted my request for help in finding the elusive Shaman's Cave and arranged for a driver and van. She asked if her tour group could join in the ceremony. Of course, I agreed! Patty and I met the group at breakfast at the airport restaurant. There was one empty chair at the table, so our guide knew that another woman who was traveling in Sedona should be called to join us as well. My heart expanded when I realized that with Patty, me, and the driver, we made a ceremonial group of eight—again the infinity frequency had appeared. Anaya did not join the group. She stayed in the hotel, since she is huge and fragile. So my five-inch crystal ball was her surrogate.

We took a van from the hotel to the plateau near Shaman's Cave, where we exited. We joined together in a circle around a stone fire pit on the plateau where I explained to the group the reason this ceremony would be unique. I asked again for their full participation. I shared that this ceremony would take frequencies beyond the twelfth dimension, to bring in purity of light and the Christ-consciousness love energy for the ascension. Anaya, by means of the surrogate crystal ball, would access the infinity portal in Shaman's Cave, creating a tunnel from the higher dimensions down the golden spiral, through my three phi Vogel crystals—which represented pure love and light—and out into the planet as a continuous stream of undistorted energy and frequency. After the fuller explanation, all the participants agreed and expressed how honored they felt to be present. I am sure we all had planned this ceremony eons ago.

The hike began with each one carrying a backpack containing ceremonial objects: crystals, drums, an ancient Tibetan crystal skull, or incense. The mile-long path led to an enormous hill covered with ocher-colored stones and dirt. My first sign of energetic resistance manifested when a cactus allowed its spikes to enter my left hand as I passed. This happened twice. But the most dramatic effort to keep me from my goal came from the cliff near the entrance of the cave. I had a water bottle in one hand and my three Vogel crystals in a leather case over my shoulder when I began to traverse this ledge. My vertigo came fully present as I saw first how high up we were, and then how steep the passage was with only footholds and shallow stone outcroppings to grasp. Shortly after I began this transit, I faced the stone and pulled the brim of my hat down in an attempt to hide the view below. My left foot was securely placed, but I couldn't feel any ledge to put my right foot on. I felt paralyzed and fearful that the ceremony wasn't going to happen.

The two men in the group came back, took my water and crystals, and either found a foothold for me or provided it with their hands. Having made it across the narrow ledge, I sat down and bumped my way slowly over the steep rocks and into the amazing cave. The cave had an enormous opening and offered a spectacular view of the distant ridges.

Shaman's Cave hole, Sedona, Arizona.

While the others went to have their photographs taken, I tried to calm my breathing.

We began the ceremony by placing rose incense in the fire pit, which was positioned in the center front of the cave. I suggested that each one present ask permission to bring in personal protection, if they felt that was appropriate. We sat watching the smoke gently billowing up, out, and around until the last gray swirl flew away.

Everyone felt at that point that we could start. I placed Metatron's seal in the center of the cave. It was a white cloth, and a bright pink sacred geometrical form, resembling lightning bolts, came together in the center of the seal. The seal had been renamed during my night's download—from Metatron's seal to the infinity seal. I placed my large crystal ball in the center of the cave and the three Vogel crystals, with their points facing the crystal ball, in a triangle on the seal. My personal crystal, with gold and amethyst embedded in its bottom, the violet ray phi Vogel, was placed in the east position in front of me (love). The 108-facet phi Vogel, purity (Raquel), was to my left, and the 9-gate dream Vogel, light (CJ), was placed to my right. The four corners of the seal were anchored with stones from sacred sites in Bolivia.

I shared with the others how the ceremony would unfold, and they gathered in a circle around the seal. While I was breathing the infinity breath to move the enormous energy contained in Anaya, drumming began. The energy rose up the golden spiral in the infinity portal. Patty later told me that in vision she saw the top of the cave disappear.

Up and up the energy went, and then something unexpected occurred. I found myself, with my hands above my head, tearing open the time matrix that divided the twelfth dimension from the purity of love and light present in the higher dimensions. This opening allowed Anaya to energetically travel through to the higher dimensions. When she had arrived, I reversed the direction of the three phi Vogel crystals [light (CJ), purity (Raquel) and love (Nina)] so that the flow from the upper realms could come down the golden spiral of the infinity portal into the central crystal and out through the three Vogels, which were resting in a triangle on the infinity seal. A flow, a stream, a river had been set in motion. I was told that there were to be no boundaries, the flow would be constant. This frequency was to be available for each person present to tap into when they did ceremony, meditated, or on any occasion in which the ascension process was to be advanced.

They were also to ethereally know that all events of love and light in the past could be up-shifted with this frequency of purity. On completion, I found tones that wished to be sounded, and then an ancient magical language came pouring out of my mouth. My hands moved up to the golden spiral, to each crystal, to each participant, then in a circle to connect the flow of pure love and light into one infinity consciousness stream.

We each shared our experiences. The group needed more time to integrate the new frequencies, so we were silent until we knew that it was time to give thanks and depart, understanding that we could return to this timeless space anytime.

With all backpacks hitched on and our hands empty, we began the decent. On the way down, our guide told me that the first ledge I crossed wasn't the scary one; that one was ahead. Then as I completed that piece of the trail, she confessed that she hadn't told the truth, and I had already safely made it across. I had been allowed, therefore, to descend in ease and grace. We gathered on the plateau to bring closure to the pilgrimage and give thanks to each other, the land, and the sacred ceremony of pure love and light, infinity consciousness.

When I was back in Santa Fe, I could see in my mind's eye the energy coming into the top of Shaman's Cave and the river of infinity consciousness flowing down the hill, into the valley and moving on.

I sent this accounting of the event to Patty, who replied:

> Thank you so much for this! It was and still is energy that makes my heart sing. When we went to the new moon drumming that evening, I was shown a picture of the ceiling of the cave taken by one of the participants, as he was the last to leave the cave. There was a very large blue orb in the center of the ceiling. Pure love and light was anchored in and the portal is open. Thank you again for asking me to join you on this part of your destiny.

After sending the same accounting to Tyb, I closed by saying:

> As you have seen, I do want to be the caretaker of Anaya. Thank you from the bottom of my heart for making this possible.

Now that I knew Anaya and I were to work together, I wrote to Tyb explaining that work.

> I just completed a distance session using Anaya with a woman from the Netherlands. Historically, my body has shaken and the infinity breath has been labored. Today with Anaya there was none of that; the energy just flowed. I am going to get big biceps holding her. I am so grateful.

Tyb replied:

> Anaya-Ra is an incredible crystal, and I am happy you are the caretaker. Ra is a term of impeccability and honor that was used in Atlantis, sort of like Sri in Sanskrit. I say her/his because I think

Anaya-Ra is above gender, existing in the nonpolar, nongender zero-point of the unified crystalline field of Mer-Ki-Va. Anaya-Ra will download the form of energy needed, always to achieve zero-point balance, and of course that means the majority of energy brought in will be what we in dualistic terms think of as the divine feminine energy. Sounds like your trip to Shaman's Cave was amazing. I'd love to see photos. Metatron told me that Anaya-Ra as well as the meteorites and gems mentioned will be of great help to you. You are achieving the things you need to achieve, Metatron added, but these tools will help you interpret it—i.e., bring the accurate transduction and step-down of the experience in higher realms more accurately from the subconscious corridors of the higher self into clearer explanation in the lower frequencies of the conscious mind. It's like a transduction of digital back into analogue.

I replied:

Tyb, Anaya-Ra is so beautiful. Thank you for the expanded name. I will send photos of Shaman's Cave when the participants send them to me. They were mostly from Europe. To summarize, Raquel, CJ, and I bonded strongly. It was difficult to say good-bye. It is because of you, Tyb, so again I acknowledge you. I hope you truly know the value you bring to so many.

~ 21 ~

Pure Love of Source Is Who We Are

The time is now, the dawn of a new era, a time for the protective cover of the ancient wisdom to be removed. "The protective cover that you and others placed over both rocks is now to be removed. Those rocks were covered when humanity forgot how to love, and only pure love of Source can unlock and release." The unveiling began for me at Enchanted Rock. Recorded history in the memory of the cosmos was also to be changed. I was asked, "If one were to rewrite history based on the new age of love and compassion, what would it look like? You can do this, dear one. Open your heart to who you are."

> Are you interested in coming to San Antonio and doing sessions? You would love Enchanted Rock.
>
> After two months away, Tyb, I haven't been able to think of much but sitting in my red leather chair. I just asked and the answer came: yes, I would be pleased to come to San Antonio and on to Enchanted Rock in December. Please describe how you would like me to participate. The energies are pouring into me still, and I know I have expanded from my experiences in Bolivia. Marijon said that Enchanted Rock connected to El Fuerte in Bolivia. At El Fuerte, I was told that by connecting to those who had chosen to enter the inner earth tunnel, they now know that love is returning to earth, and it is safe to return.

Tyberonn had arranged at the request of Archangel Metatron for the Earth-Keeper group to gather in San Antonio and later in Fredericksburg,

Texas, for the "Return of the Heart of the Dove." I had told Tyb that I would be attending, but something else was brewing that I knew nothing about until it began to unfold. Later, I realized that (as is so often the case with magical events) it was a good thing I didn't know all the details from the beginning.

The unfolding of events began in the wee hours of the morning, with such an intensity that I had to turn the computer on and share my transmission with Tyb:

> Tyb, I had to get up, turn the computer on, and write in the hope that I will be able to sleep after sharing these new insights. We have not really talked about my adventures in Bolivia, but I think they are relevant to Enchanted Rock. The best way I can summarize is to say that while in Bolivia, Marijon had a knowing and would turn to me and tell me to sit there or go there and tone. On doing so, a trance came over me. Sometimes it was gentle, and other times it was very dramatic, with voices in other languages pouring out of me and hands pointing in a very demanding way. Milton would distract the guide with conversation while these magical moments unfolded. I tell you this now because I am feeling bonded tonight to Enchanted Rock. In El Fuerte, the beings felt the love I brought down to the earth plane from the crystalline grid and knew that it was safe to return. There is some similarity at Enchanted Rock, but I think this time it is about information. Marijon believes there is a hall of records that is alive in Enchanted Rock, similar to that below the Sphinx in Egypt. What came to me tonight is that bringing the Christ-consciousness frequencies of love to Enchanted Rock will unlock those records, making the information available to humanity. I feel that I am to be a part of that. I am writing because I feel that there will be a very strong tug at me at some point, and that I will express that tug in some as yet unknown way. It is so much more comfortable as a "human" to be alone or with one or two who understand. That might not necessarily be the case.

Please check with Archangel Metatron. I don't want this to be about me.

I later wrote:

Tyb, While having coffee this morning and sitting in my red leather chair, the rest came in. I am to precede you and bring in the Christ-consciousness frequencies to unlock the veil that covers the knowledge hidden in the pink granite of Enchanted Rock. Then I am to join you and the others in ceremony to release and expand that knowledge throughout the planet in celebration. My work is not to be public. You caught me off guard in the Grand Tetons, but since I thought, "noon in Yellowstone," there was no resistance. At the time, I didn't know the true spot was Cathedral Mountain. Now I do know, and I can feel resistance when I think of many people watching. It is similar to what unfolded at the Toltec Mounds; there, too, I felt the need to first go alone before going with the group. I brought in the frequencies and was greeted warmly by the star beings from many nations. As I mentioned, apparently I had promised that I would return on the full moon of the ninth month of the ninth year, 2009. I hope this feels comfortable to you.

Tyb replied:

You realize you have the ability to code any place on the planet without your physical body being present. The other night when you "bonded" with Enchanted Rock, you were definitely in its energy. There are of course advantages to being there physically, but it is not essential. In time you will learn how to be lucid in dream state and navigate consciously, but you can and do have extraordinary abilities for astral travel. The 144 phi Vogel crystal will help in this too. Once you have the time, you can work on fine-tuning astral travel.

That morning I just happened to pick up an article Tyberonn had written about Enchanted Rock in which he mentioned Windsong, the guardian of the rock. Who better to ask for clarity on why I was to do ceremony at Enchanted Rock.

Holy Hall of Records to Be Opened–11/10/09

Nina: To Windsong, the indigenous holy man, guardian of the rock, Enchanted Rock, Fredericksburg. Am I to do ceremony at Enchanted Rock in December? Is there a hall of records in Enchanted Rock similar to that below the Sphinx in Egypt? Please tell me anything else I need to know and if I may share this information.

Dearest one, we have waited a long, long time to hear those words. Do you remember? You were with us as we veiled the vital information in this cathedral of pink granite. Do you remember? You will, dear one, as you stand with me on the central dome of Enchanted Rock at sunrise on December 10, 2009. Again you will hear the words of praise and adulation from all the sacred beings, who have been waiting for your promised return. For you carry the Christ-consciousness codes, the highest frequency of divine love, which can unlock this holy hall of records. It is to be done as the light of the sun shines on the new day. You are granted the permission you request from me, Windsong, guardian of the rock. Others will come who know they are to join us. They will come by means of their spirit's desire, joining us in the etheric with the enormous love that they radiate. That love will surround us as the wind is called in, as the songs are sung. The brilliance of this long anticipated moment will dazzle the universe. Love divine will free the records for all of humanity to receive. Yes, share this critically important information!

With my deep love,
Windsong, guardian of the rock via Anaya-Ra

How exactly does one "unlock a holy hall of records"? I no longer had the thought "why me?" My thoughts were like an organic flow now. I didn't necessarily have the answer, but I had S.T.A.R., and the universe had gifted me with another tool, which had become a part of me and of all my work, my 144-facet phi Vogel crystal.

About an hour after hearing from Windsong, inner voices said that the ceremony on December 10 would bring in the love vibration and that the gathering at Enchanted Rock by the Earth-Keepers on Monday, December 14, would signal the release of the knowledge contained in the rock's inner core. It was to be a two-part process.

Tyb wrote me this same day and asked me to be a speaker at the conference. I accepted.

On Monday, December 7, the day before I was to take off for the two-day drive to Fredericksburg, the location of Enchanted Rock, I had a prearranged remote session with Raquel (www.raquelspencer.com), a multidimensional energy specialist and intuitive, who is known by Archangel Metatron as the master healer of cellular light and the master healer in the Temple of One. The Cosmic Council of Light told me that Raquel had a profound knowledge of cosmic anatomy. The timing of this session seemed divinely coordinated to occur just before my trip to Enchanted Rock. What Raquel saw were blocks made up of distorted fire discs in my throat, which were removed and replaced to allow for more perfected sound. She identified synapse connections in my brain that were very gradually altered over a seventy-two-hour period, so as not to "put me down for three days." The work done on my new eyes allowed me to see all aspects of reality instead of blocking out the negative. The sight would be as an observer, not a participant.

In the days following my session with Raquel, I experienced cold-like symptoms—with congestion in my head and throat, clearing—and eventual coughing. I felt dizzy for several days Intuitively, I knew that I was not sick, but was detoxing and would be fine by the time I was to chant during ceremony at Enchanted Rock. I left Santa Fe on Tuesday to give myself time enough for a relaxed journey to my destination. I had learned to take better care of myself from Archangel Metatron, who cautioned me to not overdo, because of my physical age and the intensity of the work.

Five inches of snow already covered the ground as I pulled out of my garage. Near my house, a car was backing down the hill it couldn't climb. I did the same, to allow the retreating car room to maneuver. I knew I was intended to be in Texas and that the snow would not stop me, so up the hill I went with ease. Driving through Cline's Corner, New Mexico, was a different matter. It was not the road that was a challenge, but the wind. Snow blew across the road so fiercely that I was encompassed in a wall of white, unable at times to see the road or any car that might be in front of me. The drive became at this point slow and cautious. The farther south I got, the clearer the conditions became, and I eventually sailed down the road to my first stop, Carlsbad. At 4:00 a.m. on Wednesday, December 9, in the Comfort Inn, I wrote in my journal to the guardians of Enchanted Rock and El Fuerte in Samaipata, Bolivia, asking if the work I was to do would be connected by means of harmonic oscillation. The answer was, "Yes."

Is There a Connection between Enchanted Rock and El Fuerte in Bolivia?–12/9/09

Nina: To Windsong, guardian of Enchanted Rock and to the guardian(s) of El Fuerte in Samaipata, Bolivia, when I do ceremony in Fredericksburg, on top of Enchanted Rock, is there a connection to El Fuerte? Is there anything else I should know?

Beloved one, we greet you with such warmth and appreciation that you have heard our call to you in the early hours of your morning. Yes, is the answer! We are connected in soul, in form, and in purpose. You, dear one, have been to both sacred cosmic sites in your human past and have and will return again. The protective cover that you and others placed over both rocks is now to be removed. As you work on Enchanted Rock, you will be etherically working on El Fuerte, for El Fuerte knows you, knows your heart, knows the perfection of your desire. When you connected to the beings at El Fuerte and they felt the pure love of Source flowing through you, this was the moment you were granted permission to open the hall of records that lies within the granite rock covering both repositories of knowledge and ancient wisdom. They were covered when humanity forgot how to love, as Archangel Raphael has told you. You will be working simultaneously in Texas and in Samaipata for the benefit of humanity, who is beginning to remember that love, pure love of Source, is who they are and what they are to share with one another. This is the dawn of a new era, dear one: a time of joy, of peace, of harmony, of ease and grace.

You came to planet earth to upshift and recalibrate the frequency of love on the planet and in the DNA and sacred heart of humanity. It is fitting and right that you bring the key to the opening of these halls of records, for only pure love of Source can unlock and release them. Yes, it is Anaya-Ra (huge 144-facet phi Vogel crystal) who came to you for this explicit purpose, to amplify the love frequency that flows through you to ignite the granite, the rock, in such a way that the flow of knowledge will be released. You are indeed to chant. The corrections in your throat are complete and the tones will strike the rock with just the correct sounds, vibrations, and frequencies. The triad (love, light, and purity) contains this vital work, and we thank you from the supreme beings of the cosmos who are supporting you, watching you, and guarding you. You have no need to fear. You are protected by the radiant love vibration, through which no incompatible energies can penetrate. As you stand, as you walk, this radiance surrounds you, for your higher self commands this to be so, and we, dear one, join you in that command. The work you are here to perform is vital to planet earth, and thus this new emerald shield surrounds you. Know that there is more to be done, more veils to be removed—that this is a beginning, that your work is beginning. We will be with you to nudge you and to speak to you, so that your inner knowing will release the information that you need at just the right time to do the command of your higher self, who knows who you are and why you are here. This work is indeed all about love, the highest vibration frequency of the divine feminine, love of Christos energy or divine essence. You carry these codes now, and you are transferring them to the 144,000, who will indeed transfer that frequency to others, for love is returning to the earth, and the knowledge and ancient wisdom returns.

With our deep love,
The guardians of the rocks via Anaya-Ra

The old limestone and wood bed-and-breakfast in Fredericksburg was waiting for me as I ended my trip from Santa Fe. I wearily wandered into my room and lay down. It soon became clear that rest was not possible until a connection with Enchanted Rock (ER) had been made, in preparation for the next day's sunrise ceremony on the dome.

No one answered at the state park when I called to see how early one could enter, so I got back in my car and headed twenty miles out of town. The hill country in this part of Texas is serene with a gentle energy that emanates from the Edwards Aquifers in the Hydro Lay Lines. After a short while, I turned a corner and there it was: Enchanted Rock. Oh my, how steep it was. I was to climb to the dome by myself in the limited light of the early morning sunrise. Ah my, but I had Windsong to escort me:

> Boy, Tyb, ER is tall! I weighed the crystals and their cases, and I will be carrying seven pounds up to the top tomorrow. But you said Windsong is there to help.

Tyb replied:

> Are you going to ER alone? Better if you had someone to accompany you. It is a steep, steep walk in places, walkable, but can be tough in terms of stamina and physical exertion and can be slippery when you are carrying a pack. You should take at least one water bottle.

I answered:

> Tyb, Yes I am alone. I will go slowly and carry a water bottle with me. If I am to do this, I am sure the way will appear. I will sit down if I need to and inch my way up. I was told going down is the most challenging. My goal is sunrise before the park opens at 8:00 a.m. The guard told me that would be okay. Just have to put my senior citizen payment of three dollars in an envelope. El Fuerte was a challenge, but I walked in the guide's foot trail, as if he was clearing an energetic path for me. So up and down and up I went with relative ease. Windsong might do the same thing for me. I will ask. I will leave here before noon, I suspect. I know you have a lot to do. It will all fall in place, as it is supposed to. I am very calm.

Early to bed and early to rise. When I got in my car the morning of the tenth of December, the clock said 5:00 a.m. Darn, the bed would have been nice for another hour, but then I remembered that I was not in New Mexico but in Texas, where the time was 6:00 a.m. Upon arrival at the closed registration office, I found the envelope that had been described yesterday by the state park guard with whom I had spoken. I put three dollars in the envelope in the appropriate slot, hung the receipt on my windshield, and drove down to the parking lot to await the sunrise. My calculations were incorrect, or perhaps it was the time change between states. The sun was visible at 7:00, not 6:30 as I had projected. I got out and loaded myself with water and seven pounds of crystals in leather carrying cases to protect them. I did not have on enough clothes to keep me warm in the early morning temperature. No matter, off I went.

I stumbled around in the dark, unable to find the trail entrance. Finally, I went over the cement block bridge and on to the summit. The dirt path soon turned into granite rock with just enough incline to let me walk at a rather steady pace. Periodic stops allowed me to catch my breath while viewing the sun as it climbed in the east. I was amazed at how I just seemed to plow ahead, up and up the granite wall of this batholith. Then the moment came when I stopped, looked up, and declared, "I will not make it to the top. This will have to do." I backed down a bit and found a somewhat flat space where I could sit down. As I started to unpack, the wind began to blow and the temperature was so cold that I felt a twinge of fear. Worried that my precious Vogel crystals might roll down the hill, I placed the infinity seal under me, with the crystals representing pure love and light around me. Then out came Anaya-Ra, the crystal of infinity consciousness. I connected to the rock, thanked the guardians of both rocks, and began to etherically open the pink granite.

On completion, I held the huge crystal above my head and began an infinity breath to bring in the highest frequency of pure love of Source, down through the crystal into my body and down into the core of Enchanted Rock. When I was complete, I didn't close the vortex I had opened. The frequency was to pour in, I had been told. This allowed the love vibration to gently widen the hole until the rock felt safe and would allow for a release of the records it contained.

I felt as if the cold air was distracting me from the perfection I wished for during my ceremony. The cold won. After packing up everything in somewhat of a hurry, it was time for the descent. I conducted most of the

Enchanted Rock.

journey on my fanny instead of my feet. Being alone and a bit overcome by vertigo, this seemed like the wisest means of travel. My feet then found the dirt path, and I saw my car in front of me. I took one picture to record this amazing venture. Then, shivering on a park bench, I opened my journal and asked the guardians if we were complete. "Yes, but the return on Monday will be the final release." Certainly reclimbing Enchanted Rock would not be my job when the group returned on Monday! Surely, that was the gift of the others in the group.

A Gradual Process That Began This Morning–12/10/09

Nina: To the guardians of the rocks (hands shaking from the cold), are we complete with the opening of the hall of records?

Most definitely, dear one. Do you see the light pouring into the opening you made. This radiance dazzles all who are present. The hole is indeed expanding for the frequency and vibration of the Christos energy is so profound that as it enters, the walls of the granite gently recess. This will continue until you return on Monday. Pure love of Source will pour in. The result is that the rocks feel that love and, over time, begin to accept the safety that provides allowing for a release. It is a gradual process that began this morning.

With our deep love,

The guardians of the rocks via Anaya-Ra

The second day of the conference, 12/12/09, was a day of numerical significance. It was the second date for the frequencial portals of the Triad Stargates, the first being 11/11/09, and the last winter solstice. Early in the morning it came to me that the work at Enchanted Rock was not just for Enchanted Rock and El Fuerte in Bolivia, but for all the batholiths on the planet. I also learned that the participants who would gather on Monday for the second phase of the ceremony had placed the veil over the encapsulated knowledge with me in various locations around the earth. Since I was to be a speaker, I would have an opportunity to share this information.

The next day, Sunday, the schedule was changed, since Tyb wanted to take the group to Comal Springs, the source of the springs in New Braunfels, where the plasma and negative ion atmosphere is extremely vital. Tyb had already channeled Archangel Metatron for the group, so I would be the only remaining speaker, and my talk would happen in Founder's Park under Founder's Tree, a sentient being with an enormous consciousness.

After bathing or foot soaking in the river, we all gathered around the famous tree in Founder's Park. I sat on the stone wall directly in front of the tree trunk, which was so ancient that its heavy branches had to be propped up with columns of concrete. I had my suitcase, which contained my journal and crystals, by my side. CJ, who had intuitively felt the need to ground me, sat next to me as a protective force. She kept asking me how I was, knowing that the emotions and intensity of this building event were taking its toll on me. The talk began when Tyb spoke about the energy of the tree and the park, in terms not only of geology but also of botany. He encouraged all to gather in a semicircle facing me, some on the ground, some standing, and others on the stone wall.

I began by sharing my San Antonio story of becoming a receiver and transmitter in St. Fernando Cathedral two years before. I knew then, for the first time, that I was a receiver and transmitter of divine energy, which on that occasion, was going to those at the receiving end of the camera.

As I was speaking in Founder's Park, the late afternoon sun found an opening in the trees and cast its radiant beams directly into my eyes, causing me to shut them as I continued to speak. I was told later that it was as if I had a spotlight on me, with the sun illuminating my face and the diamonds in my ears and around my neck. I heard someone say, as I was speaking, that the animal kingdom was gathering as well.

When I finished speaking, both the sunlight and the animals departed. I shared with those who were to go to the ceremony at Enchanted Rock that I had been told the energies of tomorrow's ceremony would extend to all the batholiths on the planet, by means of harmonic oscillation, and that each person who would attend had participated eons ago in veiling the ancient wisdom that was contained in the rocks. It was the return of the love vibration that would allow the release: the love frequency that had been streaming into the rocks since last Thursday when the initial ceremony had taken place at sunrise.

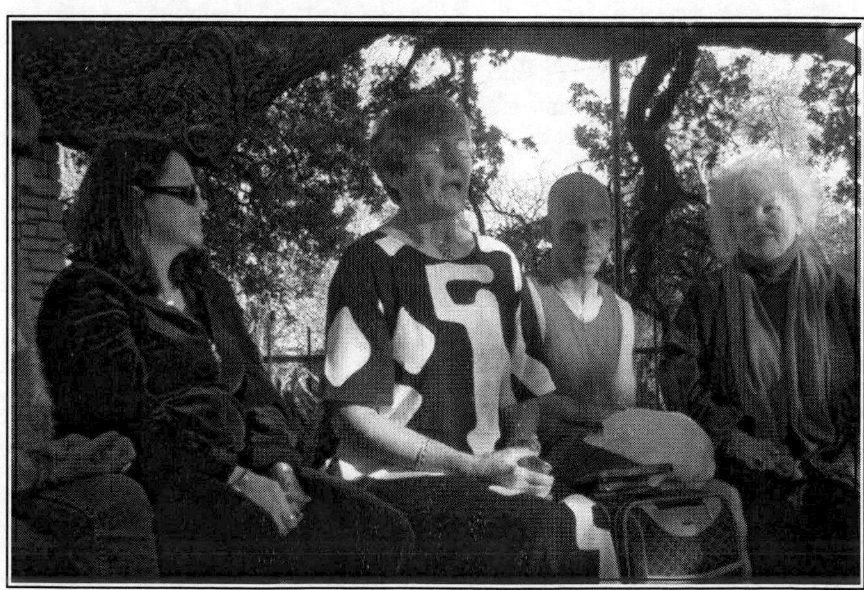

CJ, Nina, Matthew, and Marilyn at Founder's Park.

The next morning, the group gathered in the Hilton lobby for an 8:30 a.m. departure. CJ climbed aboard the bus and asked to sit next to me. Her presence was comforting, since I didn't have the vitality to engage in conversation with someone I didn't know well. CJ was easy to be with, but as soon as she asked me how I was, the tears began to well up in my eyes and flow down my cheeks. I wasn't sure that it was about anything in particular—just exhaustion and anticipation. It was the not knowing what was to transpire that gave me anxiety, and being in the presence of a group of people. Everyone was supportive, yet I would have preferred to be alone. I couldn't hide amongst a busload of people. On the other hand, it was wonderful being surrounded by people who wished me well.

As we descended from the bus in the parking lot of Enchanted Rock, Nevin, a member of the group, asked if he could escort me up the rock. Instead of being stubbornly independent, I accepted. What a difference his support made in the ease with which I moved along the steep pink granite. The group climbed together, stopping at just the right spots to regain our breath. I kept looking for the place where I had done ceremony. When I thought I had found it, there was more rock to climb. For some reason, the top of the rock didn't seem as dangerously steep as it had when I had been by myself early Thursday morning. And then, holding Nevin's hand, I was on the top. It was truly time to rest. Many of us spread out on the summit, with sweaters under our heads, using the granite as a bed. We soaked up the warmth of the sun and allowed our muscles to relax after the intense climb. I placed my Vogel crystals of pure love and light around me with Anaya-Ra on my chest; I didn't think too much about what was to transpire, for I really wasn't sure.

Tyb called us all to gather in a seated circle around what he believed to be the highest point on the rock. There had been a geological brass marker in the rock, which apparently had been removed, so we just guessed that was the one. I was facing northeast, for no reason in particular, and the others filled in the circle. CJ told me later that she had heard, with her inner hearing, "Go find Nina." So there she was again, sitting next to me—very much my protector. Tyb began the ceremony.

Behind me, there was a screeching sound, like the discordant one I remembered from the ceremony at Mount Magazine on 09-09-09. Yes, and it seemed to be the same woman making the sounds. I broke into Tyb's speaking and said, "I cannot do this with that interference!" Tyb said he agreed, and CJ jumped up in a flash to ask that her toning be postponed. The sounds stopped, but the woman chose to remain outside our circle even though she was part of our group. Archangel Metatron later said that the sounds had been unconsciously directed to interfere with the work that both Tyb and I were there to do, and that my auric field is particularly sensitive to the sound irritant. I was instructed how, in the future, to deflect incompatible energies.

The ceremony continued in peace and quiet. Tyb spoke of the Sirian ships that had gathered overhead, the underground base of the Sirians, and said that he and I were commanders of the Galactic Federation, which was also present. Next, he asked me to continue. It was then that my higher self took charge. Strong tones came out of my mouth, as they had at the Temple of the Moon on the Island of the Moon in Lake Titicaca the previous September in Bolivia. Then galactic sounds or words flowed out. It was as if I was thanking everyone present, for my hand gestured slowly around the circle in acknowledgment. I spoke to the rock with appreciation, then waved my large 144-facet phi Vogel crystal in a circle above my head to connect the sounds and ceremony to all the batholiths around the planet. The sounds, words, and actions were strong and intentional, as if I had known for a long time what they were to be, and now they were being spoken. Then Tyb invited each participant to tone, and our toning completed the ceremony.

We then stood around a small tree, which was miraculously growing on the top of the rock. We sang thanks to it; asked it to stand in for the guardian of the rock, Windsong; and then sang in gratitude and appreciation. Tyb came over and asked me if I felt complete. "Oh, yes!" I said. Everything had unfolded in a manner even fuller and richer than I had ever expected. Having the group participate and witness was so perfect. After more than a month of knowing I was to do ceremony on top of

Enchanted Rock, it was complete. How wonderful I felt. But then the fatigue set in as I released all the accumulated emotions of the month. I needed days and days of rest.

When I returned to the hotel from Enchanted Rock and said goodbye to all who had participated, I asked what tomorrow was to look like. The answer was, "the Alamo." Rainy weather was forecasted, and I knew it wasn't necessary for me to be physically at the Alamo, and that the frequency could be upshifted from the hotel room. As for the core reason, I knew it had to be more than to focus on the perspective of the Texans, who so heroically gave their lives at the Alamo. The Mexicans under Santa Ana had their story, as well. I wondered if there was a cosmic version I was to focus on.

The Alamo, San Antonio, Texas–12/15/09

Nina: To my higher self, am I to do ceremony today while in San Antonio, Texas? Is the reason more far-reaching than the history and legends of the Alamo? Please tell me what I am to know on a deep, more cosmic level. With great appreciation.

War and aggression, defense, sacrifice, loyalty, and so many other concepts are the topics about which we wish to speak. Yes, we have called you to action, to duty this day—just as the defenders of the Alamo were called to duty on that fateful day. You have said yes, as they did and even as Santa Ana's army did. We are talking, therefore, about courage and commitment. Each participant had his own reason for being present—an internal calling, a fear of command, a duty, a loyalty, a belief, whatever it was that gave him the fortitude to do his duty. There were noble intentions on both sides. Having said that, it is the manner in which each side felt obliged to execute these convictions that is the point of this message. Conflict versus compassion is the core of all that transpired. If one were to rewrite history based on the new age of love and compassion, what would it look like? That is the work we ask you to do this morning—to literally change recorded history in the memory of the cosmos—to remove hate, anger, aggression, dominance, and all the other incompatible energies to the supreme divine love of Source. You can do this, dear one. Open your heart to who you are.

With our deep love,
All who love you deeply via Anaya-Ra

After receiving the message that I was to literally "change recorded history in the memory of the cosmos," I placed the infinity seal on the floor of my hotel room, next to the desk. I moved two chairs aside and placed the three Vogel crystals representing pure love and light in the triangle within the seal. I tore a local brochure to capture just the words "The Alamo" and put them in the center of the seal. I allowed the energies to combine while I lay on the bed with my 144-facet phi Vogel crystal on my chest. There was never fear that what was asked could not be done, but rather a knowing that it was possible. After a certain point, inner voices said, "We are ready." I got up and went to the site in my hotel room designated for the ceremony. My crystal was pointed at the words "The Alamo," and I began focused breathing to connect, while I walked slowly around the geometry of the seal. Then I sat in one of the two chairs to continue the breath.

When I knew that the Alamo and I were connected energetically, I began to open the etheric site using the infinity breath. After eight counterclockwise rotations, I pointed the huge phi Vogel crystal above my head, continuing the infinity breath and allowing the highest frequencies of love vibration to pour down into my crown chakra, to my root chakra, and back to my heart chakra. With my being connected to the Alamo, the vibration that was entering me also flowed into the etheric sacred heart of the Alamo. I then pointed my crystal to the words "The Alamo" and began closure. On completion, I ran my crystal from the top of my head to the floor to disconnect from the energy of the Alamo. With several infinity breaths into the core of the earth, I grounded myself, followed by the unique toning sounds suited to this experience. I found that both my hands went up and began forming figure eights on each side of my body for several rotations. Then we were complete. I left the crystals in place, pointing toward the words "The Alamo" for about an hour, as the Christos energy poured in, my duty complete.

I sent this account to Cindy in Houston, who replied:

> Awesome! The Alamo is one big honking portal! That is what the fight was about. My friend and I did work on the grounds and inside the Alamo itself. So glad attention is once again on this enormous vortex.

Another friend replied:

> Thank you for sharing this monumental moment with me. This healing I felt went to all the battlegrounds around the world. Peace to all.

~ 22 ~

Recognize and Acknowledge Who You Are

I was told by my voices to recognize and acknowledge who I am. To recognize not just who I am but who we are is the importance of all that I have written. At the end of this amazing journey, I came to understand, with crystalline clarity, that we, as creator beings, are to raise our frequency in order to create heaven on earth, merging our hearts and souls as the true aspect of Christ-consciousness, the love, that is returning to planet earth. To share that message, a book had to be written.

Once again Archangel Metatron nudged Tyb to move me further along on my magical journey. Another invitation was extended to me.

> Nina, Can you arrange a photo of yourself with Anaya-Ra (my master crystal) and send it to me? Would you like to speak for thirty minutes in the blue pyramid in Galveston on the spring equinox in 2010?

I replied to Tyb that I didn't know what I would talk about. Then—what a surprise—Tyb sent an email to thousands of people around the planet announcing my cosmic name, that I was an ascended master, and that I would conduct an upcoming ceremony the night of March 20, 2010, spring equinox, in the blue pyramid to usher in the second phase of the cosmic trigger. Oh, my gosh! I'm not doing this alone! Then that evening, I heard myself speak with the dolphins in conversation. I imagine they were preparing me for this new assignment.

A few days later on winter solstice, December, 21, 2009—the final sequential portal of the triad stargates, which I would celebrate with James and friends at Stardreaming—Tyb called to tell me Archangel Metatron had suggested I bring in a white wolf totem for protection. He told me that when speaking in Founder's Park, my aura extended the width of Founder's Tree and beyond. Then on top of Enchanted Rock, I had opened totally as a pure love aspect. He told me that because I vibrate so fast, I needed a shield for my work. The white wolf is a totem, an angel, an enormous energy thought form, a guardian being. It is four times the size of a regular wolf, but when necessary, I could make it smaller. The wolf totem would deflect incompatible energies. Tyb told me I would see it in time and suggested that I buy a totem white wolf as a reminder. My totem would act as a mother wolf protecting her young. I was also told that if the sounds on Enchanted Rock and at Mount Magazine weren't attacking me, someone or something else would, which is why I needed to bring in a white wolf totem for my protection.

> Tyb, I am so grateful that you have written *Metatron Speaks* and said yes to its transmission. You are so filled with knowledge that no matter how often you go before a gathering of people it cannot all come out in one weekend. The book flows sequentially and fills in all the gaps that one might miss. I understand so much better what I am doing now. The description of the crystalline grid gives me such clarity. I am able to put pieces together of my experience as a result of this book. Last night, at 1:00 a.m., I received the answer to why I went to Bolivia, and what is the work I am to do on Christmas Day. In summary, just as harmonic oscillation connected Enchanted Rock to all the batholiths on the planet, so my work in the *apus*, earth tunnels, caverns, waterways, labyrinths, calderas, mounds, cathedrals, etc., has been connected to all other similar frequencies. By bringing in the love vibration, I am unveiling, or raising, the frequency of that specific planetary node or human DNA to that of the crystalline grid, clear crystalline vibration, so that humanity can create responsibly. Tomorrow, Christmas Day, with permission from my daughter's higher self

I will do ceremony to bring in this frequency, which will oscillate with the frequency of others of similar vibration, Christian and non-Christian. The pure love and light, the clear alignment of matter, and the unveiling will allow a vibration and expansion on a higher level on the spiral of life.

Thank you so much for your kind words, Nina. They are most appreciated and taken to heart. I think grids are so often misunderstood. Yes, what you do is very, very important for the planetary ascension, both for humanity and the earth and grid system. Metatron has emphasized the importance of your mission many times to me. Wishing you a wonderful Christmas and New Year's! Love and light.

I knew I was to do a ceremony on Christmas morning, but the details hadn't yet come through. In the early hours of Christmas Eve, I was sitting in my red leather chair after a beautiful day of enjoying a fire, knowing that the ground was covered with new snow, and working on my book. These are the notes I wrote to capture my feelings about the ceremony I had been called to do Christmas Day: "I feel as if all the beings in the cosmos are here watching me. Their love is palpable. Ralph, my white wolf totem, is by my side as I sit in my red leather chair. I am feeling so honored."

I slept well, and enjoyed not being awakened at 1:00 a.m. or 2:00 a.m. with voices telling me more details. On Christmas morning, I knew that I was to pull out my journal to learn more about the morning's ceremony.

Today It Begins—12/25/09

Today it begins, dear one, the opening, the merging of heart and soul, as you just read from the Akashic record[1] so beautifully channeled. The merging of the two is the true aspect of Christ-consciousness. This event has been long awaited with pockets of it appearing throughout recorded history, but because of ego, greed, pride, corruption, and the many aspects of conflict and control, the frequency has been suppressed so that its counterenergy could emerge.

Your planet earth is striving for, hungry for, balance. This is the greatest aspect of the ascension: balance, unity, the zero-point field, where all and none coexist, where there is not the removal of one vibration being replaced by the other, but the blending of both into their original form of perfection and unity. You ask about your call today to do ceremony, as you call it. This is why you are on the planet, Anaya-Ra, Crystal Singer of the divine energy of the collective. You are very much a vital force of the Christ-consciousness collective of master beings, who have been on earth many times for the specific purpose of bringing the energetics, the frequency, to humanity and all sentient matter. This moment is unusually different, for it resides in this life expression of the time of the anticipated ascension, and you are a primary component of the return of love to the planet. You found the stone, the true beginning of this journey of receiving and transmitting the Christ-consciousness frequency. Ask now in silence, in prayer, who is to stand for humanity in the frequency, the vibration, of the higher self, knowing of divine love. You will find the answer, dear one. Perhaps it is you or your daughter. We are all one.

With our deep love,
The Christ-consciousness Collective via Anaya-Ra

As I was about to go downstairs to meditate on the question "Who will stand for humanity, me or my daughter?" I heard the etheric, telepathic voice of my daughter saying, "I would like to do it for you, Mother." Tears filled my eyes as this message came through.

After walking in the very cold, crisp air, taking a bath in essential oils, and dressing for Christmas in my long black pleated skirt and sequined shirt, I knew I was ready to begin and was told, "We're ready." The grid had been in position all night, so all I had to do was take a seat. I picked up each crystal, asked permission, and thanked it. While holding Anaya-Ra, my very large 144-facet phi Vogel crystal, I heard words of appreciation and knew that all the master beings had gathered. I was not working alone. Each breath, each positioning of the crystals was in consort with the other master beings of the Christ-consciousness collective.

I turned my attention to my daughter's higher self asking permission to hold her etheric hands and to point Anaya-Ra at her etheric heart.

I picked up the surrogate crystal ball from the center of the grid and placed it on my lap. I began the infinity breath in order to bond our two energetic fields. Then I held my large crystal out in front of me toward my daughter's sacred heart and, with the infinity breath, rotated it eight times counterclockwise to open. I held the crystal above my head and again, with the same breath, reached up beyond the twelfth dimension where pure love and light exist, connected, and began to draw that energy down. Knowing that the frequency had passed through me into my daughter's sacred heart, I rotated Anaya-Ra eight times in the clockwise direction to close.

Once complete, I raised the crystal above my head and ran it down to the earth to disconnect. With six deep breaths into the core of the earth, I grounded myself and opened my mouth to allow the appropriate tones to seal the transfer. The rhythmic, gentle, and repetitive sounds were followed by cosmic words and arms gesturing in a circle above my head toward my daughter and all of humanity, as a way of acknowledging the divine in what had just transpired. I then placed my hands together at my heart and bowed to my daughter, who, along with her brothers, is the light of my life.

I was amazed at how easily the enormous energy flowed, on this occasion, and was told that the harmonious flow came from the collective working together that allowed for this particularly gentle transmission. I rose from my chair and went into the bathroom to get a tissue, and suddenly saw myself in the mirror. There were huge black streaks running down my cheeks from the kind of mascara that was not meant to be used when one cries. I went downstairs and turned on Christmas music, gathered the packages that had been sent to me, and placed them by the red leather chair. Walking to the kitchen to boil water for some tea, I noticed the sun pouring through the windows was casting light on the myriad sequins on my shirt, beaming colors all over the house. It was as if the whole house and all within were celebrating, joyous, delighted. "We are indeed," I was to write. "The world rejoices at this marvelous event in human history. And so it is."

My red leather chair.

~ 23 ~

Does All of This Matter?

Why does any of this matter? I now know the answer. It matters because it reveals the wisdom I asked for from the whales and the dolphins while sitting on the bench in Del Mar, California, three years ago. The stone that I held next to my heart and brought back to Stardreaming ended up being a focal point in my painting and in James's children's book and became my philosopher's stone, which I carry in my heart.

The wisdom I have learned by means of my alchemical journey is that we were created in the image of the Creator to be creators. We have been creating as mortals in the third dimension of duality, we are more than that. We are divine creators capable of creating heaven on earth. The ancient wisdom of who we are and why we are here is returning to planet earth. With the return of the frequency of pure love and light, we are raising our frequency and therefore raising the frequency of our manifestations.

With a higher frequency of pure love and light, we begin to live in two dimensions simultaneously. We move beyond mortality to combine our divinity into all that we are. We move beyond duality to unity: a state of zero-point, a state of perfection. Then, as creators working in both dimensions simultaneously, in unity, our intentions have a higher frequency.

When we ultimately surrender our intentions—created in pure love and light—into the space of infinity and trust that there the laws of attraction and magnetism reign, we can allow the perfection of Source. We can receive with gratitude and appreciation what we have manifested in the frequency of pure love and light, no longer in distortion or in duality, S.T.A.R.

We, therefore, are creating heaven on earth, manifesting by means of pure love and light in two dimensions simultaneously: divinity and humanity. This is the ascension. This is my truth, my beach stone, my philosopher's stone. "I am the ambassador of light, who now carries the stone of infinite light in my breast."[1] This is who we are. This is why we are here, to create—in the image of the Creator—heaven on earth. This is who we are, why we are here, and the work we are here to do.

We are perfection seeking the expression of perfection.
We are here to create heaven on earth.
We do so by means of pure love and light.
With an upshift of the vibratory note of humanity,
we manifest heaven on earth,
the ascension of the planet and humanity.

Epilogue

A few days ago, James asked, "How do you feel about all that has transpired?" I find it easy to hide my feelings, to hide behind journal entries and accounts of events, but I realize that sharing my feelings is the next step in my growth. I need to share how I feel openly to all who are experiencing their own journey of stretching into a new ascension skin. The answer is that I feel at peace and full. I have been seeking for so long to understand why I am here, and now I know. I don't have to ask another person or read another book. I don't have to go to a seminar or find a guru. I am the source of all of my answers. All I have to do is ask my higher self.

There were times in this part of my journey—for I am sure there is more to come—that I said to James, "I am so glad you are here, so that I can tell someone about the miracles that are happening in my life." I could not have traveled the path alone. I needed people to tell me, "It is OK. Go with the flow." I know I fought back, just as I did that night when Rex heard me screaming and banging on the chair. The simple route would have been easier.

Then there was the day that James suggested that it was time to "step out of the closet." That was difficult. (Ah, tears come to my eyes as I write those words.) I did it awkwardly. I upset many with my clumsy message. I didn't have the experience to explain what it was that I was feeling and knowing, so I upset and puzzled people by my new vocabulary. And I was puzzled as well.

The words from Dr. Norma Milanovich were so foreign to me. I listened to the tape repeatedly, trying to comprehend and determine what her words truly meant for me. I could have easily ignored statements such as, "You are to receive the Christ-consciousness codes from Sananda over the next several days of time." But I chose to accept and allow the flow, for I surely had no idea what to make of any of it. I jumped in with both feet as if it were just another new experience. I had no idea until months later that the work with Sananda was the precursor to that with Archangel Metatron and with the Cosmic Council of Light several months later. That was probably a good thing!

Then there was Archangel Michael, through Ronna Herman, telling me I was a crystal singer in Atlantis and so much more. I read that channel several times before I even realized that it was personally intended for me. So what did all of that mean and what was I to do with it? Nothing, was the answer. Again it was somebody else's information until it integrated into me and my experience and knowing. So I stayed quiet, until that time came.

Next there was the message from Saint Germain: "You are to ignite an electromagnetic supertunnel in Wyoming over summer solstice." There was a point where I just wanted to run away. That was the day Marijon intuitively sensed that I was in trouble and called me. (Ah, more tears as I write.) Why me? I like sitting in my red leather chair. Feelings are so difficult to write about. They make you so vulnerable.

So what about Archangel Metatron's information that Tyberonn shared with me? That was the biggest shock of all. I remember when Tyb greeted me at the breakfast table in Jackson Hole and said, indirectly, "I know who you are." I had to leave him and go back to my table where I felt safe, to get my breath. It was too much! I just wanted to be alone in Yellowstone National Park and sing my mantra that Archangel Metatron had given me.

And how did it feel to be in front of Cathedral Mountain with Tyb's Vogel crystal in my hand? I don't remember, is the answer. All I can say is that a tug in my heart told me what was happening was what was supposed to happen, and that is how it has continued, a tug that tells me I am to "be" or to "do." Waking up in the middle of the night with this tug, climbing on a steep ledge to get to a cave because of this tug, heading straight up a huge batholith at dawn, alone, because of this tug, daring to say that I had something to offer hundreds of people around the world—as I point a huge crystal at their sacred heart—because of this tug.

The tug is my higher self pulling this earthly physical being farther up the spiral of life, closer to zero-point, where I want and need to dwell. That is where my comfort is. It is a rapture of pure love and light that is impossible to describe (more tears). It is where I go after working with another and bringing in the highest frequency of the divine feminine of the Christ-consciousness codes. Our divinity is who we truly are; this is where humanity is going on the path of the ascension. We share the amazing experience of a spiritual being living as a human on this delicious journey, each in our own way, at our own pace, but ultimately we will return to our Adam/Eve Kadmon state of unity. The frequency of love is returning to planet earth so we can remember who we are, why we are here, and what work we are here to do. We need to find the philosopher's stone inside our sacred hearts, to raise our vibratory note, and to find our divinity and oneness with all that is, ultimately to allow us to manifest responsibly.

In the new year, I received a message from the Cosmic Council of Light telling me why I am working with the 144,000, who in turn will share the frequency of love with humanity. "The manifestations' glory is only possible with a very high love quotient. In order for the planet to balance—to be in unity and true harmony—the manifestation and creations of humanity have to raise in frequency. That can only occur when the frequency of their love raises. You understand now the greatest reason for the work that you are doing, dear one. With each one with whom you work, you are raising their frequency of manifestation."

Knowing this truth, I continue to allow the flow of the divine plan to course through my being and wonder, with fascination, "What's next?"

Glossary

12/21/12: The date the crystal network will be globalized. This winter solstice event, igniting the work begun on the twelve master Atlantean crystals and twelve golden sun discs initially activated on 01/01/01, will initiate the crystalline age, in which Mother Earth will increase her frequency and range of dimensionality, making higher dimensional realms available to humanity.

144: The number of facets in the geometric form of the crystalline grid; the square of 12, the sacred dimensional aspect of the expanded earth.

144,000: The number of lightworkers energetically anchoring the crystalline grid to the planet; master number of the ascension.

Adam/Eve Kadmon: The primary being of light who was created in the heavens; the nongendered image of God as expressed in humanity.

adamantine particles: A matrix of potential that precedes all energy mass; the body of God, God-consciousness particles; the irreducible, nonnegotiable, fundamental, and completely elemental particles of creation that bring divine will into manifest form; the building blocks of the universe, thought manifestation, and consciousness units; particles of light that pour forth from the heart center of the Creator in great streams of cosmic life force because of the heart center's never-ending desire to experience more of itself.

adoula: One who assists the soul of an unborn child to connect with the mother and father at the time of preconception or during early pregnancy.

ahkala: One heart; God's heart; the sacred heart.

airport (mesa) vortex: A landmark in Sedona, Arizona; the energy at this vortex enhances psychic abilities and expands spiritual consciousness.

Akash: The fifth element, ether; creative-consciousness units of life, also called adamantine particles.

Akashic record: A register of all past, present, future, and potential occurrences; a log that resides in the quantum field of human DNA.

alchemy: An ancient investigation of nature that combines chemistry, metallurgy, physics, medicine, astrology, semiotics, mysticism, and spiritualism into a force greater than the sum of the parts.

alchemy, new phase of: An era when it will be safe to embrace one's wholeness and declare one's divinity; the Age of the Golden Dolphin.

All That Is: The substance that underlies all of life's appearances and manifestations, including matter, antimatter, nonmatter, energy, nonenergy, thought, absence of thought, and all that exists beyond these.

alpha and omega: The first and the last.

Alpha Centauri: A member of the Council of Thirteen and a star in the constellation Centaurus.

ambassador of light: A representative of unconditional love from the star nations; one who, by being and exchanging energies, assists with the rapid spiritual awakening of another.

anatomy of a miracle: According to Jesus, the spontaneous appearance of that which was already given but unavailable until the moment one could receive.

Anaya-Ra: The name of Nina Brown's higher self; a Vogel phi crystal; a member of the Sirian triad.

ancient ones: The masters, angels, grandmothers, grandfathers, elementals, fairies, star beings of the light, and shining ones.

ancient wisdom: The knowledge of who we are as divine beings; the knowledge we forgot when we forgot we were divine beings.

angel: A multidimensional being of light; a conscious being of divine essence who exists at the key frequency for helping humanity to evolve and love; a nurturing guardian, messenger of God.

angel of change: One who brings light to others.

Aphrodite: Goddess of the heart and love.

appreciation: Expressed quality that feeds the beauty of our planet.

***apu*:** Inca word signifying god or supreme being; mountain deity; the most powerful of all nature spirits.

Araragat: A survivor of Atlantis who, along with Thoth and Ra, set up the unity-consciousness grid.

Archangel Gabriel: An archangel who announces changes in someone's consciousness.

Archangels Jophiel and Lady Constance: Archangels who embody wisdom and assist in receiving guidance; liaisons between God and humanity's divinity.

Archangel Metatron: A member of the angelic realm; a nurturing support for humanity; a lower vibration of Lord Metatron.

Archangel Michael: An archangel who slays the dragons of illusion.

Archangel Raphael: An archangel who counsels belief in one's power and miracles.

Archangel Uriel: The archangel of alchemy who proclaims love and self-forgiveness as catalysts to wholeness.

ascend: To move into the next lifetime without experiencing biological death; to void karma and achieve life's lessons. To transform the human body into crystal light for purposes of entering a new world where one taps into the bliss state of the higher dimensions; to participate in a natural and requisite expression of accelerating planetary consciousness.

ascended masters: Beings of enlightenment who have chosen to return to earth to assist humanity with their ascension by means of guidance and impeccability.

ascension: The planet's crystalline transition to a frequency of perfect order, or impeccability; a newly opened frequency doorway that can be passed through, depending on the individual's readiness, pure intent, and light quotient; a process that occurs one heart, one mind at a time.

Ashtar Command: An extraterrestrial government that closely monitors activities on earth and offers support to humanity.

aspects of God: The Tree of Life.

astral plane: A plane of existence—above the physical and below the angelic planes—populated by thought forms, spirits, and other immaterial beings.

astral travel: Means by which the astral body leaves the physical body.

Atla-Ra: A tall golden Atlantean race of scientist-priests characterized by very high frequencies of consciousness.

Atlantis: An ancient continent and civilization (200,000 BC–10,500 BC).

Atlantis, New: See New Atlantis.

auric field: The basic liquid, flexible, and colorful electromagnetic field of all biological life forms.

automatic writing: The act of taking pen to paper with a clear mind and allowing consciousness to flow.

awakening: The experience of aligning with the wholeness that is already ours.

axiatonal lines: Meridian lines (the equivalent of acupuncture lines) that connect with resonating star systems in the galactic body of creation. These lines are called axiatonal, in keeping with the law of harmonic oscillation, which states that when one tone vibrates, all similar tones will vibrate.

Aya: A powerful Atlantean crystal located in Santa Fe, New Mexico.

being of light: One who has walked the earth in final mastery, exuding an energy of peace and well-being, and in whose presence all of life responds and blossoms; one who effortlessly creates joy, the energy of light.

beingness: A state in which the mind communicates with everything that is real, or reality.

beings from inner earth: Life forms within the etheric realms of the earth, many of whom have been here far longer than humankind.

biodynamic farming: A method of organic farming that treats farms as unified and individual organisms.

Bioneers: A New Mexico–based nonprofit organization focused on resolving environmental and social problems.

blessing: God's love enfolding us.

Blue Lake: A sacred lake on Taos Pueblo in the Sangre de Cristo Mountains of New Mexico.

Blue Pyramid: One of the tri-pyramids at Moody Gardens in Galveston, Texas; a geometric crystalline light temple.

blue star kachina: Hopi name for the star Sirius.

blue star matrix: An array containing new light codes of innocent love, compassion, and knowledge of oneness with Source; cosmic consciousness connecting all nations, cultures, star systems, and planets.

blueprint: An original recorded plan.

body: A symbol of what we think we are.

book of records: A book containing all past, present, and future occurrences and potentialities to come; the Akashic records.

bridge between heaven and earth: Free will, the means by which humanity can create heaven on earth.

business principles: The guidelines upon which a business is created and managed.

Bwanazarias: Magician of many universes and royal guide to the stars.

caldera: A cauldron-like volcanic feature, usually formed by the collapse of land following a volcanic eruption.

Cathedral Group: A collection of most of the tallest mountains of the Teton Range, all of which are located in Grand Teton National Park in Wyoming.

Cauda Pavonis (Peacock's Tail): Alchemical term for the rebirth of matter on a more perfect or spiritual level.

cave of symbols: An etheric location within the Royal Teton Retreat of the Cosmic Council of Light in Table Mountain in the Grand Teton National Park in Wyoming.

Cayce, Edgar: An American psychic (1877–1945).

celestial cities of light: Multidimensional chambers, or nodes, on the electromagnetic grid that hold great amounts of energy. It is said that if we go to these chambers during dream states, Archangel Michael and other beings of light will assist us during the 12/ 21/12 dimensional shift.

celestorium: Sound-healing temple.

cetacean family of light: The whales and the dolphins.

Chaco Canyon, New Mexico: A major center of ancient Pueblo culture (900 AD–1150 AD).

chakras: Wheel-like vortices in the body that are focal points for the reception and transmission of energies.

Chalice Well: A sacred well situated in Glastonbury, Somerset, England.

channeler: One who translates multidimensional messages into the third dimension.

children of light: See lightworkers.

Christ: A state of awareness in which the individual has attained fully enlightened consciousness.

Christ-consciousness: The awareness of oneness with the divine while embracing one's humanity.

Christ-consciousness codes: Energy of pure love and light without distortions of duality.

Christ-consciousness collective: Masters who have been on earth many times for the specific purpose of bringing the energy of pure love and light to humanity and all sentient matter.

Christ-consciousness gateway: The cosmic opening allowing Christ-consciousness to pour down on all of humanity. This outpouring helps humanity grow in the continuous spherical fields in space-time and become part of the awareness of all.

Christ light of the earth: Pure love and light without the distortions of duality.

Christos: The higher-light expressions of Jesus, Lord of Light and Restoration; protector of all children on earth and beyond.

Christos energy: The frequency of pure love and light.

Christos humans: Humans who embrace the wholeness of who they are in their divinity.

circle of higher consciousness: The spiral of life.

city of light, crystal: A huge celestial sphere that contains a microcosm of our universe's dimensions, along with God's benevolence, as its central core (or sun); graduate schools of awareness for humanity, which are accessed by the etheric body in nightly sojourns.

clairaudient: The ability to hear voices psychically; the ability to telepathically access thoughts from another source.

collective consciousness: The shared beliefs and moral attitudes that operate as a unifying force within society.

Comal Springs: Springs composed of living water, and a vital plasma and anionic atmosphere, located in New Braunfels, Texas.

company of heaven: Beings who vibrate at or above the Christ-consciousness frequency.

compassion: Sympathetic consciousness; the birthing place of life.

compression: Arrangement of the particles of creation by means of intention, which then leads to expansion, or manifestation.

compression and expansion: The great rhythm of the universe; compression gives birth to universal order, which eventually reverses to expansion and releases created potential.

consciousness: One's eternal spark of divine essence.

consciousness, cetacean: The dolphins' advanced stellar-navigation awareness.

consciousness, cosmic: An awareness of the oneness of all of creation within the cosmos.

consciousness, golden dolphin: Awareness of one's human divinity.

consciousness, infinity: The understanding that all of creation comes from the adamantine particles within the space of infinity.

consciousness units: Adamantine particles; Akash.

consciousness, unity: Awareness of unity despite the many expressions of All That Is.

cosmic being: One who is part of the great intelligent awareness of the universe; an ascended master who has never incarnated in a human body.

cosmic center: A sacred site for humanity and otherworldly beings.

Cosmic Council of Light: An enclave of ascended masters of the earth; highly evolved nonphysical spiritual beings from all areas of our universe, who now reside in the various celestial cities of light around the world; highly advanced beings who have completed the lessons of physical duality and chosen to empathically assist humanity.

cosmic talk: Languages of the star nations.

cosmic triangle: The Grand Tetons National Park/Yellowstone National Park, Chaco Canyon, and Stardreaming in a triangle connected to Alpha Centauri; also known as the electromagnetic supertunnel.

cosmic trigger: Spring equinox cascades of energy pouring into the Great Pyramid of Giza in Egypt and the Blue Pyramid in Moody Gardens in Galveston, Texas, which are longitudinally aligned, acti vating long dormant magnetic codes that then radiate around the planet; part of the activation of the crystalline grid for 12/21/12.

cosmos: An orderly or harmonious system synonymous with the word *universe.*

Council of Thirteen: An enclave representing thirteen star nations who oversee the growth of consciousness on earth.

creation: God exploring God's self through every means imaginable.

creation codes, new: The frequencies carried in glyph form and toned at the Solar Cross at Giza Plateau in Egypt in 2008 to activate the unity-consciousness vortex.

Crimson Circle: A global affiliation of new-energy humans, including metaphysicians, healers, teachers, and counselors from all walks of life, a wide variety of spiritual backgrounds, and over one hundred countries.

crystal: A mineralogical form and also a frequency that is exuded in impeccable uniform clarity; solidified light used as a means of communication between the worlds.

crystal children: Sacred savant scientists who will, in the next generations, complete the circle of understanding and join spiritual insight with scientific knowledge.

crystal field master: Leader of the Ashtar Command.

crystal library: A body of ancient knowledge stowed within crystal skulls.

crystal singer: An Atlantean who activated healing-light frequencies from crystals by means of intonation.

crystal skulls: Keepers of humanity's perfected ancient blueprint.

crystalline: Energy of impeccability, in which there is no conflict between what one believes to be the right path and what one actuates.

crystalline age: Era in which it becomes possible to live a life of impeccability.

crystalline auric field: An impeccable auric field.

crystalline grid: A light matrix envisioned as a geodesic sphere sparkling with pentagons, triangles, and dodecadrons; a light grid covering our planet that increases its resonant vibratory rate in a series of twelve phases expected to reach their full resonant vibratory rate on 12/21/12; a light matrix, also known as Gaia's aura, carrying numeric light codes that open and activate each of its twelve major facets; a matrix sometimes referred to as the crystalline 144 grid because it is said to have 144 facets.

crystalline guild: A soul family.

crystalline light: Impeccable emanations of unconditional love from Source.

crystalline love frequency: The impeccability of love's vibration.

crystalline seed: An incarnate impeccable soul.

crystalline structure: A configuration containing nonpolar frequency, or zero-point energy.

crystallized matrix of sacred sites: Array of sacred sites built on ley lines.

curandera/curandero: A traditional folk healer or shaman who is dedicated to curing physical and spiritual illnesses.

curriculum of light: Master Kathumi's teachings for humanity.

dimension: A frequency at which energy vibrates.

third dimension: A dual mode of perception characterized by limitation and separation.

fourth dimension: A mode involving emotions, dreams, and creativity.

fifth dimension: A mode entailing reintegration with one's higher self in which one's innate spiritual abilities reveal themselves; frequency of the new earth, characterized by unconditional love and acceptance.

sixth dimension: A mode of being fully in one's light body; a magical and blessed state.

seventh dimension: A mode populated by luminous beings of light.

eighth through twelfth dimension: Modes in which luminous beings of light cease to have individuation but instead exist as soul groups.

dimension, living in two simultaneously: A state in which the higher self and the ego self work in partnership, ensuring an experience of peace and joy as one begins to manifest the new-earth reality.

discernment: The act of loving allowance and loving disallowance; the opposite of judgment.

diva: An elemental, such as a dragon, elf, sprite, rock troll, gnome, undine, or sylph.

divine blueprint: The wholeness of who we are in higher dimensions.

divine Creator: God, Source, All That Is.

divine feminine matrix: An array of inwardly focused sacred attributes such as love, compassion, nurturance, intuition, and wisdom; the sacred heart.

divine intention: A purpose that is perfectly aligned with that of the higher self.

divine masculine matrix: An array of outwardly focused sacred attributes such as will, power, and purpose; the sacred mind.

divine mind: A consciousness capable of reflection; everything that is, has been, and will be existing as a thought.

divine order of events: A flow of occurrences in alignment with one's higher self.

divine plan: Humanity's remembrance of its divinity.

divine will: The power of choice resulting in a perfect alignment of events with one's higher self.

DNA (medical): Deoxyribonucleic acid, a carrier of genetic information; our biochemical blueprint.

DNA (nonmedical): Spiritual intelligence (accessed when an individual is vibrating at a high frequency); the crossroads of God and humanity; a mixture of quantum and nonquantum energy.

DNA recoding (DNA upshift): increasing the efficiency with which DNA communicates to the body by aligning with the crystalline grid; giving energy to enhance what one already has; increasing the level of awareness of who one is.

dragon's breath: Powerful, transformational breath of blue smoke.

dreaming stone: A large horizontal stone at Stardreaming, in Santa Fe, New Mexico.

duality: A state of separation from one's wholeness or divinity; the clash of two concepts within a singular consciousness; the carnal and biological human being who also is a piece of God.

earth mound: A natural earthen formation resembling a miniature hill.

ego: Individuated aspects of Source that are experienced and expressed in duality and are not the full awareness of who we are.

El Fuerte: A batholith (large body of igneous rock) in Samaipata, Bolivia, with a tunnel to inner earth at its base.

El Morya: An ascended master of the Cosmic Council of Light; master of will, discipline, truth, and universal law.

electromagnetic supertunnel: Etheric tunnel energetically connecting three sacred sites with Alpha Centauri.

elementals: Beings representing the four elements: gnomes (earth elementals), undines (water elementals), sylphs (air elementals), and salamanders (fire elementals).

EMF: Electromagnetic field; an aura, when referring to a human electromagnetic field.

empathic: Quality of being extremely in tune with the emotions of others.

Enchanted Rock: A batholith in Fredericksburg, Texas, known as the Heart of the Dove. See **Head of the Dove, Heart of the Dove, Firmament of the Dove,** and **Return of the Dove**.

energy, crystalline: Pure light of love that creates everything in the universe, causing a shift in how we see ourselves and how much light we bring into our life and body.

enlightenment: God awareness; knowing that we are not our mind but rather our divine heart.

evolution: The advancement of consciousness; the movement of consciousness to overcome physical limitations and mindsets that inhibit the full expression of love.

exchange: The basis of life in the universe from the most elemental particles to the most complex human situations; a marvelous lubricant for life.

fairies: Little shape-shifters or shape-changers who are able to live between worlds.

faith: A soul's certainty in the fruits of right action; the cessation of fear and the surrender to all positive possibilities.

fear: A state of anxiety; the foundation of all false beliefs.

Fibonacci spiral: A geometric configuration whose growth is regulated by the numeric series 1, 1, 2, 3, 5, 8, 13, 21, and 34; also known as the Fibonacci series.

filter of duality: The distortion of pure love and light by the dense frequency of duality in the third dimension.

Firmament of the Dove: The angelic, white appearance of a dove in the sky, formed by a download of adamantine particles; a magno-crystalline configuration that will complete itself in the sky when all the master Atlantean crystals are empowered and the crystalline grid is in full function on 12/21/12. See **Head of the Dove, Heart of the Dove,** and **Return of the Dove**.

firmament, magno-crystalline: Powerful celestial energy waves transformed into a benevolent form that can be more easily received on earth following completion of the crystalline grid.

Flordemayo: A member of the International Council of Thirteen Indigenous Grandmothers.

Flower of Life: A sacred geometrical figure composed of multiple, evenly spaced, overlapping circles.

forgiveness: Amnesty, the experience of which demonstrates that one is the light of the world.

Founder's Tree: A sentient being with an enormous consciousness, located in Founder's Park, New Braunfels, Texas.

frequencial zero-point: Space of no duality.

frequency, gold and platinum: The high vibration projected by these noble metals.

frequency of manifestation: The high vibration projected by the adamantine particles forming our intention.

functional genomist: A scientist (geneticist, protein biochemist, or nutritional biochemist) who studies genes, their resulting proteins, and the role these proteins play in metabolic processes involving the prevention or treatment of human diseases.

Gabriel's trumpet: Association of the infinite with the finite.

Gaia: Mother Nature's energy consciousness.

Gaia effect: Earth's bias to create life.

galactic citizens: Members of our solar and galactic family of light; family of light members whose reunification is viewed as enlightenment.

Galactic Federation of Worlds: A large alliance of civilizations from many different planets, galaxies, and universes working together for the harmonious existence of all life; an alliance that exists in each of the inhabited galaxies of our universe.

Garden of the Goddess Retreat Center: A learning center located in the high desert outside of Santa Fe, New Mexico.

Gathering of Golden Dolphins: Two or more individuals coming together to embrace their wholeness and to declare their divinity in a safe place.

Giza Plateau: A necropolis in Giza, Egypt, on which the three great pyramids are located.

God: Father/Mother creator of life; omnipotent energy; conscious light and love; totality of all consciousness, omnipotent energy; the sum of all consciousness, whose whole is more than the sum of its parts.

God center: Sacred heart.

God force: Love.

gods and goddesses: The split-off energies of sea, air, land, crops, sun, warmth, cold, and more emanating from the divine force of Gaia (Earth).

gold vibration: The frequency of pure love of Source.

Golden Dolphin Society Trust: Name of the proposed trust instrument that will own Stardreaming for perpetuity.

golden dolphins: Star warriors who are in service to the light and to all the inhabitants of earth; aspects of the higher vibration of one's higher self; enlightened beings, formerly known as lightworkers, who assist in the ascending transition of both humanity and the planet; those who encourage the use of crystals to connect to the crystalline grid so that humanity can sustain higher frequencies to aid in DNA recoding.

golden mean: The desirable middle ground between the extremes of excess and deficiency.

golden mean spirals: Spirals that continue on in ever-diminishing whorls.

golden sun disc: Ancient blueprint of the feminine code.

grand experiment: The experiment that brought the great diversity of creation to earth and gave it free will to become a giant melting pot in order to see how long it would take for humanity to return to unity consciousness.

gratitude: Thankfulness and appreciation; a sacred responsibility.

Great Central Sun: The galactic center around which all other stars and galaxies revolve and are born; the highest vibration human mortals can use on earth.

green goddess: Goddess of the earth.

grid: Any system that organizes energy patterns supporting the intention and consciousness of the user.

grid activation meditation: A meditation given to humanity by Archangel Metatron.

guardians: Human and nonhuman beings who have agreed to protect specific sacred sites.

hado medicine: A radionics device capable of measuring various vibrations of the body at the cellular level (no longer available).

hall of records: Etheric repository of ancient wisdom.

harmonic convergence: An astrological term applied to the planetary alignment that occurred August 16–17, 1987; the beginning of the "shift."

harmonic energy oscillations: Vibratory pulses generated from a matrix of sacred sites.

harmonic gateway: A zero-point energy field for transforming consciousness on all levels.

harmonic oscillation: A frequency capable of affecting and achieving communication with all formations of identical type regardless of their location; frequencies of a low vibration incorporated into those of a higher one.

Hathor: An ancient Egyptian goddess; an interdimensional, intergalactic being who personified the principles of love, beauty, music, motherhood, and joy.

Head of the Dove: The crystalline grid or firmament appearing as a luminous angelic white dove spiraling in brief flight across the heavens, with its head sighted over Moody Gardens' Blue Pyramid in Galveston, Texas.

healer of crystalline seed: One who assists others in remembering their divinity.

healing: The knowledge that, as a spark of divine essence, we are whole and perfect; a memory of wholeness.

heart: The center point of stillness and peace from which infinity is viewed.

Heart of the Dove: The crystalline grid or firmament appearing as a luminous angelic white dove spiraling in brief flight across the heavens, with its heart sighted over Enchanted Rock in Fredericksburg, Texas.

heaven: Anywhere that love prevails in the manifesting of existence.

heaven on earth: God (each of us) expressing perfection on earth through the divinity of humanity.

Helios: A conscious earth-keeper crystal located under Peace Valley Sanctuary in Arkansas.

Herman, Ronna: Author and messenger for Archangel Michael.

higher beings of light: Spiritual entities aware of their divinity.

higher mind: Our higher consciousness.

higher self: An individualized expression of Source, which resides in the quantum field of DNA; a point of connection to the other side of the veil; the part of a person that vibrates higher than the three-dimensional human cellular structure; the absolute divinity of every person.

holy ones: Beings of Christ-consciousness or higher.

Holy Spirit: One's higher self; one's absolute divinity.

humanity: Beings of light; beings of powerful spiritual consciousness that are sparks of the divine; an aspect of the divine that evolves back into God-expansion plurality, choosing to experience free will and relearn creation through that magnanimous lens.

hundredth monkey effect: A phenomenon in which a learned behavior spreads instantaneously from one group of monkeys to all related monkeys once a critical number is reached.

illusion, the: The premise that our earthly reality is a holographic image.

incompatible forces: Dark energies in opposition to light energies within third-dimensional duality.

indigo child: Youngster who displays a new and unusual set of psychological attributes and shows a pattern of behavior generally undocumented before.

infinity: The unlimited potential of God, which first manifests as awareness, then as love, next as spirit, and finally as an immeasurable supply of adamantine particles lending themselves to an endless number of arrangements.

infinity ascension portal: A vortex-portal formed by a Vesica-Pisces flow combining, in this instance, the once separate vortexes of Grand Teton National Park and Yellowstone National Park.

infinity breath: Archangel Michael's breath meditation, which circulates adamantine particles in an infinite flow throughout the body.

infinity consciousness: Awareness of the unlimited potential of God, which eventually manifests as love, then spirit, and ultimately an infinite supply of adamantine particles that can be arranged endlessly.

infinity gate: See stargate.

infinity portal: Multidimensional gateway that is aware of itself and is fully conscious within the crystalline frequency.

infinity space: Space between the adamantine particles in all of creation.

infinity streaming: Moving consciousness out of density into the space between the particles, or infinity; allowing the pure love and intention of Source to flow through us for magnetizing and creating our reality.

inner-earth beings: Beings of lighter body form that live in the inner earth.

innocent perception: Seeing and responding without preconception.

integral sacred unity: The oneness of male and female expressions.

intent: An extremely powerful force that can change human DNA and move the particles of creation into manifested form.

internal compass: Wisdom of the higher self.

intuition: A map that can be used daily to make sense of life; energy of the higher self that is with us all the time and aware of All That Is.

Isis crystal: A crystal that, when placed in front of the lips, transforms sounds into their perfect expression.

Island of the Moon: Island on Lake Titicaca in Bolivia; site of a ruined temple to Mama Quilla.

Island of the Sun: Island on Lake Titicaca in Bolivia, known as the Garden of Eden to the Incas; site of the Temple of the Three Waters and the Fountain of Youth.

Jeshua ben Joseph: Jesus, son of Joseph.

Journey to the Fifth World Ceremony: A shamanistic ritual assisting in the development of increased spiritual alignment and nondualistic perspectives in order to transition to the fifth dimension.

Kaipu: High priestess for the *apu* Mama Quilla.

Keepers of the Temples of the Cosmos: Twelve women, each of whom cared for a specific temple at Stardreaming, in Santa Fe, New Mexico.

kingdom of heaven: Zone of perfection; the bond between God and humanity, found within the sacred heart.

kino osteopath: An osteopath who uses kinesiology, or muscle testing.

Kryon: A spiritual entity who has come to change the grid structure of the planet.

kundalini spinal cord: The path divine energy takes up the spinal cord to help expand spiritual awareness.

labyrinth: A unicursal (single-path), geometrical, magical tool; a course for walking that encourages a back-and-forth movement capable of balancing and uniting the left and right hemispheres of the brain, and the inner male and inner female principles.

Labyrinth Society: An international organization whose mission is to support individuals who create, maintain, and use labyrinths and to serve the global community by providing education, networking, and opportunities to experience transformation.

law of attraction/law of magnetism: Principle asserting that like attracts like.

law of creation: Principle often represented as S.T.A.R. (surrender, trust, allow, receive).

law of intergalactic connection: Principle emphasizing that we surrender intention based on trust in the laws of attraction and magnetism, allow for the perfection of God, and receive with appreciation and gratitude.

Lemuria: Ancient continent populated by a pre-Atlantean civilization, also known today as Hawaii; the oldest and most advanced stable human civilization, existing 50,000 years ago; a large civilization from the Pleiades, which lasted many thousands of years.

ley lines: A network of light or energy veins for Mother Earth; living energy expressed by the perfectly straight alignments of ancient holy places; energy flow of electromagnetic telluric forces.

libraries of the stars: Wisdom from the star nations.

life: Love in action.

light: Crystalline energy; the vitality that forms the integral nature of all worlds and realities.

light beings: Beings composed of light; beings from the star nations arriving on earth through special portals of entry, whose presence is increasingly felt on our planet.

light codes, new: Symbols representing structures of light and capable of awakening dormant human energies of innocent love and compassion, as well as knowledge of the oneness of Source.

light language: See cosmic talk.

lightning rod to the stars: One who can absorb the highest frequencies of love and transfer that energy safely to others.

lightworkers: Star seeds who bring light to the planet by their compassionate thoughts, thus assisting with the ascension; the next incarnation of lightworkers is referred to as golden dolphins.

Lilith: Sumerian goddess of light, truth, and shadow.

liquid light: Highly vibrating adamantine particles; love and appreciation.

Lord Metatron: Angel of light; a generator of adamantine particles.

love: A complex high frequency not to be confused with the emotional feeling usually thought of as love; an arrangement of adamantine particles that exists everywhere at the same time; a power beyond the universe; the physical form of who we are.

love, pure: Love undistorted by the dense vibration of duality.

love, unconditional: The highest form of love, which can only be grasped from the level of the fifth dimension.

love quotient: The degree to which we accept our divinity.

love vibration: Frequency of the adamantine particles of creation.

lucid dream state: Awareness within a dream indicating that one is dreaming.

magic: The extraordinary power of Source energy to create forms; the art of being in harmony with Source and serving as a conduit for its energy.

magical forest: A woodland with mounds where inner earth beings live.

magnetism and attraction: The force behind creation.

Mama Quilla: Goddess of the moon; an *apu* of Bolivia.

manifest: To command the adamantine particles to project a form.

manifest destiny: Divine purpose.

mantra: A sound, syllable, word, or group of words considered capable of initiating transformation.

master, Atlantean crystals: Enormous crystals that moved in hyperdimensional tunnel systems at the fall of Atlantis.

master beings: Those having the frequency of Christ-consciousness or higher.

master creator: One who, in combination with the higher self, commands the adamantine particles to create heaven on earth.

Master Kuthumi: A member of the spiritual hierarchy called Masters of the Ancient Wisdom who oversees the movement of humans toward higher levels of consciousness; an ascended master of the Cosmic Council of Light and a world teacher; ambassador of Archangel Metatron.

master of transmission: One whose impeccability transmits the highest vibration of love and light.

master numbers: The numbers eleven (illumination), twenty-two (master builder, cosmic law), thirty-three (Christ energy), and double numbers from forty-four through ninety-nine (with meanings yet to be revealed).

masters, the: Individuals who have lived in physical bodies, acquired the wisdom and mastery needed to become immortal and free of the cycles of karma, and attained their ascension; individuals who display peace, patience, equanimity, love, and understanding; those whose twelve layers (quantum field) of DNA are fully activated, representing the potential of all of humanity.

Masters of the Blue Crystal Skull: The Council of Thirteen.

mastery: Understanding the emotion of self-love and the energy it creates; the state of being in love with God within us.

Max: The thirteenth crystal skull of the Pleaidean-Sirian alliance; carrier of a sacred library of ancient wisdom.

Mayan (end age) prophecy: The completion (on 12/21/12) of the thirteenth B'ak'tun cycle in the long count of the Maya calendar, signifying a major change in world order.

megalabyrinth: A proposed labyrinth at Stardreaming, in Santa Fe, New Mexico; this will be the largest stone labyrinth used for healing and transformation.

Melchizedek: A person believed to have lived on earth in biblical times who is now a cosmic priest offering guidance throughout all dimensions on every sacred planet.

Mer-Ka-Bah: Eight-pointed star divine light vehicle based on a magnetic grid; a forerunner of the Mer-Ki-Va.

Mer-Ka-Ba of Earthstar: The crystalline grid around the consciousness of Gaia.

Mer-Ka-Na: Twenty-pointed star divine light vehicle.

Mer-Ki-Va: A nonpolarity-based eight-pointed star light body.

Metatronic shield: A channeled geometric design that projects a field of protection; noble metal precisely placed on the wrists and neck, as well as single and double refractive gems on the fingers, to assist in preventing the auric field from fissuring; form of protection that produces higher dimensional light waves to help hold the auric field intact.

mind, sacred: A fully functioning, perfect unit of wisdom and power that is stored within the structure of the brain.

moldovite: An olive-green or dull greenish vitreous substance possibly formed by a meteorite's impact that many believe possesses spiritual and medicinal properties.

Mu: A continent that existed in one of earth's oceans but disappeared at the dawn of human history; also known as Lemuria.

multiple consciousness: A state of awareness in which many dimensions can be accessed simultaneously.

muscle test: A method of manual testing used in applied kinesiology for medical diagnosis.

mutuality: Communication and exchange by common consent; conduct stipulated by the law of intergalactic connection.

Neptunus: Priest and king of the ancient ones; keeper of the library of Mu.

New Atlantis: A stage in the earth's evolution in which all beings will be enlightened golden dolphins.

new business plan model: Prototype emphasizing mutuality; business plan that includes and recognizes inspiration from one's higher self.

new creation codes: Sacred symbols or knowledge having the same rate of vibration as unity consciousness.

new earth: A futuristic reality signifying the transcendence of ego-based consciousness and arrival at unity consciousness; a paradigm in which humanity expresses the perfection of God.

new light codes: Sacred symbols or knowledge having the same rate of vibration as cosmic consciousness; means for awakening innocent love, compassion, and knowledge of oneness with Source.

new world order: The state of living in unity with one another as individual aspects of God.

Og: One of the three major islands of Atlantis, along with Poseida and Aryan.

original sin: The belief that we are born with a hereditary stain as a result of our descent from Adam. Also, humanity's judgment of others and themselves, due to their separation from God.

otherworldly friends: Beings from other star nations.

oversoul: The collective indivisible soul, which includes all souls; one's divine ascended soul.

Paa-Taal: Ancient language of the dolphins.

Pachamama: Mother Earth, according to the indigenous peoples of the Andes.

panaca: Brotherhood of Bolivian shamans and elders.

particles of infinity: Adamantine particles, identified by their function.

peace: A distinct energy that radiates unconditional love and compassion and acceptance of all; an inner energy that must be cultivated in the heart before it can be experienced in outer reality.

Peace Valley Sanctuary: Mystical site of the conscious earth-keeper crystal Helios; this site is a sanctuary of ancient wisdom, healing, and transcendence.

Peacock's Tail: See Cauda Pavonis.

pendulum: An amplifying tool that helps access the collective unconscious and the higher self in order to answer "yes" or "no" questions.

pendulum of life: Life's rhythm of compression and expansion.

philosopher's stone: That which transforms base metal into gold and holds the secret of eternal life, spiritual perfection, and humanity's realization of its divinity.

pillar of light: One of the 144,000 ascended masters grounding the crystalline grid for the world.

pillar of majesty: An ascended master who energetically connects a stargate to the earth.

planetary heart: Central core of the earth, identified as the proposed Temple of the Stone at Stardreaming, in Santa Fe, New Mexico, a site believed to have received the new light codes from the heart of the Great Central Sun on 08/08/08.

portal: A multidimensional gateway.

power nodes: Spots of high electromagnetic frequency, usually at sacred sites or the intersection of two ley lines.

***prana*:** Life force; also known as chi.

prayer: The expansion of oneself into a higher realm of consciousness; the medium of miracles.

precipitation: An alchemical term describing the coagulation of a purified substance following distillation.

pregnancy of intention: The slow gestation period of one's intention.

Price, John : Founder of Quartus Foundation, a research and communications organization established in 1981 to probe the mysteries of ageless wisdom and integrate those truths with spiritual metaphysics.

process of dragons: The ouroboros, in alchemy; the union of opposing energies; all in one.

Pueblo Bonito: The largest and best known great house in Chaco Canyon National Historical Park, occupied from 828 AD to 1126 AD.

pure knowledge of Source: Knowledge undistorted by duality.

pure light vibration: The frequency of light energy in human form unhampered by the dense vibration of duality.

pure love vibration: The frequency of love undistorted by the dense vibration of duality.

quantum: An aggregate, or "soup," of multidimensional attributes that have no location or place of origin but instead are everywhere entangled; a state of being at one with everything.

Queen of the Golden Dolphin: Mary Magdalene.

Ra: A survivor of Atlantis who, with Araragat and Thoth, set up the unity-consciousness grid.

Raimundo: A gem cutter from Brazil who was trained to cut crystal by research scientist Marcel Vogel (1917–1991), designer of the Vogel Crystal.

rainbow race: A group formed by nations, cultures, star systems, and planets, with the sole purpose of loving and caring for one another in peace, magic, and harmony.

reality: The presence of God manifested throughout existence.

realms: Planes of existence that, despite their varying densities and vibrations, are not separated by space or distance; states of spirit-matter that permeate one another.

receiver and transmitter: One who receives high frequencies from other dimensions and transmits them to humanity.

recoding (upshifting) DNA: Increasing the efficiency of DNA's communication to the body by working in its quantum field; increasing the level of awareness of who we are.

reconnective healing: A form of healing based on a new bandwidth of frequencies received by the practitioner via a spectrum of light;

energy healing originating in the sending and receiving of information.

Reiki healing: A method of transferring healing energy through the palm.

remote viewing: Gathering information about a distant or unseen target using paranormal means.

Return of the Dove: Completion of the crystalline grid, when long dormant magnetic codes will be reactivated, projecting the appearance of a luminous angelic white dove spiraling in brief flight across the heavens. A new age heralded in *The Keys of Enoch* by J. J. Hurtak.

rhythm of life: Compression and expansion.

sacred: A quality describing the center of one's consciousness and awareness.

sacred geometry: Universal patterns used in the design of everything in our reality.

sacred heart: The center of one's soul; the point of oneness with God.

sacred space: A place with unique electromagnetic properties that allows one to contact nonphysical realms.

Saint Germain: Ascended master and bearer of the violet flame for humanity, one of the seven main rays of the Holy Spirit, which transmutes negative karma from one's quantum DNA field.

Sampaya, Bolivia: Ancient town in which all the residents were female.

Sananda: Name used for the resurrected Master Jesus.

School of No Mysteries: Where all the sacred wisdom is taught and nothing is hidden from humanity.

Schumann resonance: A set of electromagnetic waves in the extremely low frequency portion of the earth's electromagnetic field.

Seshat: Ancient Egyptian goddess of wisdom, knowledge, and writing; wife of Thoth.

Seti I: A pharaoh of the ancient nineteenth dynasty of Egypt; son of Ramses I and Queen Sitre; father of Ramses II.

shaman: One who mediates between the visible and invisible worlds.

Shaman's Cave: The least known vortex in Sedona, Arizona, located in Red Rock National Forest.

Shambala: Dwelling place of the governing deities of earth.

Shambala Council: An ancient etheric assembly also called the Cosmic Council of Light.

shift, the: A change in the vibratory rate of human consciousness, leading to the remembrance of long dormant experiences of oneness with All That Is; a phenomenon that began in 1987 with the Harmonic Convergence and is accelerated by the reversal of the earth's poles currently under way; also known as the dimensional shift.

shining ones: Ethereal beings who appear in myths throughout the world as gods, goddesses, or creational forces of light.

Sirian-Hathor Goddess Guild: A group of enlightened beings from Sirius who display characteristics of the goddess Hathor.

Sirian Triad: Three Hathors of the divine feminine goddess energy—Crystal Star Walker, Che xel-Ra, and Anaya-Ra.

Sirius Alliance: A group of enlightened beings from Sirius; members of the Galactic Federation who are focused on the evolution of earth.

Sirius C: A star that revolves around Sirius.

smudge: Scented smoke used in ceremonies of purification.

Solar Cross: A site located at Giza Plateau in Egypt; north pole of the unity-consciousness grid.

Soqwahote: The blue crystal skull and blue star matrix of the ancient ones.

soul: One's divine self.

Source: God, or All That Is.

space of infinity: The space between adamantine particles; a continuum that comes together through love by way of spirit and that exists throughout us and beyond.

spark of divine essence: An individualized expression of Source.

Spencer, Raquel: Master healer of cellular light; healer in the Temple of One; Che xel-Ra, a member of the Sirian Triad.

spiral of life: The spiral of consciousness moving into the core of our divinity and the oneness with All That Is.

spirit: The active force employed by All That Is; energy currently expressed in separation but existing in oneness beyond the fourth dimension.

spiritual beings: Individuals awakening to the wholeness of who they arc.

S.T.A.R.: Acronym defining the law of creation (surrender, trust, allow, receive).

star beings from many nations: Life forms from the stars.

S.T.A.R. clinic: An etheric treatment facility based on the principles of surrender, trust, allow, and receive.

star codes: Adamantine particles; tools for raising the frequency of one's DNA.

star consciousness: Awareness that humanity comes from the star nations.

star nations: Communities of higher-dimensional beings from the stars, including Alpha Centauri, Alpha Draconis, Andromeda, Antares, Arcturus, Lyra, Spica, Orion, Pleiades, Sirius A, Sirius B, Sirius C, Vega, and Venus.

star path: Name for the new trajectory humanity is taking during the dimensional shift.

star seed crystalline being: Incarnate, impeccable old soul from the star nations; individual whose DNA received the seed of spiritual knowledge.

star warriors: Lightworkers—now referred to as golden dolphins.

Stardreaming: A twenty-two–acre sacred labyrinth temple complex for the new millennium, located in Santa Fe, New Mexico.

stargate: A wormhole enabling personal teleportation to complementary locations cosmic distances away; a shamanic tool of the future.

sungate: A sun halo, or natural phenomenon of light around the sun, resulting from the bending of sunlight by particles of water.

supreme beings of the cosmos: Those of a Christ-consciousness or higher frequency.

synchronicity: The simultaneous occurrence, in a meaningful manner, of two or more events that are causally unrelated.

talking stones: A complex of large stones at Stardreaming, in Santa Fe, New Mexico.

tall golden ones: Atlanteans of Pleiadean lineage living on the isle of Poseida; a race of gentle giants involved in Atlantean cultural, artistic, and educational pursuits.

Temascal: Bolivian sweat lodge.

Temple of Illumination: An Atlantean temple on the isle of Poseida.

Temple of One: An Atlantean temple on the isle of Poseida.

Temple of the Stone: The proposed largest stone labyrinth for healing and transformation, to be located at Stardreaming, in Santa Fe, New Mexico.

Temples of the Cosmos: Twelve temples of stone at Stardreaming, in Santa Fe, New Mexico.

third eye: An esoteric concept referring to the brow chakra in certain Eastern and Western spiritual traditions; a gate leading to inner realms of higher consciousness.

Thoth: A survivor of Atlantis who, with Araragat and Ra, set up the unity-consciousness grid; a manifestation of Enoch; architect of the pyramids.

thought form: An image held in the mind, which aids in the manifestation of intent; an image that takes form in prephysical realms of existence, acting in accord with the intent of its creator.

timegate: A dimensional portal allowing travel across different timelines.

timeline: A graphic design used to show events occurring over a period of time.

Tobias: An angelic being who has lived many lifetimes on earth as Tobit, a character featured in the apocryphal *Book of Tobit*.

Toltec Mounds: An archaeological state park near Scott, Arkansas, once serving as ceremonial grounds of the Plum Bayou Indians (circa 600–1050 AD); remnants of pyramids used to coordinate the natural projections of local mineral energies; a site beneath which the Sirian-Pleiadean Alliance has maintained an enormous subterranean pyramid since Atlantean times.

toning: The emanation of frequencies used to balance and stimulate a vibratory field.

torus: Any three-dimensional form, like a doughnut, which, when rotated around an axis, becomes spherical as the axis passes through its center.

transformational vortex: A funnel-shaped energy spiral with electromagnetic properties capable of raising the frequency of one's DNA.

Tree of Life: A grid that can raise the frequency in one's body or in space; the thirty-two secret paths of wisdom, interfaced with ten energy centers and the twenty-two letters of the Hebrew alphabet.

triad stargates: Three dates—November 11, 2009, December 12, 2009, and December 21, 2009—when humanity was assisted through a potent energy transition associated with the dimensional shift.

triangle of mutuality principles: A combination business plan–business model–business profits expressed as communication and exchange by common consent; a model for conducting business on the new earth based on moderation, equilibrium, and love.

triple dates: Twelve dates—01/01/01, 02/02/02, and so forth—each of which carries numeric light codes that open and activate one of the twelve major pentacle facets of the crystalline grid.

trust: Reliance on one's inner truth.

truth: An understanding of the laws of nature and the cosmos, signaled by the ringing or vibration of one's cells.

truth of the universe: That which humanity is on the planet to discover.

Tula: A great central sun referred to by Archangel Metatron via Tyberonn.

Tyberonn: A Pleiadean; member of the Cosmic Council of Light who has incarnated to serve as a messenger for Archangel Metatron.

unconsciousness: A state in which the oversoul can no longer be remembered.

unified crystalline field: A hologram of impeccability that is manifesting to encompass our planet and all twelve light dimensions around it.

unity consciousness: An awareness of unity, or All That Is.

unity-consciousness grid: Network of energetic connections between sacred temples and other sites around the globe and the crystals that link them, creating a shared unity consciousness.

unity-consciousness vortex: The funnel-shaped energy spiral connecting the north and south poles of the unity-consciousness grid—the Solar Cross at Egypt's Giza Plateau in the north and Moorea, an island in French Polynesia, in the south.

universal chakras: Force centers of the universe.

universal compression: Precursor to expansion in the universal rhythm of creation.

universal consciousness: The thread that joins all forms of human endeavor with all states of sentient and nonsentient existence.

universal field: The physical presence of spirit in the universal quantum field, allowing fundamental forces and elementary particles to be expressed in terms of a single field.

universal flow: The quantum "soup" in which all portions of the universe, each with its unique properties, exist as one.

universal knowledge: The knowledge of who we are that is contained in our DNA.

universal plan: A higher wisdom than what is known by one's earth-bound personality and ego.

universal portal: A multidimensional gateway that brings oneness, union, and expansion to planet earth.

universal song of creation: The combined frequency of each aspect of creation.

universal substance: Adamantine particles.

upshifting: Recoding specific earth energy nodes and human DNA to the crystalline blueprint.

veil, the: Invisible barrier that causes us to forget what consciousness was like before we inhabited the body.

Vesica-Pisces: A shape composed of the intersection of two circles of equal radius, in which the center of each one is on the circumference of the other.

vibrations: Oscillations around an equilibrium point.

violet flame: A life stream of energy for our galaxy, given by the ascended master Saint Germain.

vision mound: A small earthen formation in a magical forest, from which one may receive insight.

Virgins of the Sun: Ancient priestesses inhabiting Island of the Moon on Lake Titicaca, Bolivia.

Vogel crystal: A faceted crystal cut in accordance with the geometric design of Marcel Vogel, which concentrates universal life force to a higher level by duplicating the angle of the Great Pyramid of Giza.

vortex: The funnel shape created by spiraling energy.

vowel sounds of creation: Universal sounds that move the adamantine particles of creation.

vril rod: A rod that carries the knowledge and wisdom of the universe.

walk-in: One who voluntarily accepts a new soul to replace the soul that originally incarnated in the body.

walk-in, internal: One who has merged with their divine ascended soul, or oversoul, in order to complete a sacred mission of service to humanity.

walking master: One who embraces their wholeness at all times.

Walter, CJ: Crystal Star Walker, a Vogel crystal healer and member of the Sirian Triad.

warrior of light: One who comes as a lightworker into the duality-based third dimension.

watsu: A form of aquatic bodywork.

wellness: The active pursuit of health.

whales and dolphins: Cetacean beings that hold the light and love of our life force, according to many indigenous cultures.

white whale of wisdom: The ancient grandmother who will birth a new pathway of stars for the golden dolphins.

wholeness: The full integration of one's divinity.

will of heaven: The idea that active intervention from heaven will motivate us to embrace our wholeness.

Windsong: An etheric indigenous holy man; guardian of Enchanted Rock in Fredericksburg, Texas.

zero point: A state of being in perfect synchronicity with the elements, time, and space; a condition in which a person's will is perfectly reconciled with the will of God; a designation of infinity; a field devoid of electromagnetic forces.

Notes

Introduction

1. R. Buckminster Fuller, *Critical Path* (New York: St. Martin's Press, 1981), xii–xiii.

Chapter 1

1. James Tyberonn, channeling Archangel Metatron (June 28, 2009).
2. J. J. Hurtak, *The Keys of Enoch: The Book of Knowledge* (Los Gatos, CA: The Academy for Future Science, 1977), x.
3. http://www.earth-keeper.com/EKnews_4-22-09.htm.
4. Lee Carroll, channeling Kryon (April 13, 2010), http://www.kryon.com/k_channel10_melbourne_1.html.
5. James Tyberonn, "The Ascension and the 144-Crystal Grid," in *Earth-Keeper Chronicles* (July 2007), http://www.earth-keeper.com/EKnews_july07.htm.
6. Glenda Green, *Love without End: Jesus Speaks* (Sedona, AZ: Spirits Publishing, 1999), 33, 114.
7. James Tyberonn, "Metatronic Keys," in *Level 1 Course Study* (Santa Fe, NM: Earth-Keeper), 22.
8. James F. Jereb, in conversation with the author (March 15, 2010).
9. James F. Jereb, *Quest of the Golden Dolphin: In the Land of Stardreaming* (Santa Fe, NM: Stardreaming Press, 2008), 11–13.

10. William Arntz and Betsy Chase, *What the Bleep Do We Know!?* DVD (Fox Home Entertainment, 2004), http:// www.whatthebleep.com.

11. Joan Ocean, *Dolphin Connection: Interdimensional Ways of Living* (Kailua, Hawaii: Dolphin Connection Books, 1989), 42.

12. Lee Carroll and Jan Tober, *The Indigo Children—The New Kids Have Arrived* (Carlsbad, CA: Hay House,1999).

13. Lori Arviso Alvord and Elizabeth Cohen Van Pelt, *The Scalpel and the Silver Bear* (New York: Bantam, 1999).

Chapter 2

1. Dan Campbell, *Edgar Cayce on the Power of Color, Stones, and Crystals* (New York: Grand Central Publishing), 133–134.

2. Neurosensory Centers of America, http://www.neurosensorycenters.com.

Chapter 3

1. Gregg Braden, *The Isaiah Effect: Decoding the Lost Science of Prayer and Prophecy* (New York: Three Rivers Press, 2000), 160.

2. James F. Jereb, *Alchemy of the Stone* (Santa Fe, NM: Stardreaming Press, 2009).

Chapter 5

1. Drunvalo Melchizedek, *The Ancient Flower of Life* (Flagstaff, AZ: Light Technology Publishing, 1998), 108.

Chapter 6

1. George H. Williamson, *Secret Places of the Lion: Alien Influences on Earth's Destiny* (Rochester, VT: Inner Traditions, 1982), 68.
2. James F. Jereb, *Quest of the Golden Dolphin: In the Land of Stardreaming* (Santa Fe, NM: Stardreaming Press, 2008), 36.

Chapter 9

1. Glenda Green, *Love without End: Jesus Speaks* (Sedona, AZ: Spirits Publishing, 1999), 148.
2. Ibid., 74.
3. Ibid., 403.
4. Ibid., 51.
5. Baird T. Spalding, *Life and Teaching of the Masters of the Far East* (Marina del Rey, CA: DeVorss, 1924), 17.
6. Green, *Love*, 176–179.
7. Ibid., 35.
8. James Tyberonn, *Metatron Speaks* (Reno, NV: StarQuest Publishing, 2009), 173.
9. Spalding, *Life and Teaching*, 39.
10. Ibid., 40.

Chapter 10

1. Glenda Green, *Love without End: Jesus Speaks* (Sedona, AZ: Spirits Publishing, 1999), 176.
2. Baird T. Spalding, *Life and Teaching of the Masters of the Far East* (Marina del Rey, CA: DeVorss, 1924), 90.

3. Dennis W. Hauck, *The Complete Idiot's Guide to Alchemy* (New York: Alpha Books, 2008).

Chapter 11

1. Glenda Green, *The Keys of Jeshua* (Sedona, AZ: Spirits Publishing, 2003), 109.

2. James Tyberonn, channeling Archangel Metatron, "AA Metatron," in *Earth-Keeper Chronicles* (February 4, 2009), http://www.earth-keeper.com/EKnews_2-4-09.htm.

Chapter 12

1. James Tyberonn, channeling Archangel Metatron, "The Ascension Infinity Portal, Bosom of Gaia," in *Earth-Keeper Chronicles* (April 22, 2009), http://www.earth-keeper.com/EKnews_4-22-09.htm.

2. James Tyberonn, channeling Archangel Metatron, "Yellowstone, Grand Teton Grid, and the Ascension Infinity Portal," in *Earth-Keeper Chronicles* (April 22, 2009), http://www.earth-keeper.com/EKnews_4-22-09.htm.

Chapter 13

1. Celia Fenn, channeling Archangel Michael, "The Diamond Prism and the Planetary Awakening: the Energies for June 2009," http://starchildglobal.com.

Chapter 14

1. Ronna Herman, channeling Archangel Michael, "Living Your Personal Truths Revealed," in *Messages from Archangel Michael* LM-6-2009, http://www.globalmeditations.com/archjum.htm.

Chapter 15

1. James Tyberonn, "The Ascension and the 144 Crystal Grid," in *Earth-Keeper Chronicles* (July 2007), http://www.earth-keeper.com/EKnews_july07.htm.

2. James Tyberonn, "The Infinite Geometry of Sacred Sites," in *Earth-Keeper Chronicles* (October 2007), http://www.earth-keeper.com/EKnews_octo7.htm.

Chapter 16

1. James Tyberonn, "Ascension Practices: The 144 Crystal Earthkeeper-Grid" (July 28, 2007), http://www.earth-keeper.com/EKnews_july07.htm.

2. James Tyberonn, *Metatron Speaks* (Reno, NV: StarQuest Publishing, 2009), 20–21.

Chapter 17

1. www.crystalsinger.com.

Chapter 18

1. James Tyberonn, *Metatron Speaks* (Reno, NV: StarQuest Publishing, 2009), 58.

2. Ibid., 179.

Chapter 19

1. James Tyberonn, channeling Archangel Metatron, "The Triad Portals: 11-, 12-12, & 12-21-2009," in *Earth-Keeper Chronicles* (November 8, 2009), http://www.earth-keeper.com/EKnews_10-18-09.htm.

Chapter 22

1. Jen Eramith, "Akashic Records on Christ-Consciousness" (December 9, 2009), http://www.ashictransformatios.com.

Chapter 23

1. Archangel Raphael via Anaya-Ra, journal entry (February 25, 2008).

To place an order

visit www.CaudaPavonisPub.com

or email the author at:

nina@crystalsinger.com

CPSIA information can be obtained at www.ICGtesting.com
Printed in the USA
LVOW040227250412

278889LV00002B/13/P